THE COMPLETE ILLUSTRATED ENCYCLOPEDIA OF
1001 GARDEN
QUESTIONS ANSWERED

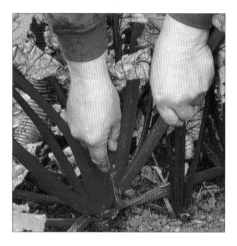

THE COMPLETE ILLUSTRATED ENCYCLOPEDIA OF
1001 GARDEN
QUESTIONS ANSWERED

EXPERT SOLUTIONS TO EVERYDAY GARDENING DILEMMAS, WITH AN EASY-TO-FOLLOW DIRECTORY AND 850 PHOTOGRAPHS AND ILLUSTRATIONS

ANDREW MIKOLAJSKI

HERMES HOUSE

This edition is published by Hermes House,
an imprint of Anness Publishing Ltd,
Hermes House, 88–89 Blackfriars Road,
London SE1 8HA;
tel. 020 7401 2077; fax 020 7633 9499
www.hermeshouse.com
www.annesspublishing.com

If you like the images in this book and would
like to investigate using them for publishing,
promotions or advertising, please visit our website
www.practicalpictures.com

Publisher: Joanna Lorenz
Editorial Director: Helen Sudell
Editor: Simona Hill
Designer: Nigel Partridge
Proofreading Manager: Lindsay Zamponi
Editorial Reader: Molly Perham
Production Controller: Wendy Lawson

ETHICAL TRADING POLICY
At Anness Publishing we believe that business
should be conducted in an ethical and ecologically
sustainable way, with respect for the environment
and a proper regard to the replacement of the
natural resources we employ.
As a publisher, we use a lot of wood pulp in
high-quality paper for printing, and that wood
commonly comes from spruce trees. We are
therefore currently growing more than 750,000
trees in three Scottish forest plantations:
Berrymoss (130 hectares/320 acres), West Touxhill
(125 hectares/305 acres) and Deveron Forest
(75 hectares/185 acres). The forests we manage
contain more than 3.5 times the number of trees
employed each year in making paper for the
books we manufacture.
Because of this ongoing ecological investment
programme, you, as our customer, can have the
pleasure and reassurance of knowing that a tree is
being cultivated on your behalf to naturally
replace the materials used to make the book you
are holding.
Our forestry programme is run in accordance with
the UK Woodland Assurance Scheme (UKWAS)
and will be certified by the internationally
recognized Forest Stewardship Council (FSC).
The FSC is a non-government organization
dedicated to promoting responsible management
of the world's forests. Certification ensures forests
are managed in an environmentally sustainable
and socially responsible way. For further
information about this scheme, go to
www.annesspublishing.com/trees

CONTENTS

INTRODUCTION

Good gardeners are always asking questions. It is one of the best ways to learn, and seasoned practitioners are very generous in giving advice. Beginner gardeners usually find that in the process of learning more about the subject, new questions keep occurring to them.

Experienced gardeners are aware that whatever knowledge they may have acquired, there is plenty about which they remain ignorant. The true experts are usually the first to admit to gaps in their knowledge. Gardening is such a huge subject that one lifetime seems scarcely enough to learn all there is to know.

The best of all ways to learn is by personal experience, but trial and error can be a costly business, not only in terms of money, but of time too. The majority of amateur gardeners (and even professional ones) acquire their knowledge in a piece-meal fashion. Reading books by trusted authorities is one way, attending a gardening course at a horticulture college is another. Talking to other gardeners is even better. If you join an allotment society or gardening club you can be sure to meet plenty of enthusiasts who are usually more than willing to pool

▲ *Adding decorative detail to paved areas, no matter how small, provides visual interest in a garden.*

▲ *Knowing when to divide congested spring bulbs and how to do it is part of the gardener's year.*

their knowledge – no gardener is ever reluctant to answer a question, if they can. Local gardeners are often a good source of information, because they

may have similar soil to yours and will know what plants thrive there. But even the most experienced gardener is sometimes stumped for a reply. With such a vast subject as this, it is impossible to know the answer to every question. While in the digital age, the Internet has become a fantastic tool, searches often yield conflicting information, or advice that is too general to be of much practical value. Besides, many sites that carry advertising may have a commercial interest in recommending certain products.

This book frames the questions that are likely to strike any amateur at some point in their gardening life. It looks not only at the what and how of gardening, but, possibly more importantly, at the why. Why do we do particular jobs at certain times of the year, for instance, and not others? The answers are intended to

◀ *This garden design, based on trimmed topiary and neat hedging, can be adapted for many garden spaces.*

▶ *Keep container plants in good health. A little know-how will see your grasses and shrubs thrive.*

be direct and practical, or point towards possible solutions (with alternatives, if appropriate). Many questions can be answered by applying certain principles. Several answers take the form of plant lists – one of the most frequently asked gardening questions is 'What plant should I grow here?'. Another feature of the book is the step-by-step sequences, which describe and show how to do specific gardening tasks.

Questions are gathered into chapters and are grouped according to specific subjects, such as annuals or bulbs in the flower garden, or bog plants in the water garden chapter. No detailed knowledge of gardening is assumed – only an enthusiasm for the subject and a willingness to learn more. What to seasoned gardeners may seem obvious, may not be so to novices, or those new to a different area of gardening, who are understandably baffled by jargon that the more experienced use freely.

▼ *Large gardens may have space to incorporate wild flower areas, but what tasks are needed to accomplish it?*

Planning and assessing

The first chapter answers many of the questions faced by gardeners who have to tackle a new garden or want to make changes to an existing one. It is remarkable how many garden 'problems' can be eliminated by making a careful survey of the site and planning the new content carefully. If you are about to make an investment in hard landscaping materials, which can be expensive, it is as well to know exactly where to site a patio or terrace. Thorough assessment will greatly help you choose which plants to grow and how to prepare the site appropriately – the ones that you like and that are naturally adapted to the site's conditions will reward you with rapid, healthy growth.

The hard landscape

Before thinking about the plants, it is sensible to get the 'bones' of the garden in place first. If you are creating a new garden, often the first job is to get all the hard landcaping – the paths and patios – established, before you can get on and plant the beds and borders. But you may be looking to replace a worn out patio, or

uneven paving, in an existing garden. You may also need to define the boundaries. Do you need to erect (or repair) a wall or fence? Should you plant a hedge or do you need to disguise a less than appealing view? This chapter will help you decide what is appropriate.

▼ *Bog gardens are determined by the landscape, but how do you make the best use of the site and what do you plant?*

▲ *Roses are popular garden plants, but many gardeners have questions on how to grow and look after them.*

▲ *Growing vegetables is a popular and rewarding pastime, but when and how do you sow your seeds?*

Lawns

A stretch of grass is an important element of the garden for many gardeners. Some devote much care and attention to a lawn's upkeep. Whether a manicured lawn that is neat and tidy is your choice, or a safe surface on which children can play ball games is your requirement, each has its own set of maintenance tasks. How do I best maintain an even sward of green? How do I deal with lawn pests such as moles and toadstools, or keep the grass in good order through the winter? Not everyone wants a high-maintenance lawn, however, and the alternatives are discussed.

The ornamental garden

For many gardeners, the over-whelming reason to garden is to grow plants that beautify the immediate environment and give pleasure on their own account, whether it is a tree that will be a strong presence for decades, or an annual that blooms for a few of weeks and is no more than a temporary resident. Consult a

plant dictionary, and it soon becomes obvious that the range is enormous – and many gardeners will feel spoilt for choice. This chapter offers answers to the questions facing gardeners when deciding how to fill beds and borders.

The kitchen garden

Of equal, if not greater, importance for many gardeners is the growing of fruit and vegetables. Others may be put off by the degree of work that they

envisage is involved in this, especially if they are new to gardening. This need be no deterrent, provided you follow a few simple principles, and you will find many of your questions answered here, including advice on making a herb garden.

The water garden

Water features appear in many gardens, whether they are still pools, more dramatic streams and watercourses, or simple bubble fountains to bring the sound of playing water into a courtyard or on

▼ *Greenhouse gardening effectively extends the growing season, and is essential for many gardeners.*

▲ *Good garden hygiene will ensure plants have the best chance of surviving through the coldest, wettest months.*

to a deck or patio. Whatever style of feature appeals, water always fascinates, and is guaranteed to attract beneficial wildlife into the garden – a host of water-based insects as well as birds, frogs and toads. This chapter will help you decide what is appropriate for the size of garden, your family and the time you have to devote to its maintenance.

Propagation methods

Few garden tasks are more rewarding than raising your own plants, either by sowing seeds or taking cuttings. But many gardeners are reluctant to try, possibly in the mistaken belief that you need to be 'green-fingered' in order to be successful. What is remarkable, in fact, is the willingness that cuttings show to root and seeds to germinate. This chapter provides reassuring advice and information on what to propagate and how to do it.

Pruning and training

Many gardeners would confess to being baffled by how they are supposed to prune plants, while at the same time acknowledging that they realize this may be necessary from time to time, as well as beneficial to the plants. This chapter aims to answer such questions as which plants need pruning, and when and how to

▶ *Garden containers can be used as a design feature to help create the garden style required.*

do it. Special attention is given to fruit trees and shrubs, which will crop abundantly if pruned and trained in the appropriate manner.

Garden problems

Gardeners' hearts sink at the visible sign that pests and diseases are prevalent in the garden. Such problems can decimate carefully nurtured plants. Learning to identify specific problems and taking action to eradicate them, or to dissuade pests from arriving in the first place, is all part of gardening. With a good mix of plants, it is possible to achieve some measure of control, even if you cannot eliminate them altogether. This chapter deals with some of the commonest garden problems that you may encounter.

Growing under cover

Many gardeners find themselves frustrated by the weather, especially during the winter months when it is too cold or wet to venture outdoors. Fortunately, many plants can be grown with success under cover, either as houseplants or in greenhouses. Greenhouses can also be used for growing tender crops in the summer that benefit from extra heat, such as tomatoes, (bell) peppers, aubergines (eggplants) and chillies.

▲ *Growing fruit is rewarding if you have the space, but how do you train and prune trees and bushes to be productive?*

Garden equipment

It is worth investing in gardening equipment that is comfortable to use, and which is appropriate for the job in hand. The right tools make many garden tasks easier and more pleasurable. This chapter guides you through the choices available, helping you to select the best tool for each job, but also providing information on how to use them safely and effectively.

CHAPTER ONE

PLANNING AND ASSESSING

Before you begin doing any work in a new garden, it makes sense to make a thorough assessment of the proposed site. This involves gauging which parts are warmest and coolest, and which are sheltered or exposed. Are there any unattractive features that need concealing? You also need to examine the soil. Is it light or heavy? What grows in it now? Does it need improving? Asking yourself all these questions will help determine whether any preliminary work needs to be done before you start making the garden, and which will be the most suitable plants to grow once you have set it out. It will indicate where to site a patio or deck, a vegetable or a flower garden, for example. It will also help you rule out plants that will not thrive, saving you from making possibly expensive mistakes.

SITE   TOPOGRAPHY   CLIMATE   ASPECT   HIDING UGLY FEATURES

SOIL   IMPROVING THE SOIL   GARDENING STYLES

◄ *A small enclosed garden with a strong focal point and limited colourscheme creates a restful and attractive vista.*

SITE

The site is the whole garden including the boundaries. The land around the exterior of the site may also affect how the garden is used, and its design. You might wish to incorporate an attractive view into the design, for instance, or screen an unappealing feature.

1 What is a site assessment?

When planning a garden, it is necessary to determine what the potential of the site is, and compare it to a realistic wish list of all the things that you would like to see included in the design. The site will in part determine what your choices are. To what extent is the garden exposed to, or sheltered from, the elements? What is the soil like? Are there any large trees that cast shade? Is the site overlooked? What grows well in the soil now? Will I be able to have a lawn, or is some alternative a more sensible option? What plants will I be able to grow? Will I be able to grow my own fruit and vegetables? Do I have space for a patio or deck?

2 Can I assess a site in the middle of winter?

Yes, but you need to project ahead. If the sun is hidden by clouds, check where it sets to determine the westerly direction. If the sun is out, remember that shadows will be longer in winter

▼ **1** *Making a quick sketch of a site can help you decide which features to retain and which to get rid of.*

than summer. Parts of the garden that are permanently shaded in winter can be well lit in summer, depending on the height of any buildings/walls/hedges or other planting.

3 What are the advantages and disadvantages of having an enclosed garden?

Enclosed gardens, with high walls, hedging or trees around them feel very private, so are excellent for entertaining and sunbathing. If the garden is small, deep shade cast by the boundary can be a problem at some times of the year if the surrounding walls or fences are high. Conversely, they will be very sheltered and provide either a sun-trap or a shady retreat. Gardens in built-up areas are often overlooked by neighbours, and the design and planting scheme needs to take account of this.

4 What are the best design solutions for a garden that is dark and enclosed?

An enclosed garden with low light levels has certain advantages in that the temperature stays relatively

constant with no searing heat in summer or extreme cold in winter. An oriental scheme that is predominantly green can be highly effective, focusing on Japanese maples (*Acer japonicum* and *A. palmatum*), ferns and hostas. To add colour, grow some of these in glazed oriental containers. Subtropical plants such as bananas (*Musa*) and tree ferns (*Dicksonia*) will also do well here. A garden of evergreens will add year round colour.

▼ **3** *Many town gardens are long and thin and enclosed by other gardens, as well as shaded by houses and garden structures. House walls, high fencing and trees are all likely to create shade. The sun will filter into the garden when it is directly overhead.*

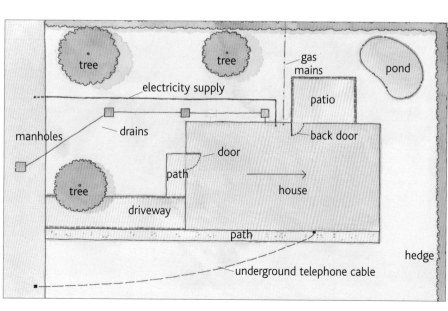

▲ **5** *A large open garden that is in full sun for much of the day is a good place to grow Mediterranean plants.*

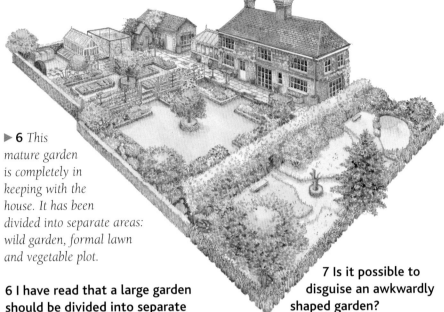

▶ **6** *This mature garden is completely in keeping with the house. It has been divided into separate areas: wild garden, formal lawn and vegetable plot.*

5 What are the advantages and disadvantages of an open garden?

A very open garden, one that is wide and long with low-growing plants, feels spacious, especially if it backs on to fields. If the garden has a view, you can integrate the landscape into the garden by concealing the boundaries with low-level planting. A downside is that the garden may well be exposed to strong winds and so you may need to plant out the view to create shelter.

▼ **5** *This garden is ideal for plants – flat and open, but sheltered by mature trees.*

6 I have read that a large garden should be divided into separate areas. Is this a good idea?

If you set out the garden so that the whole thing can be seen in a single glance you can create a sense of spaciousness – especially if you are able to 'borrow' elements, such as mature trees, from the surroundings. Dividing a large garden into 'rooms' creates mystery and surprise and allows for seasonal plantings with separate areas devoted to spring and summer bedding, or perhaps a winter garden. You can also design around different themes – a Mediterranean garden, a wild garden, a potager, etc.

7 Is it possible to disguise an awkwardly shaped garden?

Yes. Designs built on curves can be easier on the eye since those that rely on straight lines expose shapes that are not symmetrical. You can also disguise an awkwardly shaped garden with thick plantings of evergreen shrubs at the boundaries. Laurels, hollies, privets and viburnums can be highly effective when massed together, or plant carefully so that the eye is drawn to specific areas other than the boundary.

▼ **7** *Tall plants disguise the boundaries of awkwardly shaped gardens.*

TOPOGRAPHY

Topography refers to the lie of the land. Many gardens are flat, but others slope or have differing levels throughout the site. Working with the existing topography is easier than trying to change it – one of the challenges of a good garden design.

8 What is meant by the topography of a site?

Topography refers to the degree of slope, if any, as well as mounds and hollows in the landscape. Gardens attached to new-build houses in housing developments are often flat, although awkward sites are also sometimes found. The topography and the underlying soil type has a bearing on the garden design.

9 Should I attempt to alter the topography of a site?

It is usually difficult to alter the lie of the land in a garden. Earth-moving equipment such as a digger is needed, which is expensive to hire. Plus, you need to be sure that you can get the digger on and off site with ease. Excavations close to a house or other buildings can affect the foundations and possibly lead to subsidence. The best advice is to work with the site as it is and keep alterations to the minimum.

10 How do I deal with a sloping site?

A sloping site lends itself to dramatic water features, provided there is adequate room for a large tank or pool to hold the copious volume of water required. A south-facing, sloping garden can be terraced to increase the

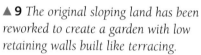

▲ **9** *The original sloping land has been reworked to create a garden with low retaining walls built like terracing.*

sun-trap qualities. This suits Mediterranean plants such as rosemary, lavender, sage, cistus and brooms, as well as succulents such as agaves, aloes and sempervivums.

To cover a bank, consider planting a climbing plant at the top and allowing the stems to trail downwards. If you pin the stems down where they touch the ground, they will root at these points and form an impenetrable ground cover. Clematis and climbing roses can be spectacular grown in this way. In a shady site, try ivies or Virginia creeper. If the garden slopes sharply to one side, you can disguise this with a thick planting of mixed shrubs at the bottom of the slope.

◄ **10** *This sloping site has been land-scaped on a grand scale to incorporate a series of pools and waterfalls that cascade into a large pond at the bottom of the slope. The building work required to produce such a setting is immense. A powerful pump is also needed to keep the water moving.*

CLIMATE

Climate varies from region to region, with some areas being much wetter, drier, windier, colder or warmer than others. It has a huge impact on garden plants, and the rate at which they grow, which is why gardens vary dramatically in different regions of the country.

11 What factors affect the climate of the garden?

Distance from the sea has a profound effect on climate. In maritime gardens, the overall temperature range is narrower than inland, with warmer winters and cooler summers. Frosts are rare. The climate is often damper, with fogs rolling in off the sea. There can be pronounced variation in rainfall depending on the latitude (degrees east or west).

Distance from the equator/poles also has an effect on day length. The farther north you go (or south, depending on the hemisphere), the longer the days are in summer and the shorter in winter. This affects when plants emerge from their winter dormancy in spring and when growth slows down in autumn. The nearer the equator, the longer the growing season. At the equator, plants can be more or less permanently in growth.

12 How does the cycle of the seasons affect plant growth?

In winter, plants are dormant, due to the combination of low light levels and low temperatures. This rest period is important to hardy plants. Many fruit trees have a specific chilling requirement – without the correct exposure to freezing temperatures they will not flower and fruit correctly. In spring, as the temperature rises and day length increases, plants start into growth, with some flowering at this time. After the spring equinox, you can observe a definite acceleration. Spring rainfall encourages plants to put on fresh growth. Late spring to early summer is a high point in the garden, with many plants flowering at this time. During the long, sunny days, pollinating insects are also active, feeding, mating and laying their eggs. During the hot days of mid- to late summer, plant growth ceases and seeds ripen. Strong autumn winds encourage plants to shed their fruits, or their seeds are carried far and wide. Wind also strips dying leaves from deciduous trees and shrubs ready for their winter dormancy, which starts some time after the autumn equinox.

13 What happens to a garden during hot, dry spells?

In hot, dry weather, plant growth above ground stops. Flowers open and are visited by pollinating insects that are usually active in dry spells. Plants set seed, which then ripen. On trees and shrubs, the bark layer thickens and hardens. Left unwatered, plants may struggle to survive.

▼ **11** *Coastal gardens have a microclimate different to any inland garden. Plants need to be salt-tolerant in order to survive in this landscape.*

▼ **12** *In the summer season when daylight hours are stretched, many plants will thrive as long as their need for water, light and nutrients are met.*

14 What happens to garden plants in prolonged dry spells?
As the ground dries out, plant roots delve deeper towards cool, damp soil, in search of moisture. Initially, there are no visible signs of the effects of dry weather on plants.

15 How does heat affect the garden?
Hot, dry spells can affect the appearance of a garden. Flowers are quickly spent, deciduous trees and shrubs can shed their leaves and perennials, annuals and bulbs can turn yellow and begin to die back. Lawns turn brown. The effects of a garden parched of rainwater are temporary, however, and a spell of rain can soon restore the garden.

16 What is meant by microclimate?
Microclimate is used in connection with parts of the garden where the configuration of buildings, walls, fences and/or plants creates shelter and the climate in those areas is more benign than in the larger garden. For instance, a west- or south-facing wall provides protection from winds and heavy rainfall as well as reflecting heat. In such a situation it is possible to grow plants of borderline hardiness that may not flourish in open areas.

▲ *16 Walls create microclimates, protecting the plants close by.*

17 What happens to a garden during periods of severe cold?
Hardy plants are adapted to cold conditions – in fact, a cold spell can be necessary to plant health. Plants rest during cold weather, and the cycle of a winter followed by a warm, damp spring promotes prolific flowering. Plants do not grow in very cold weather.

18 How does wind affect plants?
Wind is the enemy of all plants – except in autumn, when it helps strip leaves from deciduous trees in preparation for winter dormancy and carries lightweight fertile seed far from the parent plants, spreading their genetic potential over as large an area as possible. But in spring and summer, cold, drying winds can damage the soft leaves of a range of plants, particularly leafy vegetables, hostas, and Japanese maples. Newly planted conifers are also vulnerable to wind damage. Affected areas of the plant show as unsightly brown patches. A physical barrier is needed to protect them from the worst of the weather.

19 How does rain affect the garden?
All plants need moisture to grow, but prolonged wet weather can put paid to many plants, especially fruit and vegetable crops. The wet encourages leafy growth, and while in the short term this looks very lush, it tends to be sappy and is highly attractive to invertebrate pests. Diseases, especially many fungal ones, are carried in

▼ *17 Cold is essential for some garden plants, triggering growth in the same way that many seeds germinate by heat.*

23 What is a rain shadow and how does it affect the garden?

The term rain shadow is applied to the strip of land adjacent to a wall or fence about 1m (1 yd) deep. During rain showers, this area of soil always receives less rainwater than open ground, because it is sheltered. This area is therefore unsuitable for plants that prefer reliably moist ground.

24 What is a drip line and how does it affect the garden?

The drip line is the edge of a tree's canopy when it is in full leaf. The soil beneath the canopy is sheltered and receives little moisture.

25 Does snow affect plants?

Snow does little harm to hardy plants, which are usually dormant during periods of snowfall. Tall conifers, however, are more vulnerable. Heavy snow can weigh down upper branches and make them break. Regeneration in spring is often poor. To counteract this, brush or shake off snow from the tops of conifers. Conifer hedges should be cut with a batter – a gentle slope outwards from top to bottom, so that snow falls away more easily.

rainwater and will proliferate during a damp spell. Very lush growth that has not been hardened by the sun is very vulnerable to frost. If a damp summer is followed by a hard winter, there can be some losses in the garden.

20 How does wet soil affect plants?

The majority of plants do not flourish in soil that is permanently wet. Fungi and bacteria proliferate in water and will feed on plant roots, leading to the plant's death. Permanently wet conditions cause roots to rot. Plants that are adapted to wet conditions are generally referred to as bog plants.

21 Which plants tolerate wet soil?

Aruncus dioicus
Astilbe
Cornus canadensis
Cornus stolonifera
Darmera peltata
Gunnera
Houttuynia
Lobelia cardinalis
Mimulus guttatus
Pontederia
Primula bulleyana
Primula florindae
Rheum
Salix alba
Salix babylonica
Scrophularia

▲ **20** *Many plants and wildlife thrive in damp and waterlogged conditions.*

22 What is a frost pocket and how does it affect the garden?

A frost pocket is a hollow, dip or area of low ground. During cold nights, frost and cold air settle there and can kill vulnerable plants. Avoid planting frost-sensitive plants here or, if you can, raise the surface with earth.

▼ **21** *Astilbes tolerate damp.*

▼ **21** *Primulas like a cool climate.*

ASPECT

By aspect we mean the way the sun lights the garden on its daily traversal. Which parts of the garden are lit at which times of the day, and which are predominantly shady, will determine what uses you can make of it and what will be the most suitable plants to grow.

26 Why is aspect so important?

The aspect, or orientation, of a garden determines when the sun hits it and for how long. It also affects at what times of day the house and any other surrounding buildings will cast shade over the garden. A garden that is filled with light all day, or from late-morning to midday onwards, will be warm. Conversely, a garden that receives direct sunlight for only a few hours in the day or late evening will be cold.

27 How does aspect affect the garden design?

Knowing which parts of the garden will be in sun and in shade at particular times of year will help you to decide where to site patios and lawns as well as whether to build pergolas or plant trees to cast welcome shade in summer. A garden that is sunlit all day favours sun-loving plants, whereas a garden that receives only a few hours of sunlight has an aspect that favours cool-loving plants, most of which are grown for their

▼ **27** *Trees, sheds and house walls cast shade, affecting the aspect of the garden.*

foliage. Knowing how much sunlight gets into the garden will help you choose an appropriate garden style – Mediterranean and sun-baked, for instance – as well as select the most appropriate plants.

28 Does the direction in which the garden lies affect what will grow?

Gardens that face east will be lit by the morning sun, then be shaded from midday onwards, when the sun is at its hottest. Such gardens will be predominantly cool. A west-facing garden is lit from midday onwards, and will be warmer – increasing the number of plants that will thrive there.

▲ **26** *The garden's aspect affects the growing conditions of everything that is planted within it.*

29 What are the best plants for a cool garden?

North-facing gardens are cool and shady. If they are enclosed, they may receive no direct sunlight at all, or maybe just a few hours in summer when the sun is directly overhead. Shade-loving or woodland plants do well here – hostas, ferns, Japanese maples (*Acer japonicum* and

▼ **28** *Sun-worshipping plants are best for gardens that are south- or west-facing.*

▲ **29** *In a cool, sheltered, shady garden, ferns can provide a lush, even subtropical, feel.*

A. palmatum) and some of the grasses and bamboos. If the garden is paved – as many courtyard gardens are – many of these can be grown successfully in containers. Variegated plants will not do well – they need some sun to bring out the variegation in the foliage. (In summer, bring your houseplants outdoors – many are rainforest plants that are adapted to low light levels and cool ambient temperatures. Be sure to bring them back under cover as temperatures drop in autumn.)

30 What are the best plants for a hot garden?

South-facing gardens that are hot and dry are ideal if you want to grow plants that are found in scrubland or desert in the wild. This category includes most of the woody herbs – lavender, rosemary, sage and artemisia – as well as the associated flora. Brooms will do well. Cacti can also be grown in containers if you experience wet or cold winters, when they should be brought indoors. Some cacti will withstand a few degrees of frost.

▼ **30** *Gardens that are in full sun make good locations for Mediterranean plants.*

▲ **32** *A hot, dry garden can be shaded with fabric sails, an awning or by tree canopies.*

Plants with soft, delicate leaves will not do well in a hot garden. Most shrubs will bask in sunlight for some of the day, but will need watering in prolonged hot spells.

31 Are there any problems associated with a garden that gets sun early in the morning?

East-facing gardens are delightful first thing in the morning, when they are drenched with sunlight – even, occasionally, during short winter days. But they are predominantly cold, particularly if they are small as the sun's rays are not sufficiently strong to warm the ground, even though the air may feel warm.

32 How can I create shade?

In a hot summer, we all crave shade when we're outdoors. If you already have a mature deciduous tree in the garden, this is the time of year when it will be in full leaf and casting its heaviest shade. Tall hedges also create shade along certain boundaries, depending on the time of day. You can also create shade in a garden with canopies and sails – which can be moved around the garden as required.

do well, however, especially if the soil is alkaline. Hardy cyclamen also thrive in these conditions. Hostas will grow, though the soil should be improved first. They will not produce such lush growth as they would in moist ground.

35 What is the solution for a damp, dark garden?

Many town gardens are enclosed and receive little direct light, if at all. These conditions suit many woodland plants, especially those that grow beside streams. Ferns and hostas are ideal, as well as other groundcover perennials such as bugles (*Ajuga*) and many hardy geraniums. Flowering plants may be reluctant to flower prolifically with no direct sunlight for part of the day. Aim for a tropical look. It is usually impractical to create a lawn in these conditions. Mosses and lichens appear in shady, dark places, so treat these with moss killer. Plant a spring-flowering garden.

33 How can I lighten a shady area?

White reflects available light, so paint walls with white masonry paint to lighten a dark area. Terracotta pots can also be painted. Grow white-flowered plants in containers. If they need sun to flower, place them in sun until the buds begin to open, then move them into the shade.

▲ *34 Dry and shady gardens require plants such as ivy that need little moisture.*

34 How do I deal with a dry, shady area?

Without doubt, these are the least hospitable conditions for the majority of plants – most will fail to flourish and be reluctant to flower. Ivies will

36 The garden is in full sun but the soil is always damp. What should I grow?

Bog plants will thrive here – *Rheum palmatum, Rodgersia, Aruncus* and, if space allows, *Gunnera*. Bog plants are always vigorous, as there is a constant supply of moisture to the roots.

▼ *33 Damp and dark gardens shaded with a dense tree canopy can be lightened by removing the lower tree branches.*

▼ *36 Damp and sunny conditions make plant growth prolific. Lawns grow very quickly in these conditions, too.*

HIDING UGLY FEATURES

Many gardens contain ugly, but necessary, features – a brick outbuilding, for instance, or some boundary structure, or even storage bins. It is seldom possible to do anything about these directly, but clever camouflage is often an option.

37 How can I hide an outbuilding?

If the building is sound, it can support a self-clinging climber. For year-round cover, consider an ivy – especially on a cool wall – otherwise try Boston ivy (*Parthenocissus tricuspidata*) or Virginia creeper (*Parthenocissus quinquefolia*). If the wall faces the sun, an evergreen ceanothus would provide dense cover, with the advantage of striking blue flowers in spring or summer (depending on the variety). Alternatively, you could screen the building with a trellis and use this as a support for deciduous clematis or annual climbers such as sweet peas (*Lathyrus odoratus*).

38 How can I disguise an unattractive fence?

While fences can support climbing plants in the same way that walls can, there is always the possibility that vigorous growth will pull the fence down. Various screening materials, such as bamboo on a roll, are available that can be stretched over fence panels and increase their aesthetic appeal. Wicker suits a cottage garden. If you have an ugly, but structurally sound, fence, you can cover it with a bamboo or willow screen. These are often sold on the roll or as panels and can be nailed to the uprights to hold them in place. Bamboo suits an oriental scheme. Such fences can also be painted or stained. Growing tall shrubs in front of the fence is an option, though a longer-term solution.

39 How can I screen out neighbouring buildings that overlook the garden?

This is a common problem of many town gardens and new housing developments. Rather than surrounding the garden with high fences and/or hedges that cast a lot of shade, you can cut off sightlines with

▲ **37** *Fast-growing climbers will eventually screen this metal container.*

a pergola. At ground level, the eye is naturally held by the horizontal beams rather than straying above. The horizontals, if covered by plants, also screen the garden from above.

40 How do I screen a wall?

Ivies (*Hedera*), which are evergreen, provide year-round cover and are self-clinging, so need training only in the initial stages. If the wall is a sunny one, evergreen *Trachelospermum jasminoides* and *Clematis armandii* will provide flowers, but will need support, as will deciduous climbers such as other clematis and Virginia creeper. Consider planting a hedge or

▼ **38** *A large expanse of wall can be screened effectively with plants.*

▲ **41** *A purpose-built storage unit with a green roof houses essential items.*

line of bamboo to hide the wall. Choose plants that you know that you have the time to maintain.

41 In what ways can I disguise functional features?

Useful items, such as dustbins, recycling boxes, compost heaps, water butts, sheds and manhole covers, can detract from the aesthetic impact of a garden, but are necessary to the smooth running of both house and garden. You can use bamboo screens or wattle hurdles to hide unattractive working areas of the garden and large planted pots to disguise ugly manhole covers.

▼ **39** *A pergola will not stop a garden being overlooked, but will create a barrier.*

SOIL

Soil is the medium that supports plant growth. Healthy soil is of paramount importance to any gardener who loves plants and wants to grow as many different types as possible. Keeping it in good heart is one of the most important aspects of gardening.

▲ **43** *Good topsoil is free-draining and full of nutrients. It contains equal parts clay, sand, silt and humus and helps to give new plants the best start.*

42 Why do I need to assess the soil?

Certain factors in the soil affect plant growth – how quickly it drains or how effectively it retains moisture are important issues. The amount of humus – decayed organic matter – is also important. A soil that supports a wide range of invertebrate life and bacteria will be good for the majority of plants. The degree of acidity/ alkalinity can also affect plant performance. Certain plants that revel in some soils can sulk in others.

43 What is the ideal soil type?

While beautiful gardens can be made on all soil types, most gardeners prefer a soil that is moist but well drained, a well-balanced mix of clay, sand and humus. Such soil is easy to work.

44 What is meant by soil profile?

Soil is made up of distinct layers of varying depth. The upper 30cm (12in) or so comprise the topsoil. This is usually dark in colour and contains organic matter. It usually supports a host of invertebrate life – earthworms, centipedes, millipedes, slugs as well as nematodes, bacteria, fungi and other organisms that are invisible to the naked eye. Some of these are harmful to plant growth but the majority are benign, having a positive benefit. Beneath the topsoil is the subsoil – usually lighter in colour and less fertile. Below that is a layer derived from the parent (or underlying) rock.

45 What is meant by soil structure?

Soil is made up of clay, silt, sand and humus (decayed organic matter). Ideally these are present in proportions that make a fertile, free-draining, sweet-smelling soil that will support a wide range of garden plants. Coping with, or improving, soil structure is an important aspect of gardening.

46 How can I tell what kind of soil I have got?

It is important to assess your soil structure, as different types support different varieties of plant. A quick test for soil structure is to scrape up a handful. Try rubbing it through your fingers as if making pastry. If it binds into moist crumbs, you have the ideal – a free-draining but fertile loam that suits the widest range of plants. If it runs through your fingers easily without binding, it is a dry soil of low fertility – suitable for Mediterranean plants and fleshy succulents. Improve it by digging in organic matter to help retain moisture. If you can squeeze it in your hands, it is a heavy clay that will be wet and cold but potentially high in nutrients. This suits many roses, bog plants and some of the bulbs. Very stony soils are bad news for most plants, especially root vegetables whose growth can be impeded. To assess the acidity/ alkalinity of the soil, a chemical test is necessary.

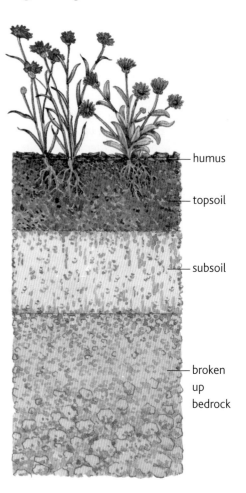

humus

topsoil

subsoil

broken up bedrock

▲ **44** *The layers of earth below the ground can differ significantly in depth and composition. Ideally, the topsoil should be a good quality, fine tilth at least one spade's depth. The quality of the topsoil can be improved.*

▼ **46** *Clay soil is heavy and contains particles that bind tightly together. It can be improved by digging in sharp grit.*

▲ **47** *Removing stones and weeds from the garden is hard work, but will make garden maintenance easier in the future.*

▲ **48** *A rotovator can be used to help incorporate soil improvers into the ground, making it more manageable.*

▲ **48** *The addition of quantities of garden compost, grit, manure and sand will improve the earth immeasurably.*

47 My soil is very stony – what is the solution?

Few plants do well in very stony soil. If possible, remove as many of the stones as you can by hand. If you have a significant area to deal with, it will be a time-consuming job and you may wish to hire a contractor to remove the top layer of earth, then buy in new topsoil as a replacement.

48 How do I improve soil and why does it matter?

Improving your soil increases the range of plants you can grow. Adding organic matter – garden compost or well-rotted farmyard manure – binds light, sandy soil into moisture-retaining crumbs, and opens up heavy soils, improving drainage. The health of the plants that you grow in the garden should improve too.

49 What does the pH scale mean?

The pH scale is an indicator of the soil's acidity/alkalinity. It runs from 0 to 14, with 7 being neutral. Lower numbers indicate degrees of acidity, higher ones alkalinity. You cannot judge the acidity/alkalinity of the soil by appearance, but there may be some indicators that provide a few clues. In a rural setting, look at what is growing wild. The presence of heathers suggests the ground is acid. Elders and ivies indicate that the soil is probably alkaline. Limestone also suggests alkaline soil, but it is possible to have an acid soil overlying limestone.

50 How does pH affect what I can grow?

Most plants have no preference for acid or alkaline soil, but some definitely do – rhododendrons, camellias, some of the heathers (*Erica*) and blueberries must have acid soil. In alkaline soil, they will die, as they are unable to absorb the trace elements they need to grow. Ivies (*Hedera*), carnations (*Dianthus caryophyllus*) and clematis seem to do better in alkaline conditions, but can often be grown – usually less successfully – in acid or neutral soil.

51 Should I do a soil test?

It is not necessary to test the soil unless you wish to include rhododendrons and other acid-loving plants, and have good reason to believe that the soil is alkaline. If you do a test, take soil from various parts of the garden. Pockets of acid soil can be present on mostly alkaline sites, and vice versa. Geological maps of the area provide information on the predominant soil type.

52 Can I permanently raise or lower the pH of my soil?

You can increase the alkalinity of soil long-term by digging in lime. This is often recommended in the vegetable garden to increase yields but is unnecessary on flower beds. Some garden limes are caustic and it may be necessary to wear rubber gardening gloves when applying them and goggles to protect your eyes.

You can dig lime into the soil at any time of year, but choose a dry, windless day – when there is less chance of the product blowing about – ideally, as far in advance of planting/sowing as possible.

Lime tends to persist in the soil over a long period, and it is easy to over-lime an area. Test the pH annually and apply lime only every two to three years as necessary to maintain the desired level.

It is possible, though difficult, to lower the pH of a soil by digging in Flowers of Sulphur or another acidifier. Add 125g per square metre (4oz per square yard) for every point on the pH scale you wish the alkalinity to drop. The application takes six months to take effect.

Any acidifying product will leach through the soil, so you should test the area every six months or so to judge whether further applications are necessary.

▼ **51** *Test the soil in different areas of your garden using a soil-testing kit because it may give different readings.*

53 How can I grow acid-lovers if my soil is alkaline?

The simplest solution is to grow the plants in containers filled with an ericaceous (acid) potting mix. Fortunately, most acid lovers thrive in containers. Alternatively, make raised beds. If made of bricks and mortar, line the beds with tough plastic (to prevent any lime in the mortar leaching into the soil) pierce the base for drainage and fill with acid topsoil. However, many would argue that acid-loving plants look out of place in a predominantly alkaline site. You need to keep testing the soil to make sure the acidity level is maintained. Most gardeners would instead choose to work with the soil they have rather than radically alter its chemical make-up.

54 Why is drainage so important?

Few plants do well in soil that is permanently wet. Moisture that does not drain away freely in soil becomes stagnant and is a breeding ground for fungi and bacteria, some of which can be very damaging to plants. Permanently wet soil is often described as 'sour' – not only do the plants not like it, but the multitude of beneficial organisms that live in soil do not like it either.

55 How can I tell if my soil does not drain properly?

If puddles of water persist on the soil surface during wet weather and shortly after, the drainage is probably poor. If you are visiting a garden for the first time during dry weather, look at the soil surface. A film of green over the soil surface is a reliable indicator that drainage is poor. The green is algae, which flourish in damp conditions. (The same algae is often seen on paving that also does not drain completely.) There are two ways to treat badly draining soil, both of which involve hard physical work or employing a professional, if you are unable to do the work yourself. Land drains and soakaways help move water away from unwanted areas.

▲ **53** *If you want blue hydrangeas but your soil is alkaline, grow them in a pot.*

▲ **53** *Hydrangeas turn pink on alkaline soil.*

Creating a soakaway and land drain

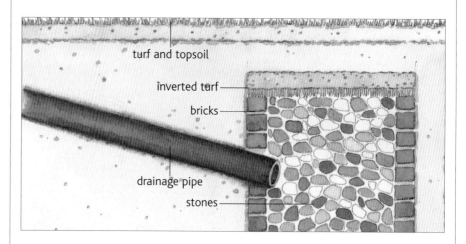

turf and topsoil
inverted turf
bricks
drainage pipe
stones

A soakaway In order to channel water away from the garden beds, dig a large hole at least 1.8m/6ft deep at a low point in the garden and fill it with clean rubble. The water from the garden should run into it, then soak away into the surrounding land.

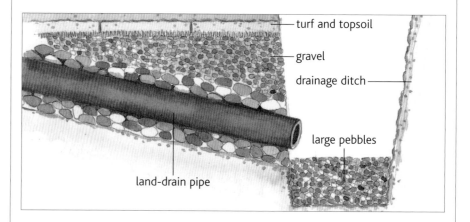

turf and topsoil
gravel
drainage ditch
large pebbles
land-drain pipe

A land drain With a land drain the water drains into a ditch, far away from any planted area. The water percolates through the soil and pebbles above and into the pipe, which then delivers the water to the drainage ditch.

▲ **56** Helenium

▲ **56** Aubrieta

▲ **56** Tagetes

56 Which plants do well on alkaline soil?

Acanthus spinosus
Acer negundo
Acer platanoides
Achillea
Alyssum
Aubrieta
Aucuba japonica
Bergenia
Buxus
Carpinus betulus
Ceanothus impressus
Cercis siliquastrum
Cistus
Clematis
Cosmos
Cotoneaster
Dianthus
Eremurus
Forsythia
Gypsophila paniculata
Gypsophila repens
Hebe

Hedera
Helenium
Helleborus
Juniperus
Ligustrum
Lychnis chalcedonica
Malus
Matthiola
Paeonia
Philadelphus
Pulsatilla
Pyrus
Robinia
Rosmarinus
Saxifraga
Sedum
Sempervivum
Sorbus aria
Stachys
Tagetes
Taxus baccata
Tilia tomentosa
Verbascum
Viburnum

57 Which are the plants that need or prefer acid soil?

Abies
Arbutus
Berberidopsis corallina
Camellia
Cassiope
Desfontainia spinosa
Erica
Eucryphia
Fagus
Gaultheria
Gentiana sino-ornata
Kalmia
Magnolia (some)
Pernettya
Pieris
Primula (some species)
Rhododendron
Stewartia
Styrax japonica
Styrax officinalis
Trillium
Uvularia

▼ **57** Erica

▼ **57** Trillium

▼ **57** Rhododendron

▲ **58** Achillea

▲ **58** Oenothera

▲ **58** Sedum

58 Which plants do well in a light, sandy soil?

Acanthus
Achillea
Anchusa
Artemisia
Ballota
Calluna
Clarkia
Clianthus puniceus
Coreopsis
Cytisus
Daboecia
Dianthus
Echinops ritro
Erica
Eschscholzia
Gypsophila
Helichrysum
Impatiens
Lavandula
Limonium
Nepeta x faassenii
Oenothera

Passiflora
Phlomis
Rudbeckia hirta
Sedum
Sempervivum
Tamarix
Tropaeolum majus
Yucca

59 Which plants tolerate or prefer a heavy, clay soil?

Amelanchier
Aristolochia
Aruncus dioicus
Aucuba
Caltha
Campsis
Chaenomeles
Citrus
Clematis
Cornus alba
Cotoneaster
Euonymus fortunei
Forsythia

Garrya
Gunnera
Hedera
Hemerocallis
Kalmia
Lathyrus latifolius
Liatris
Lonicera
Lysichiton
Mahonia
Mimulus guttatus
Passiflora
Philadelphus
Primula (some)
Pyracantha
Rheum
Rodgersia
Rosmarinus
Solidago
Taxus
Trollius
Viburnum
Wisteria
Yucca

▼ **59** Aruncus

▼ **59** Euonymus

▼ **59** Philadelphus

IMPROVING THE SOIL

All soils can be improved by additions of organic matter, preferably garden compost that you can easily make yourself. A compost heap is also an excellent means of recycling dead plant material, as well as kitchen and some household waste.

60 Why should I make compost?

Without doubt, compost is the best of all soil improvers. It has a beneficial effect on soil structure, opening up heavy clay and adding bulk to light sandy soil, thus increasing the range of plants you can grow. It also greatly boosts soil fertility – plants in soil enriched with garden compost will grow vigorously. Nowadays, as much waste material as possible should be recycled and composting is an excellent way to achieve this.
A vast range of material is suitable for composting.

61 What are the different methods of making compost?

The composting process involves the action of bacteria on organic material, which then breaks down to form humus. The secret to good compost is to make the heap large enough so that the interior is sufficently insulated for heat to build up and to be retained within the heap. If possible, make your composting bin at least 1m (1yd) square at the base. Small heaps tend to stay cool, especially if the composting material is wet, although it will break down eventually.

62 Can I make compost throughout the year?

You can add material to the compost heap all year round, but the rate at which it breaks down slows over winter. Material added to the heap in autumn can take up to six months or more to rot fully. In summer, things can break down within 6–8 weeks.

63 Where should I site a compost heap?

A compost heap can be sited in a sheltered position away from the house in sun or shade. The material will break down faster if it is in a warm place.

64 Do I need to turn the heap?

Composting is a hot process, and, being insulated, the material towards the centre of the heap heats up faster – and so breaks down more quickly than the material at the edge. Turning the heap with a garden fork allows both for the material to be redistributed, so that it composts evenly, and also aerates the heap – essential if the material is not to settle into dense layers that break down only slowly. That said, turning a compost heap is back-breaking work and can be impractical if the heap is a large one. There is also the risk of skewering frogs or other vertebrate wildlife that may be sheltering in the heap. Left to its own devices, a heap will eventually turn into usable garden compost.

◄ *63 This beehive-shaped compost bin is attractive as well as practical. A trap door at the back allows the compost to be removed. If you have a large garden and want several compost bins, dotted around the site, rather than in one area, then choosing a visually appealing composting bin such as this can enhance the garden area where it is sited.*

65 Should I use a composting bin?

A problem with many of the composting bins available is that they are too small for the appropriate temperature to build up. They can be more successful if the bin is insulated with bubble wrap to raise and maintain the temperature within the composting material. Composting bins that can be turned on a stand make it easier to turn the contents.

66 What is the difference between garden compost and potting mix?

Potting mix is the compost sold in bags in garden centres, supermarkets and DIY stores. It is sterile and contains no harmful bacteria or weed seeds. It is formulated for use in containers. Garden compost is made at home and contains a multitude of bacteria and – often – weed seeds. Its principal value is as a soil improver, either dug into the soil prior to planting or spread over the soil around plants as a mulch in spring or autumn. It is unsuitable for use in containers owing to the bacteria.

67 Can I use potting mix in place of garden compost?

In theory, yes, although the cost is likely to be prohibitively expensive. Many garden centres sell bags of soil conditioner – usually based on rotted animal manures – that are a better alternative. These are sweet-

▲ 65 Some local councils provide plastic compost bins to encourage recycling.

smelling and convenient to use. It is, however, much cheaper and more environmentally friendly to make your own compost.

68 What materials can I use to make garden compost?

Most plant material can be composted including leaves, annual weeds and lawn clippings. Perennial weeds can be used, but should be laid out in the sun for a few days to dry out first. Weeds should not be in seed, as the composting process does not destroy seeds. Lawn clippings can be added but are best mixed in among other material – otherwise they can form a dense, wet mat. From the house, vegetable peelings, egg shells, all cardboard and paper (shredded) and cotton rags and other natural fibres, hair and feathers and the contents of the vacuum cleaner can be used. Coffee grounds and used tea leaves and tea bags can also be added. These acidify the heap slightly.

◄ 68 Large quantities of greenery added to the compost bin will rot down quickly.

▶ 68 All manner of waste plant material and vegetable peelings from the kitchen can find their way into the compost heap.

69 Should any materials be avoided in the compost heap?

Meat and milk-based products and cooked vegetable waste attract rats. These can, however, be used in a wormery, in very small quantities. Diseased plant material should also be avoided. Evergreen leaves and conifer needles generally take too long to break down in the heap, though if you have plenty, you could set up a separate heap just for them.

70 What about hedge prunings?

Hedge prunings and other woody material are not suitable for composting, especially if taken from an evergreen or conifer hedge, as they break down so slowly. Shredding them finely first speeds up the rate of decomposition – alternatively, use the shreddings as an organic mulch for spreading around plants. Local authorities will recycle this material.

71 What is spent mushroom compost?

This is compost that has been used for the commercial growing of mushrooms, generally based on straw, dried blood and horse manure. Though it contains relatively few plant nutrients, it has an excellent texture so makes a good soil improver. However, most mushroom composts have a high chalk content, so this material should not be used in

▶ **72** *Brandling worms are not the same as ordinary earthworms – they live in decaying plant matter and piles of manure. They can be bought in fishing shops or by mail order.*

conjunction with acid-loving plants such as rhododendrons, camellias and blueberries. You may also find mushrooms growing in your garden!

72 What is worm compost?

Wormeries are usually more compact than conventional compost heaps or bins. A wormery uses brandlings – not earthworms – to eat material and create compost. Unlike a conventional heap, cooked vegetables can be added, as can waste dairy and meat products. It is necessary to drain off the liquid that accumulates at the bottom of the wormery as the worms work their way through the material. Most wormeries have a tap for this purpose. The liquid can be diluted to the colour of weak tea and used as a liquid feed on plants (including houseplants). The worms tend to be less active over winter, at which time you should bring the bin under cover. Severe cold can kill the worms. Some wormeries are small enough to be kept in kitchens, under the sink – actually a very practical position.

▼ **72** *A wormery needs to be insulated if it is to be kept outdoors, as freezing temperatures in winter can kill the worms.*

Wormeries produce small quantities of high quality compost and are a desirable addition to the garden.

73 Why is my compost cold, wet and smelly?

The composting process depends on heat generated by bacteria in the material to be composted to multiply and break down the material. For this, the heap has to be large enough for heat to build up in the middle and loose enough to allow air circulation. If the material is packed too densely,

▼ **73** *A compost heap made up of predominantly wet material, such as grass, will quickly turn slimey.*

moisture collects and cools the heap, making a telltale rancid smell as it stagnates. Turn the heap regularly with a garden fork and add material in layers of wet and dry clippings, avoiding too great a quantity of the same type of material. Grass clippings are notorious for compacting and are also wet material, so add them in thin layers between drier more woody material or strips of torn newspaper, or even thin cardboard. If your compost is still cold and wet by autumn, all is not lost. Spread it on the ground around plants – though take care it does not touch the stems of permanent plants, as this can lead to rotting – and allow the material to break down over winter. By spring it should have broken down.

74 Do I need to water the heap?

An active compost heap should be slightly damp but not sodden, with an earthy, not unpleasant smell. Lightly water the heap from a can during dry weather and/or when turning the heap if it seems too dry. You will need to do this more often if the heap is in sun, as it will dry out more quickly. Alternately, you could add wet material such as grass cuttings to the compost bin.

▼ **74** *You could water a heap on a hot, dry day with a fine jet of water from a garden hose.*

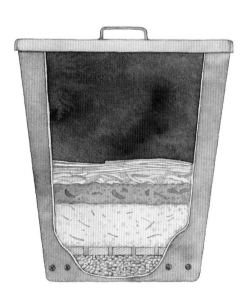

▲ **76** *Chicken manure is very rich, but it is high in uric acid, which can harm plants, so must be allowed to rot fully before use.*

75 How is farmyard manure helpful in the garden?

The manure of a range of farm animals can be used as a soil improver or added to compost. The animal must be vegetarian. If you are unsure of the animal's food source, then do not use the manure, this is particularly important if you garden organically. For use as a soil additive, farmyard manure must be well-rotted – in other words, stacked for up to 12 months before being dug into the soil. By this stage it should be crumbly in texture and odourless. If you have access only to fresh manure, add it in layers to a mixed compost heap – it makes an excellent activator. Animal manures often contain weed seed, especially if the animal has been pastured.

76 What are the advantages and disadvantages of different animal manures?

Farmyard manures are an excellent organic source of plant nutrients, but it is impossible to judge in what quantities these are present. Most manures are, however, excellent at adding bulk to poor dry soils. They can contain weed seeds that will germinate once in contact with garden soil. Pigeon and chicken manures are high in uric acid/nitrogen, often to the extent that they can 'burn' plant material on contact. These should always be well-rotted and spread around plants with caution – the manure should not actually touch the plant. They do, however, make excellent compost activators.

77 What is a compost activator?

An activator is an agent that speeds up the composting process. Commercially produced activators can be either sprinkled over the material as you layer it, or watered in. Animal manures can also be used as activators. Human urine is also a highly effective compost activator, assuming you can devise a discreet method of delivery.

78 Should I use chemical fertilizers?

Chemical fertilizers have their uses, even though many gardeners these days banish them from the vegetable garden. But if you are growing plants primarily for their flowers – such as roses, bulbs and annuals – it is difficult to find an organic product that supplies the necessary levels of potassium. Chemical fertilizers give reliable results here. They can also be used on hanging baskets and seasonal containers that are planted for their flowers.

79 What is leaf mould?

Leaf mould is made from the leaves of deciduous trees that are shed in autumn. Collect them during dry weather and fill large black plastic bags with them. Tie the bags and pierce them here and there to allow air to circulate. Put them somewhere cool and dark. The leaves are broken down not by bacteria – as is garden compost – but by fungi on the leaves. It is a cool process that takes one to two years, after which the leaves should have broken down to a crumbly, sweet-smelling mass that – unlike garden compost – is weed free. Use leaf mould as a mulch anywhere in the garden or add it to potting compost when potting up woodland plants such as clematis or camellias.

Making leaf mould

1 Build fallen leaves up into a heap, firming them in tightly so that little air is trapped.

2 Leaf mould can take a couple of years to rot down into a usable compost. Apply it to the garden in spring or autumn.

3 Leaf mould has a similar texture to pipe tobacco and smells clean, fresh and earthy.

▲ **80** *Old wool carpet can be spread over soil to keep down weeds. Hold it down with stones or bricks.*

▼ **80** *Cocoa shells, a waste product from the cocoa industry, smell of chocolate and are believed to deter slugs and snails.*

▲ **80** *Bark chippings look attractive. They make an excellent organic mulch and can also be used for paths.*

▼ **80** *Dried bracken makes an excellent autumn mulch that will break down after winter.*

▲ **80** *Newspaper can be spread on soil to prevent weeds from germinating and will rapidly break down after rainfall.*

▼ **80** *Plastic membrane makes a good weed-suppressant if you are looking for a long-term solution.*

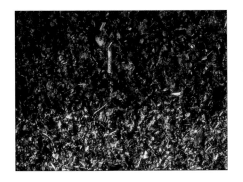

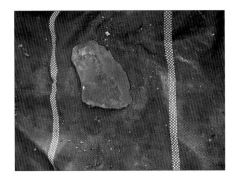

80 What is a mulch?

A mulch is a layer of material – organic or inorganic – placed around plants that can fulfil a number of functions. Organic mulches, such as bark chippings, garden compost or leaf mould, break down and are absorbed into the soil as earthworms pull them downwards, improving the

soil make-up. As part of that process, bark chippings – which have not rotted down prior to application – actually take nitrogen from the soil. To replace the nitrogen lost, it is necessary to sprinkle a nitrogen-high fertilizer over the mulch in spring. Mulches also reduce the number of weeds and prevent evaporation of moisture from the soil, helping to keep plant roots moist and cool during long, dry spells.

An inorganic mulch such as grit can do the job effectively, but like an organic mulch will tend to be absorbed into the soil over time. Decorative mulches, such as grit, pebbles or shredded bark can be laid over a membrane to prevent this. The membrane must be stretched over the area before the plants are planted through holes cut into the membrane.

◄ **81** *Peat is gradually being phased out of garden composts (soil mixes) in favour of more sustainable mixes.*

81 What is peat?

Peat forms naturally in certain wetland areas. Water in the soil acidifies and this, together with a lack of oxygen, prevents the complete decomposition of plant remains. Over time, this material compacts to create peat. This is a slow process – peat can grow at no more than 1mm per annum. Peat was traditionally used as a soil improver, though it contains no plant nutrients. It is collected from peat bogs, a valuable habitat for wildlife. Peat is used to add bulk to potting mixes and to improve the structure of soils. Its use is now frowned on, as it is not a renewable resource.

Coir, a coarse material extracted from the fibrous outer shell of a coconut, is now generally preferred by manufacturers. Coir-based potting mixes have attendant problems – they often have a loose texture and can hold excess moisture – but give excellent results if used correctly.

GARDEN STYLES

Whether urban or rural, large or small, all gardens benefit from careful planning and design.
Working out what you want beforehand as well as what your specific needs are will help you
to get the most out of your garden.

82 How can I decide on what to include when designing my garden?

First of all, you will need to think carefully about what you want from your garden and how you will use it. Do you need a space for family activities and outdoor entertaining? Items you may want to consider for this area include a patio or seating area, a water feature, a play area for children, and shrub and flower borders. Remember that any entertaining area should be close enough to the house and in a sunny position with summer shade.
Or maybe you want to grow your own fruit, vegetables and herbs in a kitchen garden?

83 How can I create a garden that has formal style?

The choice as to how formal your garden will be is a matter of taste. There are many design features to work with, but it is most likely that you will want to include a range of features and plants that reflect your own preferences. The key features of a formal garden are straight lines, a sense of order, symmetry, neatly divided garden compartments, and clipped plants such as box (*Buxus*) and yew (*Taxus*), as well as carefully chosen ornaments such as urns and statues. Your choices depend upon how much work you are prepared to do yourself or pay a contractor to do, in order to get the garden design that you want. Take into account too how much time you have to tend the garden as well as how much interest you have in the upkeep of it.

Paved gardens are formal, low-maintenance spaces, with raised beds and planted containers, as are courtyard gardens featuring large, architectural trees and shrubs and a water feature. You could also incorporate a knot garden or parterre,

a formal herb garden, or opt for a more traditional suburban approach with a rectangular lawn, straight-edged herbaceous and/or mixed borders and a rose bed, which is a popular style that suits many back gardens and is in essence formal.

▼ *83 Clipped box topiary creates a formal impression, but here the herbaceous planting softens the formality.*

▲ *82 Small gardens can incorporate features such as raised beds and seating areas to make them functional.*

84 How can I create an informal style?

Informal gardens, such as cottage gardens and wild gardens are more dependent upon the planting composition of the beds and borders than the design of plot to make a

statement. These gardens allow a certain degree of flexibility in their contents, which can change from year to year, with borders bursting with flowers of all sizes and colours, meandering paths, softly curved lines and edges. Plants are allowed dominance in this type of garden.

85 What is a cottage garden?

The cottage-garden style is recognized by its informality. A cottage garden may be a tiny yard or a large, open space with a meadow and orchard, but it is usually distinguished by an intimate atmosphere and a soft approach to the planting. Traditional features of the cottage garden, such as edible plants interwoven with ornamentals, informal mixed plantings and the use of native plants, have a universal appeal. Key plants in a cottage garden include *Campanula*, *Delphinium*, *Geranium*, *Lilium candicum*, *Lupinus*, *Paeonia*, *Papaver*, *Primula*, and *Viola*. The planting is characeristically colourful.

Other characteristics include natural materials, such as stone, cobbles or slate. And, while garden ornaments may well be found, a simple stone birdbath or sundial would be the hallmark feature.

▼ **85** *Arches covered in flowering climbers such as clematis and roses are an essential part of a cottage garden.*

▲ **84** *Although it has clipped hedging and topiary shapes, this garden has a more informal quality.*

86 What is wild gardening?

A wild garden majors on natives and other hardy robust plants that do not need staking, grown in an informal mix, usually towards the back of the garden. Some degree of control is necessary to prevent the stronger plants taking over and dominating smaller or less prolific plants.

Wild gardens are usually a haven for wildlife. The best wildlife gardens are a mosaic of habitat types – including woodland areas, meadows, hedges and water gardens – and will usually include a water feature, long grass, shrubs, trees and lots of flowers and fruit.

▼ **86** *A wild garden is one that may appear untamed, but which is carefully managed to provide colour and texture as well as food for wildlife.*

87 What is prairie planting?

A prairie planting attempts to replicate the sweeps of perennials that grow in some areas of North America. A flat or gently sloping piece of ground in full sun is the best site. Hardy plants of similar height are planted in bold drifts. Most prairie plantings major on daisy flowers – rudbeckias, heleniums, asters – and ornamental grasses, planted close enough together so as to support each other. A prairie planting is low maintenance – in fact, one of the principles is that the plants should

▲ **87** *Prairie planting has a long season of interest, and is dramatic and colourful when in bloom.*

not be fed so will not grow too lush. Most prairie plantings have a subtle colour range – fawn, beige, rust red, mauve and yellow – and are at their best in autumn.

88 What is a Mediterranean garden?

A successful Mediterranean garden has a relaxed, informal atmosphere, with rough stone slabs and rustic

terracotta tiles. Gravel suits informal areas and cobbles can be used for curved designs and path details. The overall effect is informal, but it results from the careful selection and positioning of the main elements. In cooler climates, a sun-soaked area is the wisest choice for location, making a sheltered courtyard in which tender plants will thrive. In hot, exposed situations, the inclusion of an arbour or pergola covered with vines or bougainvillea will provide shade.

Sun-loving plants, such as *Cynara cardunculus, Lavandula, Rosmarinus, Santolina chamaecyparissus, Artemisia ludoviciana, Pelargonium, Salvia officinalis* and *Thymus vulgaris* will create an authentic Mediterranean ambience. Add some large terracotta pots planted with common box (*Buxus sempervirens*) and bay (*Laurus nobilis*), or perhaps with olives, lemons and figs if your climate will allow. Also include some flowering climbers such as bougainvillea, orange-flowered campsis and perfumed white jasmine (*Jasminum*) to flourish on the sun-baked walls.

89 What is a seashore garden?

A seashore garden is in essence a relaxed space, reminiscent of fun-filled family outings and bracing sea breezes. Straight lines and neat planting beds are out of place, so opt instead for drifts of informal planting. The beds can be set among shingle. A more beautiful, though more costly, alternative is pebbles graded in size.

Planting should reflect the windswept shoreline, with waving grasses, sea thrifts (*Armeria maritima*), sea hollies (*Eryngium maritimum*), Californian poppies (*Eschscholzia californica*) and sea kale (*Crambe maritime*).

Decorate the scene with shells, strings of pebbles, driftwood, ropes, fishing nets and old lobster pots, as

◄ **88** *In a Mediterranean courtyard, heat-worshipping plants and herbs thrive. Gravel is often used to cover the ground, and the backdrop is important.*

well as areas of decking, striped awnings for shade, and hammocks to create an authentic seashore atmosphere. Remember, however, that collecting objects from the beach is illegal in many countries.

90 What is a Japanese garden?

This is a minimalist approach to gardening that uses rock, sand, water and restrained planting to create a tranquil, reflective space. Although it is difficult to reproduce this scene outside Japan, it is possible to capture its spirit. Simplicity, natural materials and a feeling of serenity are the keys to success. Use rocks, driftwood and plants such as mosses, bamboos, grasses, ferns and pines. Some splashes of floral colour can come from irises, spring blossom, camellias and autumn maples (*Acer*). You may wish to include a stone Buddha or lanterns, stepping stones through gravel areas, bamboo wind chimes and water features.

91 What are the key features of a contemporary garden?

A contemporary garden is most suited to buildings of a restrained formality. The style is essentially minimalist with an emphasis on clean lines, simple forms and the use of modern materials such as steel, concrete and granite. Glass, mirror and acrylic plastics can also be used for screening and

▲ **89** *This low-maintenance gravel garden has elements of a seashore garden, with its sparse and architectural planting, and its use of graded pebbles.*

sculpture. Natural materials such as stones and cobbles, timber and bamboo may be incorporated. Water features to provide sound and movement are also important, as are plants that make a structural statement, such as bamboos, grasses, phormiums, yuccas and cordylines. Planted containers feature in the modern garden.

▲ **90** *A traditional Japanese garden is predominantly green, with a manicured woodland setting and strong use of natural materials.*

▼ **91** *Metal, glass and stone are traditional materials that are used in a contemporary way in this garden design. The design predominates and the planting, with its minimal colour scheme, enhances it. Such a garden would be appropriate for a city garden that needs to make a strong design statement in a very small space.*

CHAPTER TWO

THE HARD LANDSCAPE

Sorting out the hard landscaping, the boundaries, and floor surfacing is usually the first part of any major garden development once you have decided on the design. The choices you make affect the look and feel of the garden as well as how different areas of the site are used. Forward planning is essential for success. Materials have to be sourced, delivered and stacked on site, with anything that is large being brought in before the boundaries are erected. Will you be doing the work yourself or hiring a contractor to do it for you? Many hard landscaping materials are expensive and will be subject to heavy use once in place, and so should be looked on as a major investment. But if the work is done properly, years of satisfaction lie ahead.

WALLS   FENCES   ARCHES, ARBOURS AND PERGOLAS   HEDGES   PATIOS AND PAVING

    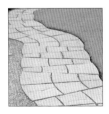

LAYING A PATIO   PATIO PROBLEMS   DECKING   STEPS   PATHS

◀ *The right choice of paving material can enhance the garden.*

WALLS

Besides their principal function of enclosing a garden, walls can be used within a garden to break up the space into smaller 'rooms' or to make raised beds. And, of course, they can be used to support and protect a range of different plants.

92 What is a retaining wall?

The function of a retaining wall is to hold back soil and prevent erosion at points in the garden where there is a change of level.

93 What materials can I use to build a wall?

A retaining wall can be built with bricks, hollow concrete blocks (in conjunction with reinforcing rods) or with large stones. A retaining wall needs to be very strong to withstand the weight of the soil behind it.

▼ **92** *Retaining walls can become an integral feature of the garden.*

Strong, but unattractive bricks or concrete blocks can be rendered with plaster. Bricklaying is a skill that needs practice to perfect. Most garden projects involving bricklaying are best left to professionals – especially freestanding walls – but if the wall is 75cm (30in) or lower, it is worth having a go yourself.

94 What do I need to consider before building a wall ?

Walls are permanent features that have an impact upon the landscape, however small or large they are. Walls take time and effort to build and can cost considerably, so proper planning

▲ **93** *Walls made of brick age sympathetically and can look attractive.*

and preparation are essential. The land on which the wall is to be built needs to be structurally sound and the wall's foundations need to be solid and secure. The choice of materials should be appropriate to the proposed function as well as satisfying any visual appeal. If the wall is to be a retaining wall, drainage of water from the surrounding land must be taken into consideration.

95 What is a dry-stone wall?

A dry-stone wall is a wall built of natural stones that are laid without mortar. For maximum strength, the stones are of different sizes and should nest closely together. In gardens, dry-stone walls are used to stabilize banks and terrace edges. Their appearance can be softened by planting trailing alpines in the small gaps between the stones.

96 How do I build a dry-stone wall?

There is an art to building a dry-stone wall. Make a footing as described for a retaining wall. Depending on the size of the stones, the first course (set below ground) can protrude above ground. For stability, use larger stones

▲ **93** *Walls can be rendered with plaster and painted with outdoor paint.*

towards the base of the wall, smaller ones above. For good water run-off, the wall should have a 'batter' – it should slope slightly away from you as you look at it from the front. Line the back of the wall with a water-proofing material such as a length of pond liner. Although a dry-stone wall is traditionally unmortared, you may prefer to mortar the stones discreetly for added strength and stability. Often dry stone walls are best left to the professionals to build, since they are time-consuming and need skill.

▼ **97** *Small plants, such as sempervivums, need very little encouragement to take root in a wall.*

97 How do I plant flowers in the wall?

Use seedlings or small rooted cuttings. Shake off old compost from around the roots and gently ease these into suitable gaps in the wall. Press equal parts of potting mix and grit around the roots, then spray with water to consolidate the mixture. Spray the plants daily until they are well established.

▼ **97** *Once established, plants can almost cover a wall.*

▲ **95** *This dry-stone wall has additional slate detailing to add interest.*

98 Climbing plants are pulling the mortar out of the wall. Should I save the wall or the plant?

It is best to repair the wall – plants can regrow. If the climber is trained on wires, trellis or some other support, it may be possible to remove this from the wall, lay it on the ground, then carry out any necessary repair work. Otherwise, cut the plant down to near ground level and see if it regrows.

FENCES

Usually made of wood, fences offer a lightweight and inexpensive alternative to walls, for screening neighbouring properties or dividing the garden. The style of fence panel that you use and the way that it is made can have a bearing on the design of the garden.

▲ **99** *Woven fences are popular and relatively inexpensive to purchase.*

99 What types of fence are there?

The most commonly used types of fence are closeboard, comprising overlapping upright planks, and waney-edged, made of overlapping horizontal planks. The former is more expensive. Most fencing panels are made of softwood (conifers). Hardwood fencing (from broad-leaved

▲ **99** *Woven willow or hazel fencing looks attractive, but is more costly.*

trees) is more expensive, but more durable. Woven willow or hazel fences are suitable for rural gardens.

100 How long will a fence last?

If properly made, using good materials, and regularly maintained, a fence should last for ten years before it needs replacing.

▲ **99** *Bamboo fencing is decorative rather than practical for a boundary.*

101 How often do I need to treat the fence with preservative?

To prolong the life of a fence, you should treat it annually with a preservative. Apply the product during dry, still weather in spring and summer, when it will dry most quickly and rain will not ruin the finish of the paint.

▼ **99** *Picket fencing is perfect for informal front gardens.*

▼ **99** *Waney-edged fencing can overlap horizontally or vertically.*

▼ **99** *Vertical overlapping boards incorporate trellis for climbers.*

Erecting a panel fence

1 Post spikes are an easy option to secure a post to the ground. Use a special tool to protect the spike top, then drive it in with a sledge-hammer. Check with a spirit (carpenter's) level to ensure it is absolutely vertical.

2 Insert the post in the spike, checking the vertical again, then lay the panel in place on the ground and mark the position of the next post. Drive in the next spike, using a mallet and a wedge to protect the top of the spike.

3 There are various ways to fix the panels to the posts, but panel brackets are easy to use. Simply nail the brackets to the posts, using an appropriate length of nail. Alternatively, use screws to bracket the panel to the post.

4 Lift the panel and nail in position, through the brackets. Insert the post at the other end and nail the panel in position at that end.

5 Check the horizontal level both before and after nailing, and make any necessary adjustments before moving on to the next panel.

6 Finish off by nailing a post cap to the top of each post. This will keep water out of the end grain of the timber and extend its life.

102 How do I fill in the gap at the base of a fence?

Ideally, the fence panels should sit on a few courses of bricks set in the ground. But it is simpler to place horizontal gravel boards at the base of each panel. The boards can be held in position with short stakes hammered into the ground, or if you left room, they can be attached to the bottom of the fence posts. A gap is not necessarily bad: plants will disguise it.

103 How do I erect a fence on sloping ground?

If you are making the fence with panels, the panels must be stepped. The uprights need to be taller than usual to accommodate the gradient. Fill in the triangular gap beneath each panel with gravel boards cut to shape. This will work if the gradient is gentle rather than a very steep rise, in which case you will end up with a very large triangular shape that needs filling

somehow. Alternatively, you can make your own overlapping vertical fencing, with each plank cut to size. Insert the uprights 1.8m (6ft) apart up the slope, then screw two or three horizontal planks, parallel with the ground and evenly spaced, between them to link them. Nail upright planks to these, following the line of the slope. This type of fencing takes longer to make, but because the planks can be cut to size there will not be an awkward gap.

ARCHES, ARBOURS AND PERGOLAS

Adding structures to the garden to walk under or sit beneath helps add height to a design and lifts the eye from ground level. Climbing plants will soon mask their supporting structure. Once covered, they provide desirable shade in summer.

104 What is an arch?

Arches are ideal for providing a focal point in a given area or for inviting visitors to pass through to reach a different part of the garden. They add height to small or flat gardens and are useful for marking the division between two sections of the garden or where two paths cross. They may frame a view out of the garden or draw attention to a particular feature within the garden itself. Arches are available preformed in a range of different styles and materials, including wood and metal. Climbing shrubs can be trained to grow up and over them. Arches can be bought ready-made from the garden centre or you can build a wooden arch yourself. Alternatively create an arch in hedging or by training tall plantings into an archway.

▼ **104** *Metal archways can be purchased at garden centres and are relatively easy to assemble. They create an instant effect that will be enhanced with planting.*

▼ **104** *This hedging has been carefully manipulated to form an arch that is tall enough to walk underneath. The arch and the path beckon the visitor.*

▲ **105** *An arbour set in a secluded area of the garden is the perfect place to eat outdoors. Hanging baskets add to the lush planting effect.*

105 What is an arbour?

An arbour has a similar function to a pergola, but is designed to shade a seating area – usually a patio or deck – creating an area of retreat in a garden. An arbour may be roofed but can also be open to the elements, functioning mainly as a plant support. Arbours are perfect for suntraps, where the planting can be used to practical effect.

106 What is the function of a pergola?

A pergola is a series of linked archways over a path. The main function of a pergola is to provide shade over a walkway, but it also makes an ideal support for a range of climbing plants – roses, wisteria, clematis, as well as grape vines (*Vitis vinifera*). Laburnum walkways are also popular.

▲ **106** *A contemporary, painted pergola makes a strong design statement.*

107 How high should I make a pergola?

If the pergola is to be used as a support for climbing plants, it should be at least 2.5m (8ft) high, to allow adequate headroom as you walk through it. If it is to be a purely ornamental feature, you can make it lower, but not less than 1.8m (6ft).

108 How do I build a pergola on the patio?

Siting a pergola over a patio and attaching parts of it to the house wall provides both privacy and shade when festooned with climbers. You can attach the overhead beams to the brick wall of the house by using joist hangers. Simply remove some of the mortar, insert the hanger, and refill with mortar. Use ground anchors and supports for the posts in order to keep the timber out of contact with damp ground, so prolonging its life.

109 What climbers can I use over a patio pergola?

Aim for a light covering of climbing plants rather than a thick canopy that blocks out all sunlight. An ideal choice is grape vines because they lose their leaves in autumn, thus allowing winter sun to reach the patio. You could also try the ornamental vine, *Vitis coignetiae*, which has vibrantly coloured leaves in autumn.

Assembling an arch

1 Establish the post positions, allowing a gap between the edge of the path and the post, so that plants do not obstruct the path. Dig a 60cm (2ft) deep hole for each post.

2 Position the legs of the arch in the holes. Backfill with the excavated earth and compact with your heel. Check that the legs are vertical using a spirit level.

3 The next stage is to construct the overhead beams of the arch. Lay both halves on a large flat surface and carefully screw the joint together at the correct angle.

4 Nail the overhead beams to the posts. In this example they slot into the tops of the posts and are nailed in place.

HEDGES

Hedges, deciduous or evergreen, can be used to mark boundaries and create divisions in a garden. They can be tall or low, depending on need, and formal or informal. Flowering hedges can be highly decorative as well as functional.

110 How do I choose the best hedging for my garden?

Think about the purpose for which the hedge is intended. Do you want a windbreak or a thick hedge to cut down road noise and pollution? Do you want a hedge that can be trimmed to a sheer surface to show off other plants or something decorative to mark the boundary of the property? Is a thorny hedge necessary to secure a boundary? Do you want to divide up the garden space into 'rooms' with hedging?

111 What is the best choice for a dwarf hedge?

Common box (*Buxus sempervirens*) is the traditional choice – it tolerates regular clipping and produces dense, even growth. It is also evergreen so looks good all year around and is faster growing than is commonly assumed, though avoid the cultivar 'Suffruticosa'. 'Faulkner' is supposed to be resistant to box blight. *Lonicera nitida* is an alternative. 'Baggesen's Gold' has bright yellow leaves.

▲ **112** *Lavender makes an attractive low-growing hedge around informal beds and borders.*

112 Can I have a dwarf flowering hedge?

Miniature roses can make an excellent dwarf flowering hedge, though they are not evergreen. A single-flowered variety in a vegetable garden will attract beneficial wildlife. Step-over apples also make an effective edging in a kitchen garden with the

▲ **116** *Berberis is an excellent choice for a low hedge. It is dense and thorny, with a show of spring flowers and autumn berries.*

advantage of fruits in autumn. Lavender (*Lavandula*) and rosemary (*Rosmarinus*) are also popular. They can be left shaggy and allowed to flower freely, but can also be trimmed closer, with sparser flowers.

113 Which are the best plants for a formal hedge?

To create a formal hedge, the plants have to be able to tolerate the severe cutting required to maintain a sheer surface. For an evergreen hedge, yew (*Taxus*) and *Thuja* are among the best. Suitable deciduous plants are beech (*Fagus*) and hornbeam (*Carpinus*). Beech hangs on to its dead leaves in autumn – a possible attraction – but on the debit side is slow growing.

114 Which are the best hedging plants for attracting wildlife?

To encourage wildlife, such as birds, small mammals and insects, you need a mix of plants, some evergreen, some deciduous, that will provide food and shelter. A mix of hawthorn

◄ **113** *Though it cuts a formal line, this beech hedge has been left unclipped.*

▶ **116** *Many roses are suitable as hedging plants.*

(*Crataegus*), holly (*Ilex*), dogwood (*Cornus*), viburnum and hazel (*Corylus*) is effective. Bear in mind that the plants will grow at different rates, so be sure to prune vigorous plants to ensure that they do not unduly shade and crowd out slower growing ones. Remember also that many insects live in tree bark – native plants support a much wider range of wildlife than imported species. A hedge will also take time to grow.

115 What are the best hedge plants for creating a windbreak?

The function of a windbreak is not to form a solid barrier but to filter wind. The best windbreak hedge, though suitable only for a large garden, is a mix of Leylandii conifers (*Cupressocyparis leylandii*) and European larch (*Larix decidua*). The larch is deciduous and will buffer strong autumn and winter gales when out of leaf. Plant the trees alternately. This type of hedge is excellent if the boundary of the garden is next to a major road that carries heavy traffic. In a small garden, try a mix of lower-growing deciduous and evergreen trees, such as hollies (*Ilex*), hawthorn (*Crataegus*) and viburnums.

116 What are the best plants for a flowering hedge?

Roses (*Rosa*), berberis and pyracantha make excellent flowering hedges. Acid-loving camellias are also excellent if you have acid soil.

117 Which are the best plants for topiary?

Yew (*Taxus*) is the best plant for topiary. With pruning, it has dense growth and a sheer surface is easily created. It can be clipped into complex shapes. Box (*Buxus*) has similar properties. Many conifers can also be trimmed into shapes such as pillars, cones or domes. Suitable evergreens include (*Prunus laurocerasus* and *P. lusitanica*) and *Viburnum tinus*.

118 I want a hedge that will grow quickly to screen an unattractive site, what is the best option?

The fastest growing hedge is undoubtedly made from Leylandii conifers, but you must be prepared to prune the plants regularly to keep them under control. A more manageable alternative is western hemlock (*Thuja plicata*).

119 Which hedging plants are suitable for a coastal garden?

Ceanothus thyrsiflorus
Cupressus macrocarpa
Elaeagnus pungens

▼ **117** *Yew* (Taxus baccata) *is the classic choice for formal hedging and topiary.*

Escallonia
Euonymus japonicus
Griselinia littoralis
Hebe rakaiensis
Myrtus communis
Olearia
Rhamnus

120 Which are the best thorny hedging plants to deter unwelcome visitors?

Berberis
Crataegus
Mahonia
Poncirus trifoliata
Pyracantha
Rosa
Rosa rugosa
Tamarix parviflora

121 I need a lot of hedging plants – what is the most economical way of buying them?

Hedging plants can be cheap – if you visit a dedicated nursery. These usually advertise in the gardening press, especially during the autumn period when many plants are available bare-root. Most will supply mail order or deliver if the order is a large one. The more plants you buy, the lower the unit cost, though you may end up buying more than you actually need if you have to buy in multiples of ten. Hedging plants supplied in pots are more expensive.

122 Do I need to plant hedging in double rows?

Only if you need to develop a thick hedge in a relatively short space of time – say within three years. In this scenario, offset the rows, so that the plants are planted in a zig-zag and buy double the number of plants.

123 When is the best time to plant a hedge?

Autumn is the best time if you are buying bare-root plants. These plants are field grown and are lifted in autumn when dormant and are usually available by mail order. They should be planted as soon after receipt as possible. Pot-grown plants are available from spring and should also be planted soon after purchase.

▲ **121** *A hedge made up of one- or two-year-old plants will take time to fill out like this, but will look attractive.*

124 How high can I allow my hedge to grow?

It is usual to keep a hedge within 1.8–2.2m (6–8ft). This is usually sufficient to create a sense of privacy in the garden depending on how thick the hedge is. Check with your local

▼ **122** *Planting a double row of hedging plants will create a thick impenetrable barrier within five years, provided the plants are looked after.*

▲ **121** *Some hedging is sold with multiple stems, to be separated out, in the same container.*

authority if any by-laws are in place restricting the height of hedges. If the hedge marks a boundary with a neighbour, a higher hedge may be acceptable provided you both agree. This height of hedge is also a manageable one to trim.

▼ **124** *A tall hedge creates privacy, but needs time spending on it to keep it neat, tidy and healthy. A trim twice a year should be sufficient.*

125 How do I calculate how many hedging shrubs I need to buy?

Measure the length of the proposed hedge, then divide by the planting distance given in the table. Add on an extra plant at the end of the line. The recommended planting distances are valid whatever the size of the plant – small plants need not be set closer together than larger ones, even though the hedge will look sparse initially.

126 What are the recommended planting distances for different hedging plants?

Berberis	45cm (18in)
Buxus sempervirens	30cm(12in)
Carpinus	60cm (24in)
Chamaecyparis lawsoniana	60cm (24in)
Crataegus	45cm (18in)
Cupressocyparis leylandii	75cm (30in)
Elaeagnus	45cm (18in)
Escallonia	45cm (18in)
Fagus sylvatica	60cm (24in)
Griselinia	45cm (18in)
Ilex aquifolium	45cm (18in)
Lavandula	30cm (12in)
Lonicera nitida	30cm (12in)
Pyracantha	45cm (18in)
Rosa (miniatures)	30cm (12in)
Rosa (shrubs)	60cm (24in)
Rosmarinus	30cm (12in)
Taxus baccata	60cm (24in)
Thuja plicata	60cm (24in)

▲ **126** *Planted at the correct distance apart hedging plants will bind quickly.*

How to plant a hedge

1 Dig over the soil and fork in a soil improver and a general fertilizer if the ground is poor.

2 Remove any weeds and large stones. Level the soil, then lightly tread it down to firm it.

3 Lightly break up the surface with a garden fork. Mark the planting holes.

4 Make a hole for each plant. On bare-root plants, look for the soil mark near the base.

5 When planting, make sure the soil mark is at the same level as the surrounding soil.

6 Wrap tree guards around the base of each plant to protect the plants from rabbits.

PATIOS AND PAVING

A patio or area of paving can be used for a variety of purposes, such as sunbathing, entertaining, sitting in and enjoying the garden, but should be planned carefully to fit in well with the rest of the garden if you are to make the best use of it.

127 How do I know where to site the patio?

Practicality normally dictates where patios are to be sited – usually just outside the house if it is be used as a standing area and for drying washing. Be sure to make it big enough for a range of uses. If you want to use the patio for sunbathing, site it in full sun and screen it from prying eyes. Having a paved or decked area next to the house is very practical, as this part of the garden usually receives heavy traffic and grass would rapidly show signs of wear. If you follow certain design principles, the patio will be pleasing to the eye, even if it is predominantly functional.

128 How do I ensure the patio links visually with the house?

You can employ a number of strategies. If the house is brick, either make the patio of brick or, if you have to use paving, consider edging it with brick. Base the proportions of the patio on one of the house's features that overlooks the intended site. For instance, if a house window measures 1.8m x 1m (6ft x 3ft), use the ratio 2:1 in the patio. Hence if the patio needs to be 10m (30ft) wide – the length of the house – consider a patio depth of 5m (15ft).

130 If I choose paving, what are my options?

Most expensive of all is natural stone. Nowadays, the quarrying of many sources of naturally occurring pavement is prohibited. Hence, much stone paving is imported. While it is very beautiful to look at, many gardeners might have a moral problem

▲ **127** *Patios are best sited in a sunny spot, if you intend to use the space for entertaining and sunbathing. You will need to ensure that you have easy access to it from the house.*

▼ **131** *Crazy paving works very well in an informal garden, and is a good way of using broken slabs.*

129 What are the advantages and disadvantages of paving?

Paving is very hard-wearing to the point of permanence, but is expensive and time-consuming to lay. Added to that, the materials needed – paviors, hardcore, sand and cement – are all heavy to use.

▶ **130** *Machine-manufactured paviours have a uniformity that makes them easier to set in position, and also makes paving a large area of land a more financially viable option for many.*

justifying the carbon emissions created by transporting such a heavy material over long distances (besides the loss to the source environment), as well as the exploitation of children who labour in the quarries.

The thickness of the stones may vary too, making them tricky to lay. Artificially produced stone is a good alternative. Paving slabs, or paviors, are available in a wide variety of sizes and colours. Cobbles and setts are designed to nest into each other.

131 I have a large area that needs paving, but a tight budget – what are my options?

Try sourcing reclaimed paving through the Internet or the small ads in your local press. Contact local contractors who are working on a garden near where you live – they may be replacing an existing paved area with new materials. They may agree to deliver the old materials for a small charge. The Internet is a good source of information for finding secondhand materials locally.

132 What is flexible paving?

Unlike rigid paving, flexible paving is laid straight on to sand – the individual paviors are not cemented into position but nest together. This means that they can be removed at will and used elsewhere in the garden should the need arise, although this is quite an arduous job. This method can also be used where the paviors are butted tight against each other.

133 What is a gravel garden?

An area of gravel in the garden is an inexpensive alternative to paving or a lawn, but it is not suitable for a patio area. Gravel blends well with plants, requires very little maintenance and can be used successfully in formal or informal designs. It can also be used to fill in areas among other hard surfaces, perhaps where paving is awkward to lay. Gravel comes in many different shapes, sizes and colours, which will all look different in sun or shade or when dry or wet.

134 How do I create a gravel garden?

Excavate the area to the required depth – approximately 5cm (2in) of gravel is ideal. Level the ground. Lay heavy-duty, black polyethylene or a mulching sheet over the area. Overlap the strips by about 5cm (2in). Cover with gravel and rake level. To plant through the gravel, draw it back from the planting area and make a slit in the polyethylene. Insert the plants,

▼ **131** *Plain square paving stones are often economical to buy and being all the same size are easy to work with.*

▲ **134** *Graded pebbles are low maintenance and blend well with other natural materials in the garden.*

feeding the soil underneath if necessary. Firm in and pull back the polyethylene before recovering with the gravel. You will need to use edging blocks to prevent the gravel from spreading beyond the designated area or ensure that it is a few inches below the grass if the gravel area is surrounded by a lawn. Adding a few larger cobbles and large stones in strategic places can enhance the natural look.

LAYING A PATIO

Laying paving can be very rewarding. It is a straightforward process, but can be physically demanding, depending on the weight and quantity of your chosen materials. For the best results, take your time. Preparation is the same for flexible paving and fixed paving.

135 How do I mark out a patio?

It is important when making a patio that the edges are straight throughout and that the angles are exact – once made, any inaccuracies are startlingly apparent. Peg out the area with strings stretched between short stakes that have been hammered into the ground. Check the angles with a builder's square. Do not necessarily aim to align the sides with boundary walls or fences that may themselves not be dead straight. The angles in the patio itself should be true. The strings should be at the height of the finished patio to act as a guide when laying the slabs.

136 How do I ensure the strings are level?

As you hammer in the pegs, check the level by laying a plank or flat piece of wood between two of them. Using a spirit level, keep knocking in the pegs until you are satisfied that the line is true.

▲ **135** *Only a few simple tools are needed for marking out a patio – wooden pegs, a set square, ruler and string.*

137 How do I stop rainwater from puddling on the patio surface?

If the patio adjoins the house, it is good practice to lay it with a gentle slope away from the house, so that rainwater will drain away from the house. A slope of 2.5cm (1in) over 2m (6ft) is adequate for good drainage.

138 How do I create a slope?

When marking out the site with pegs and strings it is easy to incorporate a slight decline away from the house. Lay a plank between pegs spaced 1.8m (6ft) apart. Over the second peg, place a chock of wood 2.5cm (1in) thick. Lay a plank between the two pegs and keep knocking in the second one (with the chock) until you achieve a level. Remove the chock. If you then run a string from the top of the first peg to the top of the second, it will show the desired drop of 2.5cm (1in) over a distance of 1.8m (6ft).

139 The patio is going to adjoin the house. How far below the damp proofing course should it be?

There should be a gap of at least 15cm (6in) between the damp course and the upper surface of the patio.

Laying flexible paving

1 Dig out the area and edge with bricks or blocks, checking the level carefully.

2 Spread a layer of builder's sand over a base of scalpings and tamp this down firmly.

3 Starting at one end, bed the paving blocks directly on to the sand.

4 Finish by brushing sand over the surface to fill in any gaps.

Laying slabs on mortar

1 Dig out the area to a depth of 20cm (8in), firm the base, and then spread a 10cm (4in) layer of scalpings.

2 Spread a 5cm (2in) layer of builder's sand over the scalpings. Tamp this down. Put blobs of mortar on the sand.

3 Place a slab over the blobs of mortar, manoeuvring it carefully into position.

4 Tamp down the slab. Check the level carefully, and lift it to add more sand or cement if necessary.

5 You can either lay each slab individually or cover the whole area with builder's sand first.

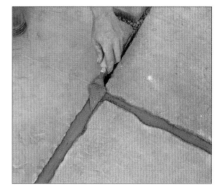

6 Mortar between each slab. Otherwise, simply brush dry mortar into the spaces between the slabs.

140 How deep a foundation should I dig for a patio?

You need to allow a foundation depth of at least 15cm (6in) below the paving slabs. Remember to allow extra for the thickness of the slabs. This depth of foundation is suitable for a patio that sees normal, light foot traffic – a much greater depth would be needed for an area of hard standing for cars and other vehicles. If the ground is soft and peaty, dig a deeper foundation to allow for a 15cm (6in) layer of scalpings.

141 How do I make the foundation of the patio?

Dig out the site to the appropriate depth. Remove all traces of perennial weeds, especially the roots of woody plants. As a further precaution, put weedkiller on the site. Put down a 10cm (4in) layer of scalpings. Tamp this down firmly with your feet or with a whacker plate, which can be hired from a tool hire company. Check the level carefully. On top of this, put a 5cm (2in) layer of builder's sand.

142 How do I lay fixed paving slabs?

Mortar the slabs in place individually. Starting in one corner, with a bricklayer's trowel, lay out four strips of mortar to create a 'box', slightly smaller than the slab. If the slab is larger than 45cm (18in) across, make a central cross of mortar or place a blob of mortar in the middle. Place the slab in position and firm it down, checking the level as you do so. Carry on laying further slabs in rows.

143 Should I allow a space between each slab for fixed paving?

Slabs can either be positioned so they butt up against each other tightly or can have a small gap between them. Use spacers about 1cm (½in) thick laid between the slabs. You can remove the spacer once each slab is in position.

144 How do I finish off the patio?

Once you have finished laying the slabs, leave them for a couple of days to allow the mortar to harden. If you have allowed spaces between slabs, brush dry mortar over the patio to fill the gaps. Brush off any excess. Either spray the patio with a light, fine jet of water from a hose or just leave to allow rainfall and moisture in the atmosphere to do the job for you.

145 Can I cut slabs?

When designing a patio it is best to choose a size that makes any cutting of slabs unnecessary. But if it is unavoidable, slabs can be cut. Lay a straight edge on the slab where you need to make the cut and score a line along it with the edge of a bolster – a special tool for cutting hard materials. Score the underside in the corresponding place. Work along the line with the bolster, hitting it with a club hammer, to deepen the cut. Place the slab over a length of timber, the cut to one side. Tap sharply with the hammer's handle to split the slab. Special powered cutters can also be hired. It is essential to wear the appropriate safety gear, as flying chips can cause serious eye injuries.

146 Can I use house bricks for paving an area of land?

Most house bricks are not frost-proof. Bricks laid horizontally absorb moisture which will expand as the weather freezes, splitting the brick. In the garden, engineering bricks (which are frost-proof) should be used.

147 Where can I find reclaimed paving materials?

Try the gardening press, the small ads in your local paper or the Internet. Visit reclamation yards for antique urns, statues and other one-off pieces.

▼ **148** *Here a large area of patio is made visually appealing with the introduction of a grid of bricks to break up the expanse of crazy paving.*

148 How do I break up a large expanse of paving?

A large paved area can look blank and uncompromising, though sometimes it can be unavoidable, for instance if you need to link the house with an outbuilding or garage. To break up the space, consider using a combination of different materials. If you are laying square or oblong slabs, replace a few here and there with cobbles set in concrete, or run lines of brickwork through the space in a decorative pattern. You can also create interest by incorporating a raised bed or water feature.

149 How do I lay concrete?

Mark out the area as for a patio, then dig out the soil to a depth of 20cm (8in). Prepare a formwork for the area to be concreted by nailing planks to stakes driven into the ground at 1m (3ft) intervals around the perimeter. The top of the planks should be at the level of the top of the proposed concreted surface. Put down a 10cm (4in) layer of scalpings and tamp this down. Pour in sufficient wet concrete to reach the top of the formwork. Work this into the corners, and level it by drawing a beam back and forwards across the top of the form-work. (To concrete a large area, divide it up into strips by creating a form-work about 1m (3ft) wide and no more than 4m (13ft) long. Cast the concrete strip by strip, waiting for the first strip to harden before making the second.)

▼ **148** *Feature areas, such as this floral pebble design that has been cemented into a path, add interest to a paved area.*

PATIO PROBLEMS

While paving is definitely a low-maintenance choice in many situations, you will still need to give it some attention periodically to keep potential problems at bay. But most are easily managed, provided you deal with them promptly.

150 The paving is sinking, what can I do?

The ground under the paving has subsided – and in all probability the paving has inadequate foundations. Your only option is to dig it up and re-lay it with deeper foundations.

151 How do I deal with weeds coming through the paving?

It is not usually practical to dig out weeds that appear in the cracks in paving by hand. They are best treated with a contact weedkiller. Spray the weeds in spring, when they are in full growth. You can help absorption of the product by stamping on the weeds first, to bruise the leaves. This allows optimum absorption of the product into the plant's system. Alternatively, burn them off with a flame gun.

152 How to I prevent green slime from appearing on my patio?

Moulds and slimes grow in surface moisture, and a green film on paving or decking is a sign that water is not draining quickly. Either the surface was laid without a slope or there are no suitable gaps through which water can run. It is not usually possible to create drainage on existing patios. Treat with an algae killer regularly.

153 How can I deal with wood stain drips on a paved surface?

Stains on paving are best dealt with quickly while they are still wet. However, it is still possible to remove them, provided the product is a water-based one. Fill a bucket with hot, soapy water, then scrub the area hard with a stiff brush. Rinse thoroughly. If the product is not water-based, wear rubber gloves, and try applying a small quantity of paint stripper or other solvent with a stiff brush to an area of the stain. If this is effective, treat the whole area before rinsing

thoroughly with clean water. Ensure that the rinsing water does not run off into the soil or on to nearby plants.

154 I have a house with an adjoining patio that is at the same level as the damp-proof course. Is there anything I can do about this?

If an existing patio was created at the same level as the damp-proof course and you cannot run to the expense of making a new one from scratch, you need to take remedial action and install a soakaway to prevent rainwater collecting and potentially damaging the brickwork. Lift the layer of slabs adjacent to the house. Trim them by 15cm (6in). Excavate a trench next to the house, 15cm (6in) across by 15cm (6in) deep. Re-lay the slabs. Fill the trench between the house and the new edge of the slabs with shingle or gravel.

155 I have an uneven patio. Can I pave over it to make an even surface?

For structural reasons, all paving and patio jobs should start by excavating

▲ **151** *Mosses and other weeds often appear in the cracks between slabs because water tends to collect there.*

the existing surfaces. It is not a good idea to lay a patio on top of what may already be there, as the reason for its uneven surface is that it is unlikely to have been compacted evenly, or to have uniform drainage. A new tightly packed sub-base reduces the chances of uneven settlement in future.

▼ **152** *A sharp jet of water can sometimes be sufficient to clear a paved area of algae.*

DECKING

Decking offers a sympathetic alternative to stone or concrete paving in many situations. It always looks stylish, working well with many different types of garden furniture, and with minimal maintenance can be a pleasure to use.

156 What are the advantages and disadvantages of decking?

Decking is much cheaper than stone, is relatively lightweight and easy to assemble and looks good straight away – hence its popularity with property developers.

Timber decking is much less durable than paving and may not age well unless regularly treated. It can become slippery when wet. Mice and rats sometimes make their home beneath a deck.

157 Are there any situations where decking is preferable to stone?

Wooden decking always looks appropriate in areas where there is already a lot of natural timber. If the house is surrounded by trees, or if it is part of a housing development that has been creating amid existing, mature trees, decking can make a sound design choice. Decking is also a good choice near water – if you live either by the sea, or if the garden backs on to a river, canal, lake or reservoir. If the garden has a large

pond decking is appropriate. Timber is traditionally used for piers and jetties, so a deck is always in keeping.

158 When is the best time to make a deck?

Decking is best laid during periods of warm, dry weather. Wood swells in wet conditions, then shrinks. All the

▲ **156** *Decking is relatively quick to assemble and looks attractive next to the house or other timber structures.*

timbers you use should also be dry to minimize the risk of shrinkage once the deck is complete. Dry wood is also easier to cut and sand. It is also much more pleasant to work in dry weather.

▼ **157** *Decking works particularly well with other wooden structures.*

▼ **157** *Decks are great for rooftop gardens because of their light weight.*

▼ **164** *Diagonal decking patterns are fiddly but economical to lay.*

▲ **159** *Maintain decking with an appropriate preservative to prolong its life and keep it looking its best.*

159 Do I need to treat the timbers?

Most wood sold for decking will probably already have been treated with a chemical preservative applied at high pressure, but you should make sure that you treat all cuts as you make them to seal them. This will prevent the timbers rotting later on. It is also important to use corrosion-resistant screws.

160 How do I prepare the site for decking?

Clear away vegetation, then mark out the area with pegs and string, making sure it is square. Dig out a foundation – you need to allow for a 10cm (4in) layer of scalpings that the supporting joists will sit on. Dig out the area and remove any large stones and the roots of perennial weeds. Compact the soil, then spread over scalpings to a depth of 10cm (4in) and tamp this down. Place over a weed-suppressing membrane and hold this down with a thin layer of grit or shingle.

161 How do I attach a deck to the house?

If the decking timbers are to butt up to the house, it is necessary to bolt a horizontal beam (or 'ledger') to the house to which you can attach the framework. Do not screw the ledger or joist directly to the house wall – insert spacers, 10mm (½in) thick, between it and the wall that will allow for ventilation. Check that the ledger is level before tightening any bolts. You need to allow a gap of at least 15cm (6in) between the damp course and the upper surface of the deck.

162 How do I construct a framework for a deck?

The framework for a deck should be slightly smaller than the finished deck. It consists of joists laid parallel to each other fixed to a plank at each end that hold the structure together. Space the joists about 40cm (16in) apart. Use angle brackets or galvanized joist hangers to ensure that the joists are square and join the end planks at right angles. Attach them to one of the end planks first, then screw the second in position. Check that the construction is square and level at all stages. If the framework is more than 3m (10ft) square, stabilize it with noggins (bracing pieces), 40cm (16in) apart, between the joists.

163 How do I lay the decking?

Lay the decking planks at right angles to the supporting joists. They should overhang slightly at the edges. It is undesirable to cut the planks, but if this is necessary, the cut ends should meet above a joist. Allow a gap of 6mm (¼in) between the planks to allow for expansion later on when the deck is wet.

164 What is the most economical way of laying the planks?

If you lay the planks on the diagonal, although more cutting is required, you will find you need less timber to complete the deck.

165 How do I prevent decking from becoming too slippery?

Decking is prone to be slippery under foot during wet weather, Clean it frequently. Treat the timbers regularly with a moss killer. You can improve the surface grip by nailing chicken wire over the top. You can also treat the timber with special paints that give a limited amount of grip.

▼ **165** *Coat decking with an aggregate to provide grip during wet weather.*

STEPS

Flights of steps create interest in gardens, allowing you to negotiate different levels. Depending on the site, you may need just a few, low steps or a steeper staircase. You can break up a long flight with larger landings.

166 How do I measure a slope for steps?

If you want to make steps on sloping ground, first it is necessary to measure the slope. To do this, use a plank of wood or other flat piece of wood. Place one end at the top of the proposed flight of steps. Hold the other end at the foot of the flight of steps. Raise the plank to the horizontal, checking with a spirit level that the level is absolutely flat. You can then measure the length of the flight and also the distance from the end of the plank to ground level at the bottom of the flight – the overall height of the steps.

167 How big should the steps be?

If the steps are to be easy to negotiate, the length of the tread plus twice the riser should equal about 65cm (26in) – the longer the tread, the shallower the riser, therefore. It is important that all the steps are the same size if falls are to be avoided. A very long flight, however, could incorporate a landing

▼ 167 *The length of these steps from front to back is deep, allowing for a full step to be taken on each level.*

▲ 167 *These steps incorporate a bridge over water before moving on to a larger decked area.*

mid-way as a resting place. Depending on the size of the landing, you may be able to add a garden seat or large container for plants.

168 How do I mark out the site?

Drive pegs into the ground to each side of the proposed flight of steps and run strings pulled taut between them. Run horizontal strings across to mark the front of each tread. Check that the horizontal strings are level using a spirit level. Keep checking the levels as you dig out earth, so that you dig out far enough for each step.

169 How do I make cut-in steps?

Dig out the steps and compact the soil with your feet. Start at the lower end of the site. Dig out a footing for the riser about 15cm (6in) deep and twice the depth of the bricks for the riser. Put in a 7cm (3in) layer of hardcore then top with concrete. Once this has hardened, lay a line of bricks for the riser, checking the level as you do so.

Back-fill with scalpings, then lay the slab for the tread over it. To allow for water run off, the tread should overhang the riser slightly and should slope down towards the edge. Lay the next riser at the back of the tread and continue until the flight of steps is complete.

▼ 167 *A steep slope will need a flight of short steps, but try and make them as broad as you can to prevent falls.*

PATHS

Paths link different areas of the garden, leading from doors and gates to patios and lawns or through beds planted with shrubs, flowers or vegetables. Often overlooked, they can receive a lot of traffic so should be made with care.

▲ **172** *Stone paving slabs with a brick detail are a practical material for a path that receives heavy wear.*

▲ **174** *Winding paths are unusual but can add interest to a flat, open space, encouraging you to take your time.*

170 How do I construct a path?
A path needs a similar foundation to a patio and should be marked out in the same way. If you are intending to use gravel or other loose material such as slate, you need to edge the path with a line of bricks or timbers held in position with short stakes.

171 How wide should the path be?
A path should be at least 1m (3ft) wide if you are to walk along it with a wheelbarrow or lawnmower. Twice that width will be sufficient for two to walk along side by side.

172 What is the best material to use for a path, and what are the advantages of each of the different types of material?
Consider how much traffic the path is likely to receive – for instance, if it is used by every family member on their way in and out of the property, then the path needs to be hard wearing, and in this instance,

paving is the best option. Paving can be economical but takes skill to set out. It may need planting to soften the harsh appearance. If a path is to be used to connect one part of a garden to another, and will receive less wear, then bricks may be used to create patterns that are practical and pretty.

173 How do I prevent paths from becoming slippery in winter?
Whenever icy weather is forecast, sprinkle salt or grit on any regularly used paths (and other paving) to keep them free of ice.

174 How do I stop an unattractive path being the focal point of a small garden?
If an existing path looks too dominant, consider paving over it with a more sympathetic material. Planting each side of the path with spreading plants, such as catmint (*Nepeta*), which will grow to flop over it will help to soften the edges. Consider erecting a pergola over the path for training climbers over. This will lift the eye from ground level. You could also try changing the shape of the path by adding in bays, or by changing some of the surface material to a more appealing type.

▼ **174** *This path has 'bays' that invite you to pause for a moment to inspect the plants. The bays could also be used to house large terracotta pots or other containers filled with seasonal displays of bulbs or other shrubs.*

CHAPTER THREE

LAWNS

A lawn – an open area of lush green grass – is a major constituent of many gardens, creating a restful oasis of colour among the planting schemes. Lawns can cover a large area of the garden and have plenty of uses, particularly if you have small children who need a play area, or if you want a space for entertaining and sunbathing, as well as being a showpiece for the keen gardener. Easier on the eye and softer underfoot than hard paving, a lawn is much less durable than paving, decking or gravel areas. A lawn can be high maintenance, but with some planning this need not take over your gardening schedule entirely. But what is the best way of making a lawn and looking after it? How often should it be mowed? And how should you deal with bare patches, moss and other problems? Are there any lawn pests you should be aware of? And what, if any, are the alternatives to a lawn?

CREATING A
NEW LAWN

ALTERNATIVES TO
LAWNS

MOWING LAWNS

OTHER LAWN
CARE TASKS

LAWN PROBLEMS
AND SOLUTIONS

MEADOW
PLANTING

◀ *Lawns are suitable for back gardens and are a perfect foil for colourful plantings.*

CREATING A NEW LAWN

If you are creating a garden from scratch, a lawn may well be at the top of your wish-list. You have several options as to how to go about this, much depending on the time you have to spend on the project, and whether you want an instant lawn or are prepared to watch it grow.

175 What is the best site for a lawn?

Grass grows best and thrives in full sun. However, it is also possible to create a lawn in a lightly shaded position, but it is essential to choose a grass type that is shade tolerant.

176 Is it better to sow grass seed or to buy turf to make a new lawn?

For an instant lawn, lay turf. If you have time on your hands, seed offers more choice as there is a range of different seed mixes available – grass for heavy wear or shade, for instance. A seed-sown lawn will need a year or two before you can subject it to heavy traffic. Sowing seed, though less convenient, is always a cheaper option than laying turf.

177 What types of lawn seed are there?

Lawn seed manufacturers create lawn mixes that fulfil a variety of purposes. Hardwearing mixes suit family gardens, where the lawn will be used as a children's play area. If you have limited time for gardening, look for a low-maintenance mix. You can also find mixes for fine lawns, drought, shade and overseeding existing lawns.

▼ **176** *Turf quickly transforms a small area of garden into a beautiful focal point upon which the eye can rest.*

▶ **177** *Grass paths need to be fairly wide and sown from hard-wearing seed or they will quickly deteriorate.*

▲ **179** *The smaller the lawn, the less time-consuming the aftercare that is needed on new grass.*

178 What is the best time of year for sowing seed?

Lawn seed is best sown in autumn or spring – ideally, during a spell of mild, damp weather, conditions that will speed up germination and encourage the emerging seedlings to grow rapidly.

179 What aftercare is needed on a newly sown lawn?

Unless rain is forecast, regularly water the site after sowing with a sprinkler or garden hose (adjusted to produce a fine spray). The soil should not be allowed to dry out. Once the seedlings have germinated, keep the ground well watered – a young lawn is very susceptible to drought.

180 How can I protect the seeded lawn from birds?

The best way to keep birds off a newly sown lawn is to suspend a net 10–15cm (4–6in) above it. Knock short stakes into the ground around the perimeter of the lawn at 1m (3ft) intervals and attach fine netting to them.

181 How do I keep cats off the site?

Deterring cats from freshly cultivated soil is difficult, but strewing thorny twigs, such as those of berberis, over the site may discourage them.

182 How long do I have to wait before I can walk on the lawn?

Newly sown lawns are extremely sensitive to wear. Until the grass is well established, it is all too easy to crush the young blades and compact the soil underfoot. You should only go on the lawn during its first year in order to mow it.

183 How do I prepare the site?

Site preparation is the same, regardless of whether you are sowing seed or laying turf.

184 The lawn has grown patchily – what can I do about this?

If germination appears patchy, the seed was probably sown unevenly. Re-sow any bare patches and, so far as is possible, thin overcrowded seedlings. It is important to deal with this problem as soon as possible – weed seeds can germinate on areas where the lawn seed was sown too thinly, and seedlings that are too close together are prone to damping off and other fungal diseases. New seedlings should soon catch up with the others.

Preparing the site for a lawn

1 Dig over the site and clear it of all weeds, rubble and large stones. Break down clods of soil.

2 Level the site – any mounds or hollows will make the lawn difficult to mow later.

3 If you know the soil to be poor quality, dig in organic matter such as garden compost or well-rotted farmyard manure. Add grit if the drainage is slow. You can also fork in a general garden fertilizer.

4 Firm the soil, then rake in both directions to create a fine tilth. If possible, let the site rest for around ten days. This allows any weed seeds brought to the surface during digging to germinate. Hoe them off.

185 What is the best way of sowing seed?

The seed box or packet should indicate what weight of seed should be sown per square metre/yard.

186 What should I do once the seed has germinated?

Lawn seed should germinate rapidly. Once the blades have reached 5cm (2in) in height, roller the seedlings to consolidate the roots. Rollering also firms the soil around the roots. If you do not roller the lawn, there is a real risk that you will rip the seedlings out of the soil when you do the first mowing. Wait a few days after rollering, then give the grass a light trim with a lawn mower.

187 What is the best time of year for laying turf?

Ideally, a turf lawn should be made in autumn or late winter. Turf dries out very quickly and this is less likely to happen at these cool times of year. However, turf can also be laid at other times, but unless the weather is mild and damp, you will have to water it regularly to ensure the turves knit together.

188 I am having some turf delivered but will not be able to lay it for some days. Will this matter?

Turf is dug up from the field in strips that are then rolled up like a Swiss roll (jelly roll), with the blades of grass on the inside. The soil is very prone to

▼ **185** *For large areas, sow the seed with a special broadcast spreader.*

Sowing grass seed

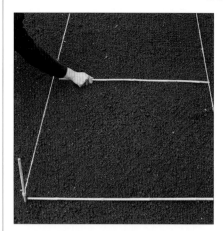

1 To calculate how much seed you will need, measure the site first. Mark out a grid with strings stretched between pegs.

2 Broadcast the seed at the rate recommended by the lawn seed manufacturer. Sow by hand or use a lawn seed spreader.

drying out and cracking. Additionally, the grass itself tends to turn yellow as it has no access to the light. Turf should therefore be laid as soon after delivery as possible. If it has to be stored, keep it somewhere cool and out of direct sunlight. Water the rolls lightly to keep them moist and cover them loosely with heavy duty plastic or hessian (burlap) to slow down the rate at which they dry out.

189 How do I lay turf?

Starting at one end and, working from outside the proposed lawn, unroll a strip of turf on to the prepared soil. Cut off any excess with a sharp garden knife. Gently firm the strip with the head of a rake held vertically. Lay a plank on this strip. Standing or kneeling on the plank, lay the second strip (the plank spreads your weight, avoiding damage to the turf). For the most economical use of the turf, use the excess cut from the first strip to form the start of the second, and always lay the turf in the same direction (left to right or right to left). Butt the second strip tightly up to the first using the head of the rake held upside down. Also butt tightly the joins between rolls. If you work systematically, the joins between the

rolls will form a zigzag pattern, spreading the joins evenly across the garden.

190 How do I finish off the lawn?

Once the turf is laid, brush over a mixture of equal parts lawn sand and garden compost, paying particular attention to the joins between strips.

191 What can I do with excess turf?

Excess turf makes an excellent composting material. When stacking, lay the turf grass side together to discourage growth and leave to rot down. Turf can also be used to line large planting holes for trees and

▼ **192** *A sprinkler can be used to water a large new lawn.*

▲ **191** *Excess rolls of turf will eventually break down to become good-quality garden compost.*

shrubs – the grass should be in contact with the sides and base of the hole. You can also use turves to line the base of aquatic baskets in the water garden. The turves help retain the soil inside the basket.

192 What aftercare is needed for a new turf lawn?

A newly laid turf lawn will not stand heavy traffic until the turves have knitted together. If the weather is mild and damp, this can happen in a couple of weeks. If it stays predominantly warm and dry, water the lawn regularly, especially if you can see the individual strips of turf.

▲ **192** *Once established, a lawn will give pleasure over many years with only a little regular maintenance.*

You should be able to use the lawn after about six to eight weeks. But you need to take care during the first year after laying a turf lawn. The less you use it during this time, the quicker it will establish.

Laying turf

1 To lay a square or oblong lawn, start working from outside the proposed area to avoid compacting the prepared soil. Starting from one end, roll out the first strip of turf, firming it down as you go. Cut off the excess turf at the opposite end.

2 Lay a plank on the turf and stand on this to lay the next strip. Starting at the same end as you began, use the excess cut from the first strip to make the start of the second strip. This is the most economical and neatest way of laying the turf.

3 Butt this up as tightly as you can to the first strip and firm the join with the back of a rake or with your hand. Continue in the same way till the lawn is laid. Finally, topdress the lawn with a mix of lawn sand and garden compost.

▲ **193** *An expanse of grass has been broken up with a brick circle.*

193 How do I make a circular lawn?

For a circular lawn, lay the turf in strips, progressively longer then shorter, to cover an area larger than the finished lawn. Decide where the centre of the circle is to be, then knock a stake into the ground at that point. Attach a string to the stake. Mark the radius of the circle on the string with a blob of paint. Hold the string in your hand, along with a can of spray paint at the point you have made the mark, and pull it taut. Keeping the can as close to the ground as possible, move around the centre, spraying the ground as you do so. Cut out the circle with a half-moon cutter. You can also use this technique to mark out a circle on an existing lawn, if you want to plant a tree or make a circular flower bed in the lawn.

▲ **194** *Use a flexible rope or garden hose to mark out an irregular shape.*

194 How do I mark out an irregularly shaped lawn?

If you want a kidney shape, use a length of hose pipe and lay it out in the desired shape. Use tent pegs to hold the pipe in position.

195 What is a turf roof?

Turf roofs offer good thermal insulation. Waterproof the roof first with a membrane to prevent damp and to encourage water retention around the roots so that the turf does not die in hot, dry weather. A special mat allows water to circulate below the turves, which are contained in netting sacks to prevent erosion.

▼ **195** *A turf roof can be planted with ground-cover plants. Grass has to be trimmed with shears.*

Marking out a circle

1 To mark out a circle for an island bed in a lawn, decide on the central spot and insert a cane in the ground at that point.

2 Attach a string to the cane. Measure the desired radius, then tie an inverted plastic drinks bottle (or plastic cup with a small hole in the base) to the string.

3 Fill the bottle or cup with sharp sand. Trace an arc, allowing the sand to trickle through, thus marking out the circle.

4 This technique can be used to 'draw' a circle on prepared topsoil in order to lay turf in the pattern of a circular lawn. If you use this method, cover the circle area entirely with turf, then repeat the marking out procedure, this time on the turf, and trim the turf to size.

ALTERNATIVES TO LAWNS

Lawns are not for everyone, and there are several alternatives that are worth considering. But it is a mistake to think that you can eliminate maintenance altogether. Even non-plant material needs some work to keep it looking good.

196 What is a chamomile lawn?

Chamomile (*Chamaemelum nobile*) is a herb with foliage that has a scent reminiscent of stewed apples. Making a lawn of chamomile as an alternative to grass is possible, but something of a romantic conceit. The plant is difficult to establish, has a tendency to die back and is never as hardwearing as grass – a chamomile lawn is not used for recreation. The site must be well-drained and in full sun. Ideally, choose a non-flowering chamomile variety such as 'Treneague'. Buy plants in quantity and plant about 30cm (12in) apart, or even closer. Peg down any long stems for good coverage and to encourage rooting. Once established, trim over the lawn with shears. It is impractical to attempt a large lawn – it can be a better idea to make a chamomile 'seat'. Make a raised bed, incorporate a square or two of decking (on which you can put a cushion later), then plant around these with chamomile. Thus, you will

be able to run your fingers through the chamomile from a seated position without crushing the plants.

197 Are there any artificial products suitable for garden use?

Synthetic grass was developed initially for sports use, as natural grasses do not stand up to extensive wear and tear. It is now sometimes used for large indoor exhibitions where a natural lawn would be impractical. Artificial grass can also be used in the garden in areas where a natural lawn

◄ **196** *Chamomile lawns are perfect for very small areas of the garden that do not receive much wear.*

cannot be established – for instance, in a very shady garden or on a rooftop or terrace. Rubber chippings made from recycled tyres are available for use in play areas.

198 Does artificial grass need any maintenance?

While you do not need to water or mow an artificial lawn to keep it looking good, you should either brush it to remove dirt and debris or hose it with a strong jet of water. In a wet area, moss can appear on the lawn. Treat this with a standard moss killer.

199 What are the alternative surfaces to grass in the garden?

Decking can look attractive, but is harder under the foot than grass. In a shady and damp garden moss is a good alternative to grass.

▼ **196** *Low-growing, non-flowering varieties of chamomile can be planted into a 'cushion', that can be sat on.*

▼ **197** *Artificial lawns can be very convincing – they are hard-wearing, resistant to cutting and non-slip.*

▼ **199** *In this shaded area, moss has been used to advantage as an alternative to grass.*

MOWING LAWNS

Many gardeners enjoy mowing the grass as it is a satisfying garden task with an instant result that transforms the garden often in little time. A freshly mown lawn looks smart and makes the whole garden look well tended.

200 How often do I need to mow the lawn?

Mow the lawn regularly during the growing season – spring to autumn – when it is growing rapidly. You can mow less frequently in winter, when growth is slower or may have stopped altogether.

201 Can I mow when the grass is wet?

It is best not to mow when the grass is wet, as wet clippings can cling to and clog up the mower blades. However, you can try setting the blades higher so you remove less of the grass.

202 Is it possible to dry the grass?

You can sweep the grass with a stiff besom broom to remove excess moisture and make the grass easier to cut. You can also use the broom to remove overnight dew if you want to mow the lawn in the morning.

▼ **200** *Regular mowing actually encourages the grass to grow – a well-tended lawn sets off neighbouring plants.*

▲ **202** *Early in the morning, a lawn may be covered in dew. Brush this off with a broom before mowing.*

203 Can I leave the grass clippings on the lawn?

It is best to collect the lawn clippings, either in a box fitted to the mower or by raking them up after mowing. If you leave them on the lawn, they will clog up the grass and prevent rainwater filtering down to the grass roots. Lawn clippings make excellent composting material but tend to compact, especially if wet. Make sure they are well mixed into the heap.

Creating a mowing strip

1 Tidy the edge of the lawn with a half-moon cutter, using a paving block or plank as a straight edge.

2 Level the ground using a plank, lightly tamping it down all over with a mallet or lump hammer. Set the first of the blocks in place.

3 Continue placing blocks along the edge so that they are flush with the lawn.

▲ **205** *If you need to cut a new edge, stand on a plank to spread your weight.*

▲ **206** *Stripes on a lawn always give the garden a professional look.*

204 What is a mowing strip?

If the lawn adjoins flower beds, edging the lawn with a line of bricks or small paviors will make mowing easier. There is less risk of damaging the plants in the beds and the bricks give a neat edge to the lawn. If you decide to use brick, they should be engineering bricks, not ordinary house bricks, which can split during freezing weather.

205 How do I keep the edges of the lawn neat?

Trim the edges of the lawn – if there is no mowing strip – with a half-moon cutter, a dedicated tool that is used for cutting turf. Trim the grass edges with shears.

206 How do I create professional looking stripes on a square or rectangular lawn?

To achieve classic lawn stripes, it is necessary to have a lawnmower that is fitted with a roller. First, mow a strip at each end of the lawn to allow you to turn the mower (on a rectangular lawn, it is usual for these to be at the shorter sides). Then, starting at one side, mow the length of the lawn. Turn the mower in the turning area,

then mow the next stripe, overlapping the first stripe slightly. Success depends on having a good eye for a straight line. Reverse the direction of the cut on alternate mowings, so that the grass grows evenly.

207 How do I create stripes on an irregularly shaped lawn?

First, mow a strip all around the perimeter of the lawn. Stand at the edge of the lawn at a point where the centre of the lawn is directly in front of you. Choose some spot on the far side of the lawn that will be easy to keep in view – a tree, shrub or statue, or maybe a particular plant. Mow a stripe down the middle of the lawn first, focusing on the spot you have selected. Turn the mower and mow a strip next to it, overlapping it slightly. Continue until one half of the lawn is cut. Return to your starting position and mow the other half of the lawn in similar fashion.

208 How can I create interest in a large lawn?

By altering the height of the blades, you can create low-relief patterns in a lawn, leaving some areas higher than others. Owing to the speed with

which grass grows, you can alter the look of the lawn repeatedly throughout the growing season.

209 I have not been able to mow the lawn and now it is much longer than usual – how should I mow it?

Set the mower blades higher than usual, so that less is removed the first time you cut. If the grass is too long use a strimmer, then mow the grass.

▼ **208** *Cut a swathe through an area of rough grass to make a path.*

OTHER LAWN CARE TASKS

To keep a lawn looking good, a regular maintenance regime is required as well as regular mowing, otherwise bare and brown patches can appear, and weeds may start to take root. As you mow the lawn take note of any areas needing attention.

210 Should I use a fertilizer on the lawn?

Applying a fertilizer will greatly help the appearance of the lawn and keep it looking lush and healthy. Use a dedicated lawn fertilizer rather than a general garden variety. Some lawn fertilizers also contain moss and weedkillers, thus eliminating the need for separate applications. Apply fertilizer twice a year, first in spring-summer, then again in autumn, after you have carried out annual maintenance.

211 Can I make the grass look greener?

Surprisingly, yes. Use a fertilizer that contains iron (Fe) – the packet will list it as a component. Iron does not actually feed grass but will darken the green, making it appear lusher.

212 What is thatch?

Throughout the growing season, dead material accumulates around individual blades of grass. With the wear and tear a lawn receives, this material compacts down to form a thick layer, which prevents rainfall from penetrating the ground and weakens the grass. The lawn can lose its lush appearance and start to show bare patches. Left untreated, thatch will prevent the grass from growing evenly and make way for weeds. Thatch should be raked off regularly throughout the growing season.

▼ **211** *A beautiful green showpiece lawn is grown from a seed that will not withstand much wear and tear. It needs to be fed and watered regularly. Products are available to make the grass greener and this will enhance its appearance.*

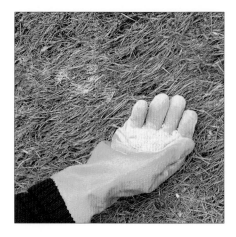

▲ **210** *Lawn fertilizers can be applied by hand. Follow the manufacturers' instructions regarding how much to use, and do not be tempted to add more, even if you think your lawn is in a particularly bad state. Most lawns will regenerate quickly, but it takes time to transform a parched patch into a showpiece lawn.*

▲ **212** *Thatch is a build-up of dead material that accumulates around grass stalks. Rake it off every year as it appears and add it to your compost heap.*

213 What annual maintenance do I need to carry out on my lawn?

Apart from the regular mowing and raking of the lawn that you do throughout the year, lawns benefit from an autumn maintenance programme comprised of scarifying, spiking and top-dressing.

214 What is scarifying?

Scarifying is a method of removing thatch that has built up around the blades of grass that will adversely affect drainage if left in place. Scarifying is hard work, so it is best to use a proper scarifying or lawn rake, which has flexible tines arranged like a fan, rather than an ordinary garden rake. Pull the rake all over the lawn in one direction, then again in the other. The thatch can be added to the compost heap.

Annual maintenance

1 Rake over the lawn with a scarifying rake to remove thatch and other dead material such as leaves from neighbouring plants. Apply a strong even pressure.

2 Make holes in the lawn to improve drainage. Either use a special tool, or spike the lawn using a garden fork. Make the holes approximately 15cm/6in apart.

3 Mix together equal parts lawn sand and garden compost or a peat substitute until evenly combined, then distribute a thin layer over the whole area using a spade, or shaking it from a bucket.

4 Brush over the lawn briskly with a hard outdoor brush so that the top-dressing fills the holes, rather than sitting on top of the grass. If the weather stays dry, lightly water the lawn.

215 What is spiking?

Spiking a lawn allows excess water to drain away from the surface rapidly and allows air into the soil, promoting good root growth. Use a garden fork to make holes all over the lawn surface. Alternatively, use a specialized tool that removes long plugs of soil.

◀ **213** *If you have a large area to maintain, products can be applied with a spreader that will distribute them evenly.*

216 What is top-dressing?

Prepare a mixture of lawn sand and garden compost, with added peat substitute or leaf mould if available, and spread this over the lawn. Brush over the lawn so that the mixture fills the spiked holes.

217 Does a lawn need watering?

As a general rule, no. But you may want to water it during a dry period to improve its appearance.

LAWN PROBLEMS AND SOLUTIONS

Even the best-kept lawns can suffer problems from time to time. Fortunately, there are simple remedies for nearly all of them. Regular maintenance and an annual routine should keep the grass in good condition and looking fresh all year round.

218 My lawn is looking worn in places and is very untidy. Should I dig it all up and start again?

Perhaps surprisingly, no. It is perfectly possible to refresh an existing lawn and much less trouble than creating a new one from scratch. Feeding, weeding and replacing patches where the grass has died are the answer.

219 Why has my grass turned a yellowish colour?

Yellow grass – unless it is drying out as a result of drought – indicates a nitrogen deficiency in the soil. Apply a nitrogen-high lawn feed to promote fresh growth.

220 My lawn is full of weeds. How do I get rid of them?

Common plant weeds include dandelions, daisies, clover and plantains. You can use a spot lawn weedkiller that will kill the weeds, but

▼ **218** *If you need to dig out an area of lawn, mark out the edge with a spade, then lift off the turf.*

leave the grass unharmed. Many weedkillers also contain fertilizer. These are most effective if they are applied while the weed is still young, before flowering. On a small lawn, you can remove weeds individually. Common lawn weeds such as daisies and dandelions are deep-rooted, so care needs to be taken when lifting them so that you do not snap the root, leaving a portion in the ground. The portion left in the ground will produce a new plant. Use either a long-bladed garden knife or a daisy grubber – a specialized tool like an elongated trowel – to remove the weeds. It may be necessary to reseed areas that have been heavily infested.

221 My lawn is dying off in patches. What is the problem?

Chafer grubs are increasingly becoming a problem in gardens. The larvae – fat, white grubs – feed on grass roots, causing yellow patches to appear. Further damage is caused by foxes, badgers, magpies and crows, which scratch at the lawn in search of

▲ **221** *A brown patch on a lawn is a sure indicator that all is not well.*

the grubs. Larvae can be treated with a chemical in mid-summer or controlled with a pathogenic nematode, *Steinernema carpocapsae*.

222 What can I do about a moss-infested lawn?

The presence of moss in a lawn is a clear signal that the drainage is poor. Water collecting at or near the soil

Removing weeds

1 To remove a weed from a lawn, use a special tool or a knife with a long blade.

2 Dig out the weed, taking care not to leave any part of the root behind. Fill in the hole.

▲ **222** *Moss appears in damp areas with poor drainage.*

surface will support moss spores, which then grow to the detriment of the grass. You need to treat not only the moss but the underlying cause. Apply a mosskiller locally as required. Wait for the moss to turn brown, then rake off with a lawn rake. Fork over the remaining bald patch and improve the drainage by working in horticultural grit. Reseed the area.

223 Is moss always bad news?

Not necessarily. On persistently damp soil, it is possible to create a moss lawn – attractive to look at though not as hard-wearing as grass. Moss can also be dug up and used to line hanging baskets.

224 How do I deal with bumps in the grass?

Cut a cross in the grass over the bump with a half-moon cutter. Fold back the turves, then use a trowel to dig out excess soil. Fold back the turves. Keep the spot well watered to help the cuts heal.

▶ **223** *You could replace your lawn with moss, planting up moss mats, if you are surrounded by trees.*

225 How do I deal with small hollows in the grass?

Cut a cross in the grass with a half-moon cutter and fold back the turves. Sprinkle in a mix of topsoil, garden compost and sharp sand. Water this well, then fold back the turves. Keep well watered so that the joins will knit back together again.

226 My lawn is covered in worm casts. How do I deal with the problem of worms?

Earthworms are generally valued in the garden. They eat through decaying plant material under ground and open up tunnels in the soil that improve drainage. However, where active under lawns, they occasionally throw up casts on to the surface – especially during warm, wet weather in spring and autumn – and these can smear in patches and provide a seed bed for weeds. As a healthy worm population is good for the garden, the simplest solution is to brush the casts on to nearby flowerbeds with a broom. Avoid walking on the lawn during wet weather, as this can compact the casts, smearing them over the grass. This will affect drainage.

227 My lawn has patches of yellow-brown in summer. What causes this?

Crane flies – or daddy-long-legs – lay eggs that hatch into larvae known as leatherjackets. These can be a lawn pest, feeding on the turf roots underground and causing die-back. They can be controlled either with a chemical pesticide or by use of the pathogenic nematode *Steinernema carpocapsae*. Alternatively, cover affected areas with black plastic over night (preferably after rain). During the night, the leatherjackets come to the surface. The following morning, remove the plastic and dispose of the pests by hand.

228 What causes bare patches to appear in the lawn?

Bare patches on a lawn represent a vicious circle – unless dealt with, they will keep getting worse. If a lawn, or part of a lawn, sees heavy traffic, the grass will wear out. Once this happens, the soil will begin to compact and may begin to puddle during wet weather. In this scenario, the grass can never recover. The first step is to improve the drainage in the area of compacted soil. Fork this over and add grit. Level the surface and rake it over, then sow with grass seed. Use a hardwearing seed mix to minimize the risk of the problem recurring. Water the seedlings. Keep off the area until the new grass is well established.

229 A large deciduous tree is overhanging the lawn. Is this likely to cause any problems?

Grass that is shaded by a large tree will not grow with the speed and vigour of grass in full sun, unless you have chosen a shade-tolerant variety. It is necessary to rake up any fallen leaves in autumn, as these can encourage disease if left on the surface and allowed to rot down. They will add to any thatch that tends to build up around grass stems.

230 My lawn puddles in wet weather – what is the solution?

If water sits on the lawn surface during wet weather, you have a drainage problem – possibly caused by a build-up of 'thatch'. Wait till the lawn is dry, then rake it thoroughly with a lawn rake. Spike the lawn, then top-dress with a mix of loam and lawn sand. Repeat annually, ideally in autumn. Treat any moss – usually associated with damp soil – with a moss killer. If this does not solve the problem, you could have a high water table. In this case, you may need to consider an alternative surface such as paving or decking.

Repairing bare patches in the lawn

1 Cut a triangle or square around the bare patch using a spade or half-moon cutter. Lift off the turf.

2 Lightly break up the soil underneath the turf with a garden fork. Remove any large stones.

3 Sprinkle topsoil mixed with garden compost over the area to raise the level.

4 Holding a garden rake vertical, lightly firm the soil using the back of the head.

5 Lightly rake over the soil surface both to level it and to create a fine tilth for sowing.

6 Sow with grass seed, then water the ground well. Keep well watered till the seedlings are established.

Repairing a ragged edge

1 If a lawn develops a ragged edge, cut out a square of turf around it, using a spade or half-moon cutter.

2 Holding the spade horizontally, cut through the under-side of the turf to free it, then lift.

3 Reverse the section of turf, so that the straight side is now at the edge. Fill the jagged area with topsoil.

4 Fill in the hole with garden compost, then sow with grass seed. Water the seed well.

231 Should I water my lawn during hot, dry spells?
The answer depends on how keen a gardener you are and how important a lush green lawn is to you. Lawns can be watered with a sprinkler attached to a hosepipe that spins round to deliver the water in a fine spray over the lawn. However, this is extremely wasteful of water, as much is lost through evaporation and not all the water will fall on the lawn. Although a lawn rapidly turns dry and brown during a hot spell, watering is not necessary. The grass will soon turn green again with the next spell of rain.

232 How do I deal with a ragged edge to the lawn?
Cut a rectangle that incorporates the ragged edge. Turn this round so that the straight edge becomes the edge of the lawn. Reseed the ragged side, which should now show as a bare patch in the lawn.

233 What is the best way of getting rid of moles?
Moles tunnel under ground and leave piles of excavated earth on the lawn. Control them with traps or with smokes introduced into their burrows. You could try to discourage them by putting a child's windmill in the holes.

▲ **233** *Moles are among the worst lawn pests. Their tunnelling can ruin the appearance of a lawn.*

234 What causes rings of toadstools on the lawn and how do I deal with them?
Gradually expanding rings of brown toadstools are seen on lawns in summer and autumn, usually in wet weather. Underground, the fungus is creating a water-repellent mat, so the grass inside the ring turns brown and dies back. Treating fairy rings is time-consuming. Brush or rake off any toadstools to prevent the fungus spreading any further. Dig up the area where the grass has turned brown, extending it by 30cm (12in) on all sides. Excavate the soil to a depth of 30cm (12in), then replace with fresh topsoil before reseeding.

▼ **234** *Toadstools are actually growing on decaying matter – often old tree roots – that are under the lawn.*

MEADOW PLANTING

A flowering meadow will attract wildlife into the garden – birds, butterflies and bees as well as a whole host of other pollinating insects. A grassy area filled with wild flowers is relatively easy to achieve although it needs as much maintenance as a conventional lawn.

235 What is a meadow planting?

A meadow planting involves growing flowering plants among grass. The grass is allowed to grow tall and is only cut once the flowers have set their seed.

236 What are the ecological benefits of meadow planting?

A meadow planting uses native flowering plants that will attract a host of beneficial pollinating insects. The long grass will shelter a range of larger creatures – frogs, toads, hedgehogs, dormice and shrews – providing a cool retreat during hot summer weather.

▼ **235** *A bank of wild flowers at the edge of a garden will attract wildlife.*

◄ **235** *Flower meadows contain a mixture of wild flowers and grass. They need careful management.*

▼ **236** *Frogs like long grass because it helps keep them cool in summer. They also feed on the insects that nest there.*

237 Is a meadow self-maintaining?
Up to a point – the principle is that the plants are allowed to flower and set seed, which will germinate and flower the following year. Over a period of years, certain species will start to dominate at the expense of others. So, a meadow that presents a diversity of flowers in year one may have only a couple of types of plant by year three. In this case, it may be necessary to remake the meadow every couple of years.

238 Why does soil fertility matter?
A meadow relies on a happy balance of grasses and flowering plants. If the soil is too fertile, the grasses will grow lush and the flowering plants will be unable to compete with them – hence there will be no flowers.

239 What types of meadow planting are there?
You can plan for either a spring or summer meadow. It is not possible to create a meadow that flowers during both seasons.

240 Can I create a meadow from seed?
You can buy wildflower seed mixes (with spring- or summer-flowering plants) that also contain grass seed from garden centres. These can be used on bare soil if you are making a meadow from scratch.

241 How do I prepare the site?
Prepare the site as for making a conventional lawn, but do not incorporate organic matter or add fertilizer. If the meadow is to be successful, the soil should not be high in nutrients.

242 When should I sow the seed?
Sow the seed either in spring or autumn. On light soils, autumn sowing is preferable, as the seedlings will germinate and grow away strongly the following spring. On heavy soils, delay sowing till spring – a lower proportion will germinate in autumn, and there is a risk that the young plants will rot off during cold, wet weather.

▲ **238** *A patch of wild flowers will thrive on soil with low nutritional value.*

243 Are there any alternative methods other than seed?
Plug plants are available that give more predictable results – at a higher cost. Remove squares of turf, then plant the plugs directly in the soil. Preseeded mats can be rolled out and laid directly on bare earth.

244 Isn't it the case that a flowering meadow will only look good for a few weeks each year?
This is certainly true, as the plants are only in flower for a short time and have to be allowed to run to seed to produce new plants next year. Against this must be set the benefits, both aesthetic and ecological. Nevertheless, it is usual to create a meadow at the end of a garden, if your garden is big enough, rather than in a more prominent position where you are looking for longer-term interest. You could always scatter wild flower seeds in awkward areas of the garden too.

245 Can I create a meadow in an existing lawn?

Yes, but it is necessary to remove the turf first. You can either strip away all the turf in the desired area, or, if you are using plug plants, just remove small squares of grass within the proposed site. Alternatively, apply a systemic weedkiller to kill off the grass.

246 What are the advantages of the methods of creating a meadow in existing lawn?

If you strip turf from land then the soil beneath it will be low in fertility. Low-nutrient soil is ideal for a flower meadow. The alternative option is to kill existing areas of grass with weedkillers. This is a quick and effective method of site creation.

247 Is a flower meadow less work than a conventional lawn?

Not necessarily – like a lawn, a meadow planting has to be managed. It cannot be mown with a conventional lawnmower, but must be cut by hand with a scythe.

248 When should I cut a spring meadow?

Wait until after the plants have flowered and shed their seeds. Then scythe to about 8cm (3in) from the ground. Cut again at three-weekly intervals, or, if you do not have time for this, in late summer. It is important to remove the clippings – if they are left in place and allowed to rot down, they will raise the soil fertility.

249 When should I cut a summer meadow?

Cut a summer meadow in spring to about 8cm (3in) above ground. One to three cuts may be needed, but make no cuts after late spring to allow the flowering plants to develop. Cut again in autumn after the seed has been shed. Remove the clippings after every cut.

Creating a wild flower meadow in an existing lawn

1 Start by marking out the area you intend to convert to a wild flower area. Use a rope or garden hose to establish flowing lines and curves.

2 With the edge finalized, cut the line in the existing turf using a half-moon edging iron and following the line made by the rope.

3 Lift the existing turf, removing all grass plants, as plants growing in wild flower meadows prefer nutrient-poor soil.

4 Once the turf has been lifted, lightly cultivate the whole area with a fork, before raking it to produce a light, crumbly seed bed ready for sowing.

5 Mix the wild flower seed into the grass seed prior to sowing to make it easier to distribute. Lightly sow the mix at a rate of 15g/m² (½oz per sq yd). Sow by hand or use a spreader.

6 The grass and wild flower seedlings will soon emerge, and the light sowing rate ensures that the grass does not swamp the developing wild flowers.

Planting bulbs in a lawn

▲ **251** *Bulbs planted under turf will naturalize if left to their own devices.*

250 Can I achieve the effect of a meadow with perennials?

Some perennials are tough enough to compete with grass and can be grown in a lawn to create the look of a wildflower meadow. They include such plants as cowslips (*Primula veris*), primroses (*Primula vulgaris*), peonies (*Paeonia*), acanthus, golden rod (*Solidago*), *Echinops ritro* and yarrow (*Achillea*). On damp soil, try kingcups (*Caltha palustris*).

251 Can I plant bulbs in a lawn?

Snowdrops (*Galanthus*), crocus and daffodils (*Narcissus*) are commonly grown in grass. If the soil is reliably damp, fritillaries (*Fritillaria*) can be successful. For later flowers, try *Gladiolus byzantinus* with magenta flowers – more robust than it looks.

252 When can I mow the lawn?

Allow the bulbs to complete their life cycle before mowing – six to eight weeks after flowering. Remove the faded flowers to prevent the bulbs from setting seed. Allow the leaves to turn yellow and wither. If the bulbs are in clumps in the lawn, you can mow round them, but removing the leaves prematurely means the bulbs will not flower to their full potential next year.

1 With a half-moon edger, cut an 'H' shape into the lawn.

2 Peel back the turf to both sides, exposing a square of soil.

3 Loosen the soil with a hand fork.

4 Scatter the bulbs over the soil.

5 Plant the bulbs, using a trowel to dig holes to the appropriate depth.

6 Fold back the turf and lightly firm down with your hands.

7 Alternatively, simply scatter the bulbs over the lawn to determine where to plant them.

8 Remove plugs of soil with a bulb planter, place each bulb at the base, and then replace the plug.

CHAPTER FOUR

THE ORNAMENTAL GARDEN

A garden filled predominantly with trees, flowering shrubs and foliage, arranged into a design scheme for its aesthetic value, is said to be ornamental. Trees and shrubs are the backbone of any garden and have a permanent presence. Against this backdrop the annuals, herbaceous perennials, roses, bulbs and alpines combine to add colour, texture, form and structure that provide a sensory treat.

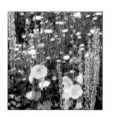
BUYING PLANTS

DESIGNING WITH PLANTS

TREES

CONIFERS

SHRUBS

CLIMBERS

ROSES

PERENNIALS

ANNUALS AND BIENNIALS

BULBS, CORMS AND TUBERS

ROCK GARDEN PLANTS

CARE AND MAINTENANCE

GROWING IN CONTAINERS

◀ *For many gardeners, flowers are the whole point of making a garden.*

BUYING PLANTS

Ranks of plants in flower in garden centres always look tempting, but this is not by any means the only way of acquiring new plants. Plant fairs, garden shows and the Internet are also a good source, as well as trading plants with friends and neighbours, of course.

253 What should I look for when buying a plant or shrub?

It is easy to choose a plant that you like the look of, but is it appropriate for the place where you wish to plant it? Garden centres provide labels with plants that describe each plant's preferences for soil type and level of sun required, as well as the ultimate height and spread of the plant, so that you can work out if it is a suitable purchase. Choose healthy looking plants with balanced, even growth, and with roots contained within the pot, rather than growing through the hole in the base. Check the leaves for signs of pests or other problems.

254 Should I be wary of buying plants mail order?

Not if you are buying from a reputable nursery. They may pack the plants well and will usually agree to replace free of charge any plant that suffers in transit or that fails to establish well. Mail order is often the only way to get hold of rare plants. Collections are sometimes advertised in the press. While this is a cheap way of acquiring plants, they are usually nothing special.

▼ **254** *Mail-order plants are often sold as 'plug' plants to ensure their maximum chance of survival. Pot them on or plant them in the garden as soon as they arrive.*

255 Where can I buy unusual plants?

Internet searches can help you find plants that are out of the ordinary. However, it is best to buy from a nursery near to where you live. Not only can you check on the plant before you buy, but the plant will have been raised in a climate – and possibly soil type – similar to the one in your garden. Gardening clubs and allotment societies often organize plant sales – a good way of picking up seedlings if you do not have time to raise your own. Private gardens that open for charity during the summer often sell plants propagated from the ones that are actually growing in the garden, so you can see what any plant you buy will look like in a garden setting.

256 What is a pot-bound plant?

Plants that have spent too long in their containers in the nursery develop roots that fill the container, coiling round. You may find on removing the plant from its container that there is very little potting compost left. These plants often prove difficult to establish in the garden – the roots may not grow very much, so the plant fails. When you are buying plants, slip them carefully out of their containers to check the root system, before putting them back.

▲ **253** *A garden centre near your home should sell those plants that will thrive in your soil type.*

257 Do plants need any aftercare once planted?

When planting, sprinkle bonemeal in the planting hole, before adding some compost. Plants need time to adjust to their new environment before they 'establish' and begin to grow away happily. During the period immediately after planting, there may not be much visible growth, but the roots should be growing beneath the soil, anchoring the plant in its new home. Water plants well during the first few months after planting, making sure that the soil does not dry out, to help them establish. In subsequent seasons, supplementary watering should not be necessary unless there is a shortage of rain.

◄ **256** *A pot-bound plant does not make a good purchase. If you have a choice, choose a plant where the roots are not congested and visible as a thick mat at the base of the pot. A less congested plant should grow away quickly.*

DESIGNING WITH PLANTS

Gardeners are often puzzled about how to display plants to their best advantage – and which plants go with each other, so that there is a succession of flowering plants through the growing season. There are rules, but a few basic principles can be useful.

258 How do you begin designing with plants?

Combining plants is to some extent a hit-and-miss affair. You cannot be sure of a plant's colour until it flowers, and it may not flower at the expected time and contribute to the intended scheme in the way you expected. Be prepared to be flexible and to experiment. Most plants can easily be moved if you make any mistakes, even when they are in flower. No planting you make needs to be permanent and mistakes are easily rectified.

259 What factors should I take into account when putting plants together?

When planning any grouping of plants, try to create as much interest and variety as possible in order to avoid producing a dull, uninteresting design. Considering carefully the form and shape, texture and pattern, and colour of the plants will help you to produce a pleasing, dynamic planting scheme. Once you have chosen your selection of plants, check the ultimate growing height of the plant so that you plant it in the correct space in the garden.

You may wish to hide boundaries or block out eyesores with climbers or put taller plants in larger spaces. Position small plants where they will be seen, either at the front of a bed or edging a path. Group plants with similar growing requirements in an appropriate part of the garden.

Use plants to create bold drifts. Try to create a rhythm to the border by repeating the same plant along its length. You can also include plants with a similar form or shape – phormiums and yuccas, for instance – to create rhythmical patterns. Use weaving paths and naturally flowing shapes to create visual interest. Consider the view of the garden

▲ **261** Gunnera maculata *is an architectural plant that grows near water. It is good in large gardens where there is space to allow it free rein.*

from inside the house. Will certain planting schemes help to link the house and garden?

260 What is meant by form and shape?

Plants have a natural habit or shape that can be exploited by the gardener to create a sense of excitement in a planting scheme. Plants with a narrow, columnar shape include delphiniums, lupins, verbascums and upright conifers, while horizontally growing plants include *Viburnum plicatum*, *Cornus controversa* and achilleas, as well as a range of groundcover plants. Add further interest, perhaps, by incorporating a weeping plant such as salix, *Pyrus salicifolia* 'Pendula', laburnum or *Garrya elliptica*. Energy and movement are further created with spiky-leaved plants such as yuccas, phormiums, cordylines, aloes, pampas grasses and ornamental grasses, while punctuation points in

▲ **261** *Many tall grasses have architectural qualities that can be used to good effect in a garden design. Grasses also make a gentle noise in the breeze.*

the garden are provided by rounded plants such as euphorbias, potentillas, clipped santolinas and clipped topiary such as box (*Buxus*).

261 Which are architectural plants and how do I use them in the garden design?

Some plants are said to have strong architectural qualities. This means that they have a clear, defining shape, making them good plants to use as focal points. The following all work well as architectural plants:
Acanthus for its spiny shape.
Agave americana for its cacti-like quality.
Euphorbia characias for its mound-like shape and growth habit.
Gunnera manicata for its huge leaves.
Kniphofia caulescens for its colourful flower spikes.
Phormium tenax for its spiky leaves.
Phyllostachys nigra for its attractive stems and foliage.

262 What is meant by groundcover?

Groundcover plants create a thick carpet of vegetation over a large area. Not only do they cover the ground but they also suppress weeds. Groundcover need not be evergreen to be effective – many herbaceous flowering plants form impenetrable mats of roots just below ground level. Being quick spreaders, many can be invasive to the extent that they become weeds. Climbers and some spreading shrubs can also be used as groundcover. In the short term, annual flowering plants can make effective groundcover.

▼ **266** *Choosing plants with colours that are next to each other on the colour wheel ensures a harmonious scheme.*

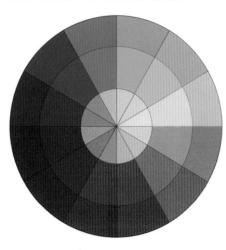

▲ **267** *Pinks, whites and blues work well together and are easy on the eye.*

263 Which plants can be used as groundcover in sun?

Alchemilla mollis
Campanulata glomerata
Ceanothus thyrsiflorus var. *repens*
Cornus canadensis
Euphorbia cyparissias

264 Which plants can be used for groundcover in shade?

Ajuga reptans
Bergenia
Convallaria majalis
Epimedium
Euphorbia amygdaloides var. *robbiae*
Geranium
Hedera
Heuchera
Hosta
Lamium
Pachysandra terminalis
Polystichum setiferum
Tiarella cordifolia
Vinca

265 How can the texture or pattern of plants enhance a planting scheme?

You can add further interest to any kind of planting scheme by considering the texture or pattern of the plants, as well as their overall shape. Leaf texture may be prickly (eryngiums, *Acanthus spinosus*, *Onopordum acanthus* and mahonia); smooth (cannas, pittosporums, hippeastrums and bergenias); or furry (*Stachys byzantina*, *Amaranthus caudatus* and *Salvia officinalis*). Foliage plants with distinctively coloured leaves such as berberis or cotinus, as well as plants with variegated or patterned leaves such as pulmonarias, *Salvia officinalis* 'Tricolor', *Arum italicum* 'Pictum' and *Lamium maculatum* 'Beacon Silver' add interest.

266 What is the colour wheel?

The colour wheel is an arrangement of the primary, secondary and tertiary colours. It places complementary tones opposite each other. There are three primary colours: red, yellow and blue. To find the complementary of any of these, mix together the other two. The complementary of red is green, that of yellow is violet and that of blue is orange. Complementary colours, when used with sensitivity, create some very exciting, dramatic schemes. Harmonizing colours, usually considered restful, lie next to each other on the wheel – blue and violet, yellow and orange, for instance.

▼ **267** *Colour affects each of us in different ways. 'Hot' colours such as red and orange create a lively colour scheme.*

◀ **269** *Cottage gardens are filled with herbaceous plantings. They are usually bare in winter, coming to life in spring.*

270 What is meant by a mixed border?

A mixed planting combines a number of plants with a permanent woody framework – such as flowering shrubs (evergreen or deciduous), dwarf conifers and small trees – with perennials, bulbs and annuals to fill any gaps in summer. If the bed or border is in front of a wall or fence, you can incorporate a climber to cover this. Alternatively, climbers can be grown over upright frames within the border. Mixed plantings always appear relaxed and are usually low maintenance once the permanent plants have established.

271 What is an island bed?

Low-growing seasonal plants – that is, spring and summer bedding plants – are traditionally grown in island beds cut into the lawn, so that they can be viewed from all sides. The tallest plants usually go in the centre and the smaller ones around the edge. Island beds are ideal for breaking up and adding interest to a large expanse of lawn.

▼ **271** *This island bed, incorporating mixed plantings, is surrounded by a grass path and can be enjoyed from all sides.*

267 How can I use colour in the garden?

The most restful effects are created by using tones of the same colour – a range of lilacs and purples, for instance – perhaps with accent plants of the complementary, yellow in this case. Combining complementary colours with white – the most dominant of all colours – is rarely successful: the eye finds no resting place. Blue-flowered plants tend to recede, white-flowered ones appear to loom – especially at dusk. It is best not to get too hung up on colour. Many flower colours are not 'true' (there are few clear blues or reds, for instance) and many flowers combine two or more colours. Besides, in any garden, it is impossible to banish green. Plants have a habit of seeding themselves in random places, so often the best design intentions may be thwarted, or provided, by nature, depending on your view point.

268 Is it true that silver-leaved plants always look restful?

No, a garden composed solely of silver foliage plants can look dull. Put silver next to red and it appears green. Next to purple the eye picks up the yellow in silver. Nevertheless, gardeners are often tempted to use silver in the garden to soften colour clashes. Using a grass with beige or fawn flowers may be more successful.

269 What is an herbaceous border?

This is a border planted with herbaceous plants. In large, traditional gardens, there is a clear distinction between herbaceous borders and shrub borders, but few gardens today can accommodate separate borders for different types of plant in this way. The compromise is a mixed border. Herbaceous borders die back to ground level in the autumn, so having mixed planting ensures winter interest.

TREES

A well-placed tree gives the garden an air of maturity, provides a landing place for birds and lifts your gaze skywards. Even the smallest garden should include at least one specimen tree. Make sure it fulfils a variety of functions.

272 How do I use trees in my garden design?

Trees bring height, texture and colour to a garden design. Some produce beautiful flowers and edible fruit, and in the process attract wildlife. A tree will become a dominant feature so should be chosen with care. You may have a practical need for a tree, such as to screen an area from view, or to create shade. But even a small tree gives a garden a sense of permanence and maturity. Use it as a focal point, perhaps at the end of a path or in the middle of a lawn. Trees are the largest plants in the garden and, unlike most perennials, they are visible throughout the year. Where space permits, they are impressive planted in avenues. Many gardens have space for one tree.

273 How do I choose a suitable tree for the size of my garden?

The final height of the tree is a major consideration. Other criteria include when it flowers, whether it has fruits, how much shade it will cast, and whether it is deciduous or evergreen.

274 How far should I plant a tree from the house?

You need to bear in mind the final height and spread of the tree – most have root systems that balance the canopy and stabilize the tree. To be sure that the roots will not interfere with the house's foundations and drainage, plant as far away from the house as possible – ideally at least

▲ 272 *Here, two small, willow-leaved pear trees* (Pyrus salicifolia) *are used in a formal scheme to flank a sheltered seat.*

10m (30ft) away (ensure that the tree is not planted too close to any bordering properties). Checking the final size of a tree in a plant dictionary can be alarming because many trees can top 30m (100ft). However, many

Planting a tree

1 To prepare the site, dig over the planting area, removing weeds and stones. Dig a hole at least twice the size of the root ball and dig organic matter into the hole.

2 Remove the tree from the container or packaging, without touching the roots if you can. The tree needs to be sited in the hole at the same depth as it is in its container.

3 Back fill the hole with topsoil and compost (soil mix). Firm the tree in place with your heel. Add a stake and tie it loosely but firmly to the main stem. Water well.

stay reasonably compact within a 20-year span, after which you can have it pruned by a tree surgeon. Many decorative trees are modest in growth.

275 What makes leaves change colour in autumn?

The leaves of deciduous trees contain various pigments. In nearly all cases, green predominates, masking the other colours. In autumn, the green pigment breaks down as the tree goes into its dormancy, and the other colours – red, orange and yellow – are revealed for a brief period before the leaves fall. Autumn leaf colour depends on soil type and how wet or dry the preceding summer was.

276 What is a bare-root tree?

In many tree nurseries, trees are grown in rows in open fields rather than in containers. This keeps the cost of the trees down, as they need far less maintenance than do trees grown in containers. They can only be sold when dormant in autumn or winter. During this period, they are lifted from the ground and the roots are shaken free of soil. They are then packed for sale. This process is suitable for deciduous trees. Roses and fruit trees and bushes are often sold bare root.

277 What is a root-balled tree?

Root-balling is a technique that is used for conifers and palms that are vulnerable to root disturbance. They are field-grown but are dug up with their root ball intact. These are held together either in hessian (burlap) bags or wire cages.

278 How can I be sure that the tree will survive when I plant it in my garden?

All trees and shrubs that have to be moved (including during the purchasing process) are vulnerable to transplant shock – there is always a risk that they will not grow away happily in their new situation. Young trees transplant very well, but older trees are more susceptible. Undercutting is a technique that helps mature trees establish quickly. Each year in the nursery, the roots are undercut with a spade, shortening them drastically. This encourages the tree to produce fibrous roots that are more efficient than the thicker cut roots at absorbing moisture. If this is done systematically, quite large trees with relatively small, very fibrous root systems result. Not only are such trees easy to transport, but the fibrous root system enables them to settle into the new situation more quickly.

279 How do I plant a tree?

Prepare the site for the new planting by weeding the land and digging in organic matter. Dig a hole large enough and deep enough to accommodate the tree. Carefully remove the tree from its wrapping and tease out the rootball. Set the rootball so that the top of it is level with the surrounding soil. Hold the tree straight and backfill the hole. Firm it well with your heel. Add a stake if necessary and water well. Continue to water well until the tree is established.

280 How do I move a tree?

Moving an established tree can be quite an undertaking. Prepare the new site before you dig up the tree to be moved, so that the tree suffers least from the move. Dig around the tree first before digging out a largish rootball. Inevitably some roots will be severed. Aim to move the tree with as much earth and root system as you can. Slide fabric underneath to keep roots and earth together. Transport it to its new site and remove the fabric once in situ. Ensure the top of the rootball is level with the surrounding earth. Hold straight and back fill with topsoil and organic matter. Firm in and water well and regularly. The tree may take time to recover.

Moving a small tree

1 Prepare the new site as for Planting a Tree. Dig a trench around the specimen to be moved, allowing for a sufficiently large rootball. Dig under the roots of the specimen.

2 With help slide a large piece of hessian (burlap) or some other strong material underneath the root ball. Tie the material securely around the stem of the plant.

3 If the plant is large it may take two people or more to lift it. Tie the plant to a post to help move it to its new site. Remove the fabric and continue as for Planting a Tree.

▲ **282** Pyrus calleryana *is an ornamental pear, grown for its mass of spring flowers. The fruits are inedible.*

▲ **282** Gleditsia triacanthos *'Sunburst', has attractive bright golden yellow young foliage that turns green in summer.*

▲ **283** Acer palmatum *produces spectacular spring and autumn colour and is perfect for a small garden.*

281 Which trees are winter-flowering?

Prunus subhirtella 'Autumnalis' is sometimes marketed as the autumn or winter cherry. Its flowers start to open in late autumn, but its flowering peak is reached early the following spring. Mimosa (*Acacia dealbata*) flowers just after the winter solstice but needs a very sheltered site in cold areas.

282 Which trees are suitable for a small garden?

If you have a small garden choose a tree that will not outgrow the space.
Acer capillipes
Acer griseum

Acer palmatum
Amelanchier
Arbutus
Betula albo-sinensis var. *septentrionalis*
Catalpa bignonioides 'Aurea'
Cercis siliquastrum
Cornus kousa
Crataegus
Fagus sylvatica 'Dawyck Gold'
Gleditsia triacanthos 'Sunburst'
Laburnum x *watereri* 'Vossii'
Malus
Prunus 'Amanogawa'
Pyrus calleryana 'Chanticleer'
Sophora microphylla
Sorbus aria
Vitex agnus-castus

283 Which are the best trees for spring leaf colour?

All trees are a delight in early spring as the leaves and buds begin to unfurl – usually a bright, fresh green. Some of the Japanese maples (*Acer japonicum, A. palmatum*) are especially valued for their new leaves. Those of 'Butterfly' are edged with cream and shrimp pink, while 'Sango-kaku' has soft butter yellow leaves, but there are many more to choose from. The new growth on any plant is delicate – these trees, especially those that are first to put on growth, need a sheltered spot in the garden if the young leaves are not to be damaged by frosts.

▼ **284** *Hawthorn (Crataegus) trees produce a mass of red berries in autumn, bringing birds into the garden to feed.*

▼ **284** *The summer flowers of* Lagerstroemia indica *stay on the plant for a long time.*

▼ **284** *Laburnum trees produce racemes of bright yellow flowers that hang from the tree in spring.*

▲ **284** *Most magnolias flower in late winter or early spring on bare stems. A large tree looks spectacular.*

▲ **284** Prunus cyclamina *has dangling, pink flowers and is an attractive sight in the spring.*

▲ **284** *In a sheltered garden,* Acacia dealbata *will delight with its showers of soft yellow flowers at the end of winter.*

284 Which are the best flowering trees?

Acacia dealbata
Aesculus
Amelanchier
Arbutus
Catalpa bignonioides
Cercis siliquastrum
Cornus
Crataegus
Eucryphia
Genista aetnensis
Laburnum x vossii
Lagerstroemia indica
Liriodendron tulipiferum
Magnolia
Malus
Paulownia tomentosa
Prunus
Pyrus
Robinia
Sorbus
Sophora

285 What are the best trees for autumn leaf colour?

Leaf colour depends to some extent on the season – how hot and dry the previous summer was, for instance. Soil pH also plays a part. Some plants produce much better colour on acid soils. Maples (*Acer*), the Katsura tree (*Cercidophyllum japonicum*) and Persian ironwood (*Parrotia persica*) are among the best and most reliable performers in the autumn months.

286 Which are the best trees for autumn fruits?

Crataegus
Ilex (female selections)
Malus 'Golden Hornet'
Malus 'John Downie'
Prunus sargentii
Sorbus

287 Which trees have attractive bark?

Acer capillipes
Acer griseum
Acer pensylvanicum
Arbutus x andrachnoides
Betula albo-sinensis var. *septentrionalis*
Betula utilis var. *jacquemontii*

▼ **286** *Many hollies (*Ilex*) are grown for their attractive autumn fruits. Branches can be cut for floral decorations in winter.*

Eucalyptus pauciflora subsp. *niphophila*
Luma apiculata
Pinus bungeana
Prunus serrula
Salix alba 'Britzensis'
Stewartia pseudocamellia

288 Which trees are most suitable for a large garden?

Aesculus
Betula
Carpinus betulus
Corylus
Davidia involucrata
Fraxinus
Ginkgo biloba
Magnolia

▼ **287** Pinus bungeana *is a conifer with attractive bark – this can be a pleasing feature in winter.*

CONIFERS

Conifers are unfairly neglected in the garden. Often a handsome presence, they give substance and weight to the overall garden design and usually have a very well-defined profile. They add a sense of permanence to any planting.

289 What is the difference between a broadleaf tree and a conifer?

A conifer is coniferous – it bears cones. Actually, there are a couple of conifers whose 'cones' are more like berries – juniper (*Juniperus*) and yew (*Taxus*). Conifers have needle-like leaves, unlike other trees that are usually referred to as 'broadleaf'. Conifers include some of the oldest living organisms on the planet.

290 My conifers have brown patches on them. Why?

Conifers turn brown if they have insufficient light (check the back of one planted close to a wall or fence), if they are affected by cold wind, or by very dry conditions. Conifers need plenty of water and in dry weather can quickly deplete that available, so remember to water them well.

291 Are all dwarf conifers really dwarf?

Many conifers that are sold as 'dwarf' would actually be better described as 'slow-growing'. Although they stay compact for the first five to ten years,

▲ **289** *Conifers are identifiable by their foliage, fruit and distinctive shape.*

they can then get into their stride and put on rapid growth. They can become massive trees.

292 Can I move an established conifer?

Conifers are highly susceptible to transplant shock. If you need to move a conifer, choose a mild, damp day in

▲ **290** A conifer that turns brown may be dying or suffering from scorch.

autumn to minimize the shock. Prepare the new site first, digging it over well and incorporating well-rotted organic matter. Dig a hole that will comfortably accommodate the rootball. Conifers are heavy plants, often with prickly stems that can cause eye injuries. Wearing suitable protective clothing, dig up the conifer, cutting through any long, thick roots. Lift the conifer on to a piece of hessian (burlap) and wrap this around the rootball to prevent the roots from drying out. Move it to its new home and be sure to plant at the same depth as that from which it has been removed – the 'soil mark', which indicates the earlier soil level and should be clearly visible. Backfill the hole. Keep the conifer watered well throughout the following growing season to ensure it establishes well.

◄ **291** *These dwarf conifers look like small, well-clipped topiary specimens. They will eventually grow large.*

SHRUBS

Shrubs, of which there is a vast choice, are the mainstay of many plantings, whatever the style. Plant them in groups (of the same type or mixed) or use them as specimens in lawns or large containers, for all-year-round interest in the garden.

293 What is the difference between a tree and a shrub?

In botanical terms, there isn't any. Both are plants with a permanent woody framework. We think of trees as being large plants with a single, thick trunk, while shrubs are more compact – usually within 3m (10ft) – and with a number of stems shooting at ground level. However, certain trees, such as birches (*Betula*) and eucalyptus can be multi-stemmed, and shrubs can become tree-like with age.

294 How do I use shrubs?

In a small garden, a shrub can be used in place of a tree. Some are stately, well-boned plants that make excellent specimens. Or they can be mixed with perennials, bulbs and annuals in a mixed border. Architectural shrubs make good focal points in containers or to give impact to a mixed border.

295 Which are the best architectural shrubs?

Chamaerops is a palm with huge fan-like leaves that is perfect for a coastal location. *Cordyline* has a clearly defined rosette of large leaves on a stem making it perfect for a focal point planting. For a hot climate

▲ **294** *Planting several of the same shrub can be very effective.*

Dracaena has interesting foliage and a compact habit. *Eriobotrya japonica is a small tree with very long leaves.*

296 Which are the best shrubs for covering a large area?

Many shrubs, if planted in proximity, will grow into each other to create companionable mounds of greenery, enlivened by flowers, as each individual shrub comes into season. To maintain once mature, simply shear over in spring and late summer. Suitable plants include cherry laurel (*Prunus laurocerasus*), viburnums, mahonias, berberis, cotoneaster and *Lonicera nitida*. It is sometimes possible to buy these in bulk.

▼ **296** *Shrubs make an excellent backdrop to many other garden plants.*

▲ **297** *The climbing rose,* Rosa *'Albertine' is one of the most popular and will happily cover a wall.*

297 What is a wall shrub?

While all shrubs can be grown freestanding, some are suitable for training against a wall. This is a good method of growing shrubs that are not reliably hardy in your area as the wall provides shelter from cold weather and harsh winds. The shrub can be loosely pinned to the wall or trained more formally to show off one of its ornamental features, usually the flowers or berries. When training a shrub, aim to pull the stems as close to the horizontal as possible. This encourages the production of flower-bearing side shoots. A wall-trained shrub can be very impressive.

298 Which shrubs are suitable for wall training?

Abelia
Abeliophyllum distichum
Abutilon
Acacia
Azara
Buddleja crispa
Callistemon
Camellia
Ceanothus
Cestrum
Chaenomeles
Cotoneaster horizontalis
Fremontodendron
Itea ilicifolia
Pyracantha
Solanum laxum

299 Which shrubs flower in spring?

Berberis darwinii
Camellia japonica
Chaenomeles speciosa
Cotoneaster
Cytisus
Forsythia (spring-flowering species)
Kerria japonica
Mahonia aquifolium
Pieris japonica
Pittosporum tobira

Ribes sanguineum
Rosmarinus officinalis
Skimmia
Spiraea (spring-flowering species)
Viburnum

300 Which shrubs flower in summer?

Buddleja alternifolia
Ceanothus
Cotinus coggygria
Escallonia
Fuchsia
Hebe
Hydrangea
Leycesteria formosa
Lavandula
Olearia
Perovskia atriplicifolia
Philadelphus
Potentilla
Syringa
Vinca
Weigela

301 Which shrubs flower in autumn?

Abelia x grandiflora
Aralia elata
Callicarpa
Hebe 'Autumn Glory'
Hypericum
Viburnum bodnantense
Viburnum fragrans
Yucca filamentosa

▼ **299** Spiraea *produces a frothy mass of flowers in spring and summer.*

▼ **300** Ceanothus *is a large evergreen shrub, suitable for growing up a wall.*

▼ **300** Philadelphus *is prized for its most delicious scent.*

302 Which shrubs flower in winter?

Abeliophyllum distichum
Calluna
Camellia
Daboecia
Daphne
Erica
Hamamelis mollis
Mahonia x *media* 'Charity'
Sarcococca
Viburnum tinus

303 Can I grow shrubs in containers?

Most definitely – the majority of shrubs will thrive in containers, and this is a good way of restricting their growth. All the plants that tolerate regular clipping – box (*Buxus*), bay (*Laurus nobilis*), evergreen laurels (*Prunus laurocerasus, P. lusitanica*) – are suitable. Hydrangeas seem to thrive in large wooden half barrels. Containers can also be used to grow acid-loving rhododendrons and camellias in alkaline gardens. Use planted containers to add interest to the site.

304 Which is the best potting mix to use when planting a shrub in a container?

A nutrient-high soil-based compost (John Innes No.3) will give the best results. Multi-purpose composts can be used, with added grit and fertilizer.

▲ **301** Abelia x grandiflora *is an autumn-flowering shrub.*

305 Do shrubs in containers need any special treatment over winter?

Shrubs in containers are more sensitive to cold – including cold, drying winds – than those growing in the open ground. To protect their roots from freezing, wrap the containers in hessian (burlap) or bubble wrap whenever a hard frost is forecast. Tenting the plant with a length of horticultural fleece will prevent damage to the top-growth. Alternatively, move the plants into a sheltered area – such as in a porch. Ensure that container plants that stand in troughs do not get waterlogged over winter, and do not dry out.

▲ **302** Daphne *species flower in late winter. Choose a scented variety.*

306 How do I plant a shrub?

Dig over the soil removing weeds. Dig a hole twice the size of the rootball and partially fill with a mixture of potting mix and compost. Position the shrub so it is at the same depth as it was in the pot. Back fill and firm well with your boot. Water well.

307 Can I move an established shrub?

Yes, spring or autumn is the best time. Dig the new hole before digging up the plant, and incorporate organic matter into the hole. Water in well.

▼ **305** *In cold weather, use horticultural fleece to protect shrubs that are not hardy.*

▼ **303** *Shrubs are perfect for growing in containers.*

CLIMBERS

Climbers are ideal for creating a sense of height in a restricted area. Train them against walls, fences and trellises or up and over pergolas and arches. Then the plants will present their flowers or scent at eye level.

308 How do climbers climb?

Climbing plants are natural woodlanders competing for light with taller trees that might be in leaf. In the wild they creep along the forest floor until they meet a suitable host plant. They then ramp up this towards the light, attaching themselves in one of a number of ways. On reaching the leaf canopy, they spread out and push out flowers towards the sun. Climbing plants have the following features in common:

Climbers are plants of great vigour. They like to have their feet in the shade but their top growth in the sun. They have flexible stems that are only sparsely clad with leaves.

They tend to produce a mass of strongly upright shoots with flowers only at the tops of stems – a habit that most gardeners aim to thwart.

Climbers have five different methods by which they climb: suckering pads, climbing leaf stalks, twining stems, tendrils and thorny grips.

309 What is a self-clinging climber?

A minority of climbers have special suckering pads or aerial roots that attach themselves to their support – either a fence, wall or host plant. Commonly grown examples include ivies (*Hedera*), the climbing hydrangea (*Hydrangea petiolaris*) and Virginia creeper (*Parthenocissus quinquefolia*).

310 What is a leaf-stalk climber?

Look closely at the leaves of a leaf-stalk climber and you will see that the stalks have a little kink. The stalk is designed to grip twiggy growth, thus helping the plant to climb. Most clematis attach themselves to host plants by this method.

311 What are twining climbers?

Twining climbers corkscrew their way up through the narrow branches of a host plant. Among the most commonly seen in gardens are honeysuckles (*Lonicera*) and wisteria. Often, where there is no adequate support – or the support is already covered – new stems will twine their way around existing stems, leading to a very congested and unproductive plant.

312 How do tendril climbers grow?

Besides their regular leaves, tendril climbers produce short, corkscrew-like growths on their stems that wrap around the twiggy growth of host plants. Passion flowers (*Passiflora*) and sweet peas (*Lathyrus odoratus*) climb by means of tendrils.

313 What do thorny climbers do?

A number of climbers have thorny stems – notably roses, but also the spectacular, though tender, bougainvilleas. Thorns grip into the bark of trees, like cats' claws, enabling the flexible stems to grow upright towards the light.

▲ **309** Hydrangea anomala *subsp.* petiolari *clings with special aerial roots.*

▼ **310** *Clematis have special leaf stalks that wrap around stems.*

▲ **310** Humulus lupulus *climbs by means of leaf stalks.*

▼ **313** *Roses have thorny stems that allow them to climb.*

▲ **316** *Many honeysuckles (Lonicera) have a delicious fragrance.*

314 How does the way a plant climbs affect the support that I choose to grow it on?

Self-clingers will cover a wall without any additional means of support. All other types need some form of support. Trellis panels can be used for twining climbers, but all are best on a system of wires or lengths of pigwire or chickenwire, which can be attached to a wall or fence. You can buy suitable wire in hardware stores and from agricultural suppliers.

315 How should climbers be trained?

The natural habit of climbers is to produce masses of vigorous upright growing stems, which then produce their flowers at the top. To produce a vertical 'carpet' of flowers, tie in the stems as close to the horizontal as possible as they grow, to build a framework of stems. This encourages them to produce short lateral shoots that will bear flowers, especially where the stems bend.

316 What are the best climbers for scent?

One of the most highly scented climbers is the evergreen *Trachelospermum jasminoides*, with a long flowering season throughout summer–autumn. Many of the honeysuckles (*Lonicera*) also have a rich scent. Many climbing and rambler roses are fragrant.

317 Which climbers can be grown in shade?

Akebia quinata
Clematis
Codonopsis convolvulacea
Hedera canariensis
Hedera colchica
Hedera helix
Hydrangea petiolaris
Jasminum nudiflorum
Lonicera x tellmanniana
Lonicera tragophylla
Muehlenbeckia complexa
Parthenocissus henryana
Parthenocissus quinquefolia
Pileostegia viburnoides
Schizophragma integrifolium

318 Which climbers do well in full sun?

Actinidia
Campsis radicans
Clematis armandii
Clianthus puniceus
Convolvulus
Eccremocarpus scaber
Ipomoea
Jasminum
Passiflora caerulea
Rhodochiton atrosanguineum
Solanum jasminoides 'Album'
Trachelospermum jasminoides

▼ **318** *Clematis is rightly known as the queen of climbers.*

ROSES

Roses are plants with a long history in gardens and many varieties still grown today are rich in historical associations. Roses deserve a place in every garden. Most have a long flowering season, and the flowers are often sumptuously scented.

319 Why are roses so popular in gardens?

Roses have always been valued as the flower of high summer, many having a delicious scent. Nowadays, extensive breeding has resulted in a vast number of plants with diverse garden use. Some are climbers useful for clothing walls or growing through trees, but the majority are shrubs for use as bedding, in mixed plantings or as specimens, with some more recent introductions being excellent for containers or as groundcover. Many modern roses have an extended flowering season – from summer until well into autumn.

320 What are old roses?

Old roses are mainly of European or Middle Eastern origin and do not have the capacity to repeat flower. Instead they flower prolifically, putting on an appealing display for a few weeks of each year. They tend to have large,

▼ **319** *Roses are plants of high summer, filling the air around them with a bewitching fragrance.*

▲ **320** *'Old Blush China' is a long-flowering rose that can be grown as a shrub or a rambler.*

many-petalled, flattened flowers, often sweetly fragrant, in a restricted colour range – white, pink and dusky red. Old roses usually make rangy shrubs in the garden.

321 What are modern roses?

Modern roses were bred from oriental roses – so-called China and tea roses. Plants introduced to the West in

▲ **321** Rosa x odorata *'Mutabilis' has flowers that change colour from peachy yellow to pink as they age.*

the middle of the 18th century were not hardy, so were grown only by wealthy connoisseurs in conservatories (sun rooms). They were crossed with European types in the 19th century to produce a range of hardy roses that have inherited the repeat-flowering capacity of the oriental roses. Their characteristically pointed buds open to high-centred flowers throughout summer or in two distinct flushes. Some are fragrant and all need pruning in spring.

322 What are the recent developments in rose breeding?

During the last few decades, rose breeders have concentrated on producing compact plants with glossy leaves that are disease-resistant, suitable for small gardens and/or growing in containers. These are the so-called patio and groundcover roses. Rugosa roses, of which there are a growing number, have been bred from the Japanese *Rosa rugosa* – a tough plant, tolerant of shade, poor soil and urban pollution, with large fragrant flowers and large, tomato-like autumn hips.

▲ **323** *Many ramblers produce their flowers in a single flush in early summer on long, arching stems.*

323 What is the difference between a climber and a rambler?

As in other areas of gardening, lines of demarcation are blurred and there is no agreement even among rose breeders themselves. As a general rule, ramblers are extemely vigorous, with arching, often thorny, canes. The flowers, usually in clusters, appear in one spectacular flush in early summer. Climbers are more variable, some

▼ **324** *Hybrid teas have urn-shaped flowers, inherited from the oriental roses from which they were bred.*

▲ **323** *A climber can scale the walls of a large house, provided the stems are carefully tied in as they grow.*

being rampant, others more compact – and not all are thorny. They flower either in two distinct flushes or intermittently over a long period over the summer.

324 What is a hybrid tea rose?

Hybrid teas – hybrids of the oriental tea roses and hardy Europeans – were first produced in the latter half of the 19th century. They have large flowers,

▼ **325** *'The Fairy' is a dainty rose that is suitable for growing either in a border or in a large container.*

carried singly at the ends of upright-growing stems. Many are excellent as cut flowers, but can be difficult to place in the border – the plants are often ungainly and flowering can be sparse. They are sometimes called 'large-flowered bush roses'.

325 What is a floribunda?

Floribundas, bred in the 20th century, have large flowers – but these are smaller than a hybrid tea's and carried in clusters. Well-grown floribundas are covered in flowers in summer in a way that hybrid teas seldom are. These roses were bred primarily for use in public gardens to provide sheets of colour over a long period. Sometimes called 'cluster-flowered bush roses', they have lost ground in recent years to patio roses, which are usually more compact.

326 What is a patio rose?

Patio roses – or dwarf cluster-flowered bush roses – were bred to meet the need of gardeners for smaller plants than the old-fashioned floribundas that would be more disease-resistant and easier to prune. They are tough, hardy plants, well-clothed with glossy green leaves and clusters of small flowers over an extended period in summer. Groundcover roses are similar, but with a more spreading habit.

▼ **326** *Rosa 'Apricot Summer' is a patio rose with a neat, compact habit, perfect for growing in containers.*

327 What is a shrub rose?

Rose classification is not an exact science – essentially, all roses are shrubs. But over the years, breeders have produced varieties that do not fit easily into any of the usual categories. Shrub roses are usually large, vigorous roses that are bigger than hybrid teas and floribundas. 'Nevada', with a single but sumptuous display of semi-double, creamy white flowers in early summer, and 'Buff Beauty', with two flushes of soft apricot, double flowers, are two tried-and-tested shrubs. They make excellent border plants or can be grown in splendid isolation.

328 What are English roses?

Around the middle of the 20th century, David Austin set about breeding a new range of plants that would combine the flower shapes and fragrance of the old roses with the robust habit and extended colour range – as well as the ability to repeat flower – of more recent introductions. The result was the English roses.

329 What is a miniature climber?

A miniature climber has small flowers like a miniature or patio rose but produces longer stems. They are suitable for training against walls or fences or on arches, trellis or pillars up to about 2m (6ft) or less. They are excellent for a small

▲ **334** *The flowers of 'Constance Spry' are almost globular, bright pink and with a strong fragrance, providing a spectacular display.*

garden or in containers on a patio. They can also be used to trail in large hanging baskets and are suitable as groundcover, especially cascading over a bank.

330 What is a bare-root rose?

Bare-root roses, like bare-root trees, are field grown and lifted from the soil when dormant in late autumn. They are usually available throughout autumn and winter. Most growers supply them mail order, and this is the best way of acquiring rare varieties. They are cheaper than pot-grown roses, which are usually only available in summer.

Bare-root roses should be planted as soon as possible after arrival. But if conditions are unsuitable – for instance, if the ground is frozen or temporarily flooded – they can be stored unopened in a cool, dark place such as a shed or garage. To plant, prepare the planting hole first, forking over the soil and digging in organic matter. Soak the roots for around an hour. Trim back any weak, straggly growth and cut back any damaged topgrowth before setting the plant in the hole and back-filling.

331 How deep should I plant my roses?

At the base of the stems you will see a knobbly, woody bit – the grafting union. When you plant the rose, this should be just below ground level. This creates a more stable and better-looking plant. If you plant with the grafting union above ground level, there is a danger that the roots will be exposed and strong winds will pull the plant from the ground. The graft union should only just be covered, though, or the stems may rot.

332 What is the best way to make sure a new rose gets off to a good start?

Nowadays, it is widely believed that good root growth is dependent on fungi in the soil that attach themselves to plant roots, thus enabling them to take in more moisture – and hence nutrients from the soil. Products containing the fungi are available from rose growers for incorporating into the planting hole. Make sure that individual roots are in contact with the product.

333 Which types of rose have the strongest scent?

It is commonly assumed that so-called old roses have the strongest scent, while their modern descendants have lost this attribute. This is not entirely true. While most modern roses have

▼ **334** *'Céleste', or 'Celestial', produces clusters of light pink fragrant flowers.*

▲ **334** *The scent of 'Apricot Nectar' is strong and fruity.*

▲ **334** *The open flowers of 'Escapade' have a sweet, musky fragrance.*

▲ **334** *'Fragrant Cloud' has one of the strongest scents of any modern rose.*

been bred for health, vigour, length of flowering season and depth of colour, many also have a rich scent comparable to that of their forebears.

334 Which varieties are particularly valued for their scent?

'Albertine'
'Ambridge Rose'
'Apricot Nectar'
'Blue Moon'
'Buff Beauty'
'Céleste'
'Charles Darwin'
'Constance Spry'
'Escapade'
'Evelyn'
'Fantin-Latour'
'Fragrant Cloud'

'Gertrude Jekyll'
'Golden Celebration'
'Harlow Carr'
'Jude the Obscure'
'Lady Emma Hamilton'
'Lady Hillingdon'
'Mme Hardy'
'Mme Isaac Pereire'
'Margaret Merril'
'Memorial Day'
'New Dawn'
'Reine Victoria'
Rosa rugosa
'Scepter'd Isle'
'Sharifa Asma'
'Sheila's Perfume'
'Tea Clipper'
'Whisky Mac'
'Wild Edric'

335 Which varieties show resistance to disease?

Note that not all roses will show the same degree of resistance to disease in all areas – for the best information, contact a local rose grower. The following have some of the best disease-resistant qualitites.

'Alpine Sunset'
'Apricot Nectar'
'Champagne Moments'
'Dainty Bess'
'Elina'
'Fragrant Cloud'
'Ingrid Bergman'
'Mountbatten'
'Polar Star'
Rosa rugosa
'Sexy Rexy'

▼ **334** *As well as its intriguing colour, 'Whisky Mac' has good fragrance.*

▼ **335** *'Sexy Rexy' is an excellent rose that is resistant to disease.*

▼ **335** *'Mountbatten' is a vigorous and extremely healthy variety.*

◄ **338** *Floribunda roses are excellent for use in mixed borders.*

to help build new flowers. Water plants well in mid-summer, especially during dry spells.

338 Can I grow roses in mixed flower borders?
Yes, in fact this is a good way to incorporate those roses that tend to go leggy at the base – their bare stems can be disguised by other lower-growing plants. Roses combine well with a range of herbaceous plants such as peonies, hostas, geraniums and lavenders.

339 Which rose varieties are thornless?
'A Shropshire Lad' (shrub)
'Amadis' (rambler)
'Belle de Crécy' (shrub)
'Bleu Magenta' (rambler)
'Cardinal de Richelieu' (shrub)
'Charles de Mills' (shrub)
'Complicata' (climber/shrub)
'Empress Joséphine' (shrub)
'Goldfinch' (shrub)
'Ipsilante' (shrub)
'James Galway' (climber/shrub)
'John Clare' (shrub)
'Kathleen Harrop' (climber)
'Mme Legras de St Germain' (shrub)
'Mortimer Sackler' (climber)

336 Which roses have the longest flowering season?
So-called remontant roses repeat flower – either in two distinct flushes, or intermittently over a long period. The majority of new introductions flower over a long period, producing their blooms throughout summer.

337 How do I persuade my roses to keep flowering?
Feed roses well with a rose fertilizer in early spring, immediately after pruning. In summer, deadhead them rigorously to encourage further flower production. After the first flush of flowers, feed again with rose fertilizer

▼ **339** *'Cardinal de Richelieu' is richly scented and thornless.*

▼ **339** *Thornless* Rosa gallica var. officinalis *is the apothecary's rose.*

▼ **339** Rosa *'Veilchenblau' is a rambler with lilac flowers and mid-green leaves.*

▲ **341** *Patio roses have a small, compact, upright habit.*

▲ **341** *Rosa 'Lancashire' grows into an attractive container shrub.*

▲ **344** *A* Rosa rugosa *hedge is an appealing sight in autumn.*

'Président de Sèze' (shrub)
Rosa gallica var. *officinalis* (shrub)
Rosa officinalis (shrub)
'Rose-Marie Viaud' (rambler/shrub)
'Snow Goose' (rambler)
'Tea Clipper' (shrub)
'The Generous Gardener' (climber)
'Tuscany Superb' (shrub)
'Veilchenblau' (rambler)
'Violette' (rambler)

340 What is rose sick soil?
This is an urban myth. It is an oft-repeated piece of gardening 'wisdom' that if you need to replace a rose, you cannot replant in the same soil – fresh soil has to be imported or the new rose should be planted some distance away from the original one. It was assumed that a rose 'exhausts' the soil so that a replacement will fail to thrive. This may be true if the original rose has been neglected without regular feeding or mulching, but in most cases there will be no problems with replacing a rose. Commercial rose growers regularly replace stocks in fields without changing the soil. In any case, when a plant is removed, the soil where it is sited needs to be dug over and prepared for the new planting with the addition of compost.

341 Which roses can I grow in containers?
Patio roses have been bred to thrive in containers. Groundcover roses and miniature climbers can also be used.

342 Can I grow roses organically?
With difficulty. Some rose fertilizers are described as 'organic based', but this is not the same as being totally organic. Most roses are highly bred plants that need high levels of

▼ **344** *Rosa 'Alexander' is a hybrid tea rose that is perfect for hedging.*

potassium to flower to their optimum. There are not many naturally occurring sources of potassium apart from wood ash and banana skins, which can be dug in around the roots.

343 What are 'bedding' roses?
Bedding roses were bred for use in public parks and gardens to provide flowers over a long period in summer. They were intended to be planted *en masse*. Many groundcover and patio roses are suitable for bedding and are usually compact.

344 Which are the best rose varieties for hedging?
'Alexander'
'Anne Harkness'
'Buff Beauty'
'Charles de Mills'
'Chinatown'
'Harlow Carr'
'Hyde Hall'
'Little White Pet'
'Queen of Sweden'
Rosa gallica
Rosa mollineux
Rosa rugosa
'Super Star'
'The Queen Elizabeth'
'Wild Edric'

345 My soil is poor and dry – can I still grow roses?

Roses appreciate fertile soil, but a few will tolerate less than ideal growing conditions. *Rosa rugosa* and its hybrids (e.g. 'Agnes') are reliable, but the best advice is always to improve the soil as much as you can by digging in organic matter before planting. Mulch the plants generously in spring or autumn.

346 Can I incorporate roses in a wildlife garden?

Yes, but concentrate on so-called wild roses, which produce single flowers in summer followed by ornamental hips. The open flowers will attract bees and other pollinating insects while the hips will be a food source for birds in the autumn.

347 Which are the best varieties for cut flowers?

'Ingrid Bergman' (shrub)
'Just Joey' (shrub)
'Louise Odier' (shrub)
'Mamy Blue' (shrub)

▼ **346** *The scent of roses attracts bees and butterflies into the garden. Later in the season the rosehips will attract garden birds.*

'Michèle Meilland' (shrub)
'Perle Noire' (shrub)
'Saint-Exupéry'
'Sweet Juliet' (shrub)
'Terracotta' (shrub)

348 Can I use roses for groundcover?

So-called groundcover roses are a relatively new introduction. They are tough, hardy, compact plants with a tendency to form low, spreading mounds. To grow them as ground-cover, plant them in groups. Peg down flexible stems as they grow to develop seamless coverage. The stems will root where they touch the ground. Thorny stems can make weeding difficult , but should eventually form a weed-proof mat.

349 How do I prune established groundcover roses?

A strict pruning regime is not necessary. Simply shear over the plants in early spring. If the roses are repeat-flowering, clip over them again in mid-summer.

350 Can any roses be grown in a shady garden?

No rose will do well in deep shade, but many flower in light shade

provided the soil is not poor and dry. Red-flowered roses are particularly worth trying in shade. The flowering may not be prolific, but the flowers will hold their colour better than in full sun.

351 Which roses tolerate light shade conditions?

'Agnes' (shrub)
'Albéric Barbier' (rambler)
'Ballerina' (shrub)
'Blanche Double de Coubert' (shrub)
'Crimson Shower' (rambler)
'Danse du Feu' (climber)
'Félicité Perpétue' (rambler)
'Frühlingsmorgen' (shrub)
'Golden Showers' (climber)
'Laura Ford' (miniature climber)
'Mme Alfred Carrière' (climber)
'Mme Plantier' (rambler)
'Maigold' (climber)
'Mermaid' (climber)
'New Dawn' (climber)
'Rambling Rector' (rambler)
'Seagull' (rambler)
'Veilchenblau' (rambler)
'Wedding Day' (rambler)
'White Pet' (shrub)

352 How do I train a rose to cover a framework?

Roses can be trained, like other climbing plants, to cover fences and structures and to grow through other shrubs and trees. Tie the rose in carefully and loosely at regular intervals so as not to restrict its growth, but sufficiently to support the stems. Prune the whole plant to support the required shape.

353 Which roses have the best autumn hips?

'Francis E. Lester' (rambler)
'Kew Rambler' (rambler)
'Pleine de Grâce' (rambler)
'Rambling Rector' (rambler)
Rosa filipes 'Kiftsgate' (rambler)
Rosa forrestiana (shrub)
Rosa macrophylla (shrub)
Rosa mulliganii (rambler)
Rosa officinalis (shrub)
Rosa rugosa (shrub)
Rosa setipoda (shrub)

Training a rose

1 To train a rose to cover a trellis or other structure, tie strong stems to the structure with string, allowing sufficient space for the rose to grow. Prune judiciously to create the shape required and continue to tie in the stems as they grow to create a dense and strong framework.

2 To train a rose along a wire, attach the main stem first to an upright post, tying it in securely. Once the rose has grown sufficiently, start to train the horizontal shoots along wires, tying them in every 30cm (12in). Remove any crossing stems and side shoots that are too large.

3 To train a rose through a tree, plant the rose 30–45cm (12–18in) from the base of the tree, angling it slightly towards the tree. Stick canes in the ground near the rose and angle them towards the tree. Tie the rose to the canes, and continue tying in as it grows to the tree.

354 Can I train a rose through an old apple tree?

This is one of the most effective and romantic ways of growing climbers and ramblers – breathtaking once established and in full flower – but you have to choose your varieties with care. A mature tree will have exhausted the soil around its roots. It will be prone to dryness and low in nutrients. Only naturally vigorous rose varieties can cope with this. Conversely, if the tree is very old or weakened through disease, a vigorous rose can pull it down, or weaken it further. Thorny rose varieties are best, as these will cling to the tree bark, allowing the stems to climb to the canopy.

355 How do I plant and train a rose up and through the branches of a tree?

Plant the rose at least 1m (3ft), or more, away from the tree's trunk. Angle the stems towards the tree. Insert long canes around the planting hole angled towards the tree and tied into suitably placed lower branches. Tie the rose stems to the canes. Continue to tie them as they grow. Once the stems have reached the tree

branches and the thorns have started to dig into the bark on the stems, you can remove the canes. Pruning a rose grown in this way is not practical. In time, you may need to remove woody, old stems by cutting through them at the base.

356 Which are the best rose varieties for growing into a tree?

'Albéric Barbier'
'Bobbie James'
'Cécile Brunner'
'Complicata'
'Crimson Shower'
'Félicité et Perpétue'
'Francis E. Lester'
'François Juranville'
'Kew Rambler'
'Rambling Rector'
Rosa wichurana
'Wedding Day'

357 Which varieties are suitable for arches and pergolas?

'Adelaide d'Orléans'
'Climbing Iceberg'
'Crépuscule'
'Crimson Shower'
'Flora'
'Malvern Hills'

'New Dawn'
'Open Arms'
'Paul Noël'
'Phyllis Bide'
'Princesse Louise'
'Rambling Rosie'
'Snow Goose'
'Super Dorothy'
'Super Fairy'
'The Generous Gardener'

▼ **351** *'White Pet' is suitable for lightly shady conditions.*

PERENNIALS

A plant or shrub with a long life span is known as a perennial. After the tall trees, these shrubs form the background against which fleeting annuals perform. Choose them for their colours, textures and leaf shapes as well as for their blooms.

358 When is the best time to buy perennials for the flower garden?

Evergreen perennials, such as hellebores (*Helleborus*), can be bought and planted at any time of year when the ground is workable – not during freezing periods in winter or prolonged hot dry spells in summer. Mild, damp weather in spring or autumn is ideal.

Herbaceous perennials – which die back in winter – are not usually sold in winter, but are usually available only during the growing season.

359 What are tender perennials?

This is a whole group of plants that have become popular on account of the seemingly unending succession of flowers they produce throughout the summer and on until the first frosts. Many are of South African origin, including such plants as the osteospermums and felicias, or other warm temperate parts of the globe, such as the heliotropes. In sheltered areas, they can flower throughout the winter. They are excellent in sunny borders, provided the soil is well-drained, and can also be used in

containers and hanging baskets. In cold areas, either discard them at the end of the growing season, overwinter them in frost-free conditions, or – if they have become woody at the base – take cuttings for use the following year.

360 How do I choose the most suitable perennials for my site?

When choosing which perennials to grow, it is obviously important to consider the conditions that you have to offer them. In a well-drained soil in full sun peonies (*Paeonia*), Oriental poppies (*Papaver orientale*), lamb's ears (*Stachys byzantina*) or springtime pasque flowers (*Pulsatilla vulgaris*) will all flourish. Conversely, primulas, pulmonarias and the bleeding heart (*Dicentra spectabilis*) are best for planting in a damp, shady hollow.

361 How should I plant herbaceous perennials?

You should plant herbaceous perennials in either spring or autumn. The advantage of autumn planting is usually noticed on drier soils as the plants establish well and are

▲ **364** *'Cool borders' are predominantly soft blue, white, pink and lilac.*

potentially more drought-resistant. Those planted on heavier soils may benefit from spring planting, as heavy soils may be wet and cold, which can cause newly planted specimens to rot. Pot-grown specimens should be watered, and the ground dug and manured, before planting. A base dressing of bonemeal or fish, blood and bone may also be applied. Dig a hole larger than the rootball and ensure that the plant is firmed in well, taking care not to compact the soil.

362 Can I buy perennials bare-root?

Certain popular perennials, such as hostas, delphiniums and poppies, are sometimes available bare-root in late winter to early spring. Depending on how long they have been out of the ground, they can be difficult to establish. They need regular and careful watering after planting.

◄ **363** *'Hot borders' are cheering with their bright and colourful hues.*

363 What perennials can I use for a hot-coloured border?

Achillea filipendulina (bright yellow)
Anthemis sancti-johannis (bright orange)
Coreopsis grandiflora 'Early Sunshine' (bright yellow)
Crocosmia 'Lucifer' (red)
Dahlia 'Bishop of Llandaff' (bright red)
Gaillardia x *grandiflora* 'Dazzler' (bright red and yellow)
Geum 'Red Wings' (bright scarlet)
Helenium 'Butterpat' (bright yellow)
Helenium 'Moerheim Beauty' (copper red)
Hemerocallis 'Christmas Is' (red)
Hemerocallis 'Scarlet Orbit' (bright red)
Kniphofia 'Prince Igor' (deep orange-red)
Ligularia 'The Rocket' (yellow)
Lobelia 'Dark Crusader' (deep red)
Lobelia 'Queen Victoria' (scarlet red)
Lysimmachia nummularia (bright yellow)
Lychnis chalcedonica (scarlet red)
Rudbeckia fulgida var. *sullivantii* 'Goldsturm' (bright yellow)
Solidago 'Goldenmosa' (golden yellow)
Verbascum olympicum (golden yellow)

◀ **365** *Christmas roses* (Helleborus) *do well in winter.*

364 What perennials can I use for a cool-coloured border?

Achillea 'Anthea' (pale yellow)
Artemisia absinthium (soft yellow)
Campanula lactiflora (pale blue)
Delphinium 'Princess Caroline' (pale pink)
Galium odoratum (white)
Gentiana asclepiadea (bright blue)
Geranium pratense 'Mrs Kendall Clark' (violet-blue)
Gypsophila paniculata (white)
Hemerocallis 'Gentle Shepherd' (creamy white)
Kniphofia 'Little Maid' (pale yellow)
Lupinus 'Chandelier' (pale yellow)
Nepeta x *faassenii* (pale lilac-blue)
Pulsatilla vulgaris f. *alba* (pure white)
Scabiosa caucasica 'Miss Willmott' (white)
Verbena peruviana 'Alba' (white)

365 Are there any perennials that flower in winter?

Winter-flowering perennials are few, but among the best are the hellebores (*Helleborus*). White-flowered Christmas rose (*Helleborus niger*) flowers in the depths of winter, but is

▼ **366** *Grasses need little attention, and the evergreen ones will add presence to the border for much of the year.*

difficult to establish. Easier are the many plants that go under the name Lenten rose (*Helleborus orientalis*). In a mild season, these will start flowering at the turn of the year and should be well into their stride by the end of winter. Winter heliotrope (*Petasites japonicus*) produces attractive flowers in mid-winter, but is invasive so suitable for only the largest gardens.

366 How do I groom a perennial grass?

Many perennial grasses provide interest over winter, showing appealing shades of beige and bronze and giving life to the garden as they move in the breeze. Spring is the time to tidy them up. Cut back any faded flower stems and any leaves that are showing signs of brown. Beware – some of the leaf edges can be as sharp as knives. If the growth is very congested, dig up the whole plant and cut it into smaller sections.

367 Should I cut back my perennials every year?

Some shrubby perennials (often referred to as sub-shrubs), such as *Phygelius* and *Penstemon*, benefit from being pruned annually in early spring. The older twiggy and unproductive growth is cut hard back to promote the growth of new shoots that will flower in summer and autumn.

▲ **369** *Dahlias grow from tubers. They need to be dug up in the winter and can be replanted the following year.*

368 What is 'stopping' as applied to herbaceous perennials?

This is the removal of the growing tip of a stem in order to encourage the side shoots to develop. The tips may be pinched out when the plant has attained a third of its ultimate height. This encourages the buds on the leaf axils to develop and leads to more flowers being produced, although these will be smaller than if the one terminal bud had been allowed to flower. This technique is successful for a range of plants including *Helenium, Rudbeckia, Chrysanthemum* and *Dahlia.*

369 Can I transplant perennials?

Most perennials can be transplanted fairly easily. This should be done in the dormant season, which is usually in autumn or early spring. Some plants dislike cold, wet conditions and these should be moved once the soil has warmed sufficiently to encourage growth. This is particularly true of any plants that are not fully hardy. Some plants that are relatively long-lived, such as peonies (*Paeonia*), resent being disturbed and will take a few years to establish again after transplanting.

▲ **373** Buddleja *varieties attract butterflies into the garden all summer long.*

370 How can I encourage my perennials to repeat-flower?

After flowering, many herbaceous perennials such as hardy geraniums, delphiniums and lady's mantle (*Alchemilla mollis*) respond well to cutting back to ground level. Give a light dressing of a general-purpose fertilizer and a generous watering in dry seasons, and the plant will respond by producing a secondary flush of foliage and flowers.

371 Which are the best perennials for cut flowers?

Achillea
Aster
Astrantia
Callistephus
Campanula lactiflora
Clematis
Delphinium
Dianthus
Geum
Kniphofia
Lupinus
Osteospermum
Paeonia
Rudbeckia
Scabiosa
Schizostylis
Solidago

372 Which perennials produce the best flowers for drying?

Achillea
Amaranthus
Astrantia
Bracteantha
Centaurea
Consolida
Cortaderia selloana
Echinops ritro
Hydrangea macrophylla
Limonium
Nigella
Sedum spectabile

373 Which are the best perennials for attracting bees and butterflies?

Ajuga reptans
Allium schoenoprasum
Asclepias incarnata
Aster
Echinacea purpurea
Echium vulgare
Eryngium planum
Lamium orvala
Lunaria rediviva
Mentha longifolia
Monarda
Origanum
Papave orientale
Papaver rhoeas
Penstemon
Prunella
Sedum
Tagetes
Trachelium

ANNUALS AND BIENNIALS

If you are looking for a feast of flowers in summer, annuals provide a speedy answer. Whether you grow your own from seed in a greenhouse or buy bedding plants from a garden centre, weeks of continuous colour in the garden are guaranteed.

374 What is an annual?

An annual is a plant that completes its growth cycle within one calendar year – the seed germinates in spring, produces leaves and roots, flowers, then sets seed and dies.

375 What is a biennial?

Biennials germinate in summer to autumn, the seedling overwinters, then flowers the following spring. Essentially, annuals and biennials are the same thing – plants that complete their life cycle within 12 months. You can sow the seed of many annuals in autumn for early flowers the following year – and some biennials, if sown in early spring, will flower the same year.

▶ **378** *A formal border with annuals planted in rows takes time to plan and plant up but is worth the effort.*

▼ **374** *A rock garden planted with annual pelargoniums and busy Lizzies* (Impatiens) *provides a riot of colour. An entirely new look can be achieved the following season with different plants.*

376 What is meant by hardy and half-hardy annuals?

A hardy annual is one that is capable of surviving frost. In practice, this means that they can be sown outdoors in spring before the last frosts. Half-hardy annuals cannot withstand frost. Early sowings need protection from frost – or they can be sown outdoors once all danger of hard frosts has passed.

377 Should I grow my own annuals?

Although garden centres are filled with bedding plants (low-growing annuals used to fill up garden beds) at various times of year, it is easy to raise your own from seed. You will also have a much wider choice of varieties, especially if you order your seeds from a seed merchant. It's best to order well in advance of sowing, as popular or unusual varieties can sell out rapidly.

378 Annuals sound like a lot of work – is it worth growing them?

Despite their short life, annuals have a longer flowering season than most other plants. Planted in drifts, they are unrivalled for producing sheets of colour throughout summer. Use them as summer bedding, to fill gaps in beds and borders, and in containers, window boxes and hanging baskets. They can also be grown in a kitchen garden to supply cut flowers for the house and to attract beneficial pollinating insects. Growing your own is more economical than buying them in plugs, too.

▲ **384** *Round flowers provide an ideal landing platform for bees and butterflies, from which they collect pollen.*

▲ **385** *Sweet peas* (Lathyrus odoratus) *have an old-fashioned scent, and the flowers are also excellent for cutting.*

▲ **385** Agastache foeniculum *is an attractive spreading plant with a scent of licorice.*

379 What are strains and series?

Annuals and biennials have been bred to produce plants with as much uniformity as possible. All seeds in any particular packet should grow into plants of a similar size with similar characteristics. Sometimes, however, there can be a variation in flower colour – or some other attribute – and these seeds are usually marketed as strains or series. For example, the Rocket Series of snapdragons (*Antirrhinum majus*)

produces reliably vigorous plants that flower profusely in a range of colours. Occasionally, it is possible through careful selection to isolate seeds that will produce flowers in a particular colour. This is the case with certain tobacco plants, such as *Nicotiana* x *sanderae* Domino Series 'Salmon Pink'.

380 What are F1 and F2 hybrids?

F1 hybrids are the result of the deliberate crossing of two seed strains that have been successively inbred to consolidate certain desirable characteristics. The resulting plants combine the uniformity produced by inbreeding with the vigour produced by cross-breeding. They are the first filial (F1) generation of plants. F1 hybrid seeds are usually more expensive than other seeds, but are often preferred by gardeners because they germinate so easily and produce such good plants.

Four selected parents can be used to produce a second filial generation

◄ **381** *Annuals need plenty of prepared soil into which their roots will spread easily as they grow.*

(F2) hybrids. The four strains chosen are effectively the grandparents of the F2 seed.

381 How do I prepare the soil before planting annuals?

Annuals do not need soil of high fertility, but it should be free-draining. Dig over the soil and add grit if it is heavy. Rake the surface to a fine tilth.

382 When should I plant annuals?

Plants should be bushy, sturdy and well-developed, with a good root system before they can be planted in their flowering positions. Hardy annuals can be planted in mid-spring when the ground is workable. Delay planting out half-hardy annuals until there is no longer any risk of night frosts – usually in late spring.

383 Can I scatter seeds on bare soil?

If you like your garden to be a relaxed riot of colour, by all means scatter seeds wherever you want summer flowers in late spring. However, there is a risk that you will mistake the emerging seedlings for weeds and hoe them off by accident. It is best to raise annuals either in pots or trays or in a seed bed in the vegetable garden. But if you appreciate scent in the garden, then sprinkle seeds of night-scented stock (*Matthiola longipetala* subsp. *bicornis*) among other plants.

384 Which types of flowers will attract bees?

Bees prefer flowers that open wide and flat to display their pollen-laden stamens. This includes single roses, plants belonging to the buttercup family (Ranunculaceae) and many annuals such as the poached egg plant (*Limnanthes douglasii*). Autumn-flowering *Sedum spectabile* is excellent. Ivies provide an excellent food source for bees in autumn–winter. Many annuals have flowers that are attractive to bees.

385 Which are the best annuals for scent?

Agastache
Centaurea moschata
Cheiranthus cheiri
Exacum affine
Lathyrus odoratus
Lobularia maritima
Matthiola incana

▼ **385** Nicotiana *flowers have a warm, incense-like fragrance in the evening.*

▶ **387** *Deadheading annuals promptly ensures that they will carry on producing new flowers.*

Nicotiana alata
Primula
Reseda odorata
Scabiosa atropurpurea
Verbena

386 How do I ensure a succession of flowers from summer to autumn?

Annuals can flower for up to six to eight weeks. To extend the flowering season into late summer–autumn, make a second sowing at the same time as you plant out the first batch of seedlings. As these begin to exhaust themselves, replace them with the second sowing, which should by now have reached flowering size.

387 How do I persuade annuals to keep on flowering?

Keep deadheading plants as the old flowers fade. This encourages the plants to produce a fresh crop of flowers. If you wish to collect a specific plant seed at the end of the season, leave a few flowers on the plants to produce seedheads.

▼ **388** *Cleomes are among the stateliest of annuals, with white or pink flowers.*

388 Which are the best annuals and biennials for cut flowers?

Amaranthus caudatus
Ammi majus
Antirrhinum
Cerinthe major
Cleome
Cosmos
Helianthus annuus
Lathyrus odoratus
Moluccella laevis
Nigella damascena
Scabiosa
Tithonia rotundiflora

▼ **388** *Scabious* (Scabiosa) *are attractive annuals with pincushion-like flowers.*

BULBS, CORMS AND TUBERS

Few plant groups can match the vivid colours of bulbs. Spring bulbs provide carpets of flowers at the start of the year, often in tones of white, yellow and blue, while summer-flowering ones are more majestic. A precious few produce their flowers in autumn.

389 What are bulbs, corms and tubers?

A bulb is a perennial plant with a special underground storage organ that allows it to go dormant when conditions are unfavourable for growth – usually during freezing weather in winter and hot dry spells in summer. Bulbs comprise modified leaves fixed to a basal plate from which the roots grow. A corm (e.g. *Crocus, Gladiolus, Anemone blanda*) has a similar function but is solid. Tubers (e.g. *Dahlia*) are knobbly roots.

390 What are the best spring bulbs for growing in a lawn?

You need early-flowering, robust bulbs that can compete with the grass. *Crocus tommasinianus*, with silvery lilac flowers, is a good choice for late winter. Daffodils (*Narcissus*) can provide flowers throughout spring if you pick and choose among the many varieties. Crown imperials (*Fritillaria meleagris*) need moist soil to flourish.

▼ **390** *Plant bulbs with a bulb planter in lawns in small groups.*

▲ **391** *Drifts of English bluebells provide a glimmer of blue in light woodland.*

Leave lawn areas containing bulbs for eight weeks after the last bulbs have flowered before mowing, so that the bulbs have time to die back.

391 What is meant by 'naturalizing' bulbs?

The aim of naturalizing is to allow plants to spread and set seed where they will, so that after a few years they create a carpet of flowers. Only species are suitable, as they usually set copious amounts of seed. Among the best are *Crocus tommasinianus* and *Fritillaria meleagris*.

392 Which are the best bulbs for growing under deciduous trees?

The majority of spring-flowering bulbs need full sun, so choose early varieties that will flower and die back before the tree's leaf canopy above them is fully developed. Snowdrops

▲ **391** *Snowflakes* (Leucojum) *thrive in damp or heavy soil and naturalize easily.*

(*Galanthus*), winter aconites (*Eranthis*), crocuses and early daffodils (*Narcissus*) are suitable. Most tulips flower too late. Among the summer bulbs, some of the lilies (such as *Lilium martagon*) tolerate dappled shade. The autumn crocus (*Colchicum sativum*), (which is related to the lilies) can be planted towards the edge of a leaf canopy.

393 My daffodils have stopped flowering – why?

If daffodils suddenly fail to flower, it may be because they are congested. Dig up the clumps when the leaves are above ground and separate them out. Replant, allowing adequate space between each bulb for good growth. Feed the bulbs with a general garden fertilizer in the autumn and again in spring. They may need a year or two to recover and build up their reserves before they flower again.

▲ **395** *Grape hyacinths (Muscari) are best planted in bold drifts.*

▲ **396** *Summer bulbs add extraordinary colour and variety to the borders.*

397 What are the best bulbs, tubers and corms for autumn?

Dahlias and gladioli are among the easiest of autumn flowerers, with a vast range of hybrids in all colours except blue. There are also many South African bulbs that flower at this time of year – nerines, amaryllis and crinums. None of these are reliably hardy and all need a sheltered spot in cold gardens.

394 Do I need to lift bulbs after they have flowered?

No. In the past, tulips were commonly grown in spring bedding schemes, then lifted after flowering to make way for summer annuals. Because the flowering potential of many modern hybrids is much reduced in

▼ **396** *Alliums are some of the most spectacular summer-flowering bulbs.*

subsequent years, they are best replaced with fresh bulbs annually each autumn. Very vigorous bulbs can be left *in situ*. If you wish to lift the bulbs to protect them from mice, it is easiest to plant them in mesh plastic pots such as are used for water plants, then lift the whole pot after flowering. This avoids possible damage caused by forking up the clumps, or even digging into them later in the year.

▼ **397** *Dahlia tubers need lifting and storing once they have flowered.*

395 When is the best time to plant spring bulbs?

It is best to plant spring bulbs in mid- to late autumn, when the weather has already started to cool significantly. Plant too early, and there is a risk that the dormant bulbs will start into growth – meaning that any flowers will be lost.

396 Which bulbs flower in summer?

Queens among the summer bulbs are the lilies (*Lilium*), but be careful when making a choice, as not all of them will grow in every garden. Some need acid soil, others alkaline. Some tolerate shade, while others need full sun. *Galtonia candicans* produces spires of white flowers in mid-summer.

ROCK GARDEN PLANTS

Many plants are adapted to harsh conditions, including extreme cold, wind and poor, stony soil. Sometimes called rock garden plants, they usually need to be grown in a dedicated area of the garden or an alpine house. They can be stunningly beautiful when in flower.

398 What are rock garden plants?
Rock garden plants are plants that in the wild are found growing among rocks. Here, there is not much soil around the roots and rainwater drains away swiftly. The rock surface reflects light back on to the leaves, which can be succulent.

399 Do rock plants need to be grown in full sun?
Contrary to popular belief, some rock plants are shade-loving. These naturally occur growing among rocks that line streamsides, with a constant flow of fresh water running over their roots and sheltered by larger rocks and/or overhanging trees. Rocks in this situation tend to be moss-covered, as the prevailing conditions are cool and damp. Many ferns and hostas enjoy similar conditions. For this reason, rock gardens are often combined with cascading water features.

▼ *399 Large planters can be sited in the best available space to suit the needs of the rock plants they contain.*

400 What are alpines?
Alpines are a special group of hardy plants that grow in mountain areas between the tree line and the line of permanent snow. Here, the prevailing climate is cold and dry, and sometimes windy. Summers are short. Alpines are dwarf plants that often have relatively large, brilliantly coloured flowers. In winter they may be covered by snow. In the warmer growing season, their roots are washed by melted snow from above running through them. Some are shrubs (deciduous or evergreen), others are perennials. Dwarf bulbs are sometimes treated as alpines, as they need similar growing conditions.

▲ *400 Alpine plants will thrive in rocky ground. In the wild, they survive above the tree line.*

401 What is a scree garden?
A scree is effectively a rock garden made on a flat or, preferably, slightly sloping site, with a few larger rocks set in a deep layer of grit or gravel chips mixed with potting mix. Scree gardens suit spreading and mound-forming alpines and dwarf conifers. They are usually made in full sun.

402 What is an alpine house?
An alpine house is like a greenhouse, but usually has more vents and panels that can be opened. They can be kept

open for most of the year and closed only in the very coldest weather. Insulation is not necessary – the main function of an alpine house is to protect the plants from excessive wet rather than cold.

403 Where should I site the alpine house?
An alpine house should be sited away from fences, walls, tall buildings and trees that may shade the plants. While the site should be open and sunny, there should also be shelter from strong winds.

404 How do I grow alpines?
Alpines are usually grown in individual pots that are sunk into sand-filled raised beds in the alpine house. The sand helps keep the roots cool. Use a very free-draining, gritty potting mix and top the surface with grit so that water does not collect around the neck of the plant. Good ventilation is critical. Doors can be left open, except in high winds or heavy rain, to maximize air circulation. Shading may be required in hot weather to prevent the temperature rising too high.

▼ **401** *To encourage mosses to take a hold on large rocks in a scree garden, paint the rocks with yogurt or sour milk.*

405 What routine maintenance do the plants need?
Check your plants for dead foliage and remove this promptly. Treat all outbreaks of pests and diseases effectively and swiftly. When watering, aim to water around the base of the plants, not directly overhead. (Water can collect in the leaves and lead to rots and other diseases.) Ensure that the potting mix stays moist but is never too dry or too wet.

406 Can I grow alpines in troughs?
If you do not have room for a rock garden, scree or dedicated alpine house, you can grow them in troughs or sinks. Fill these with gritty potting mix topped with a layer of grit to ensure good drainage. During prolonged periods of wet weather, protect the plants with a sheet of glass supported on short stakes inserted in the corners of the trough.

407 I do not have an alpine house. Can I still grow alpines?
Many alpines can be grown in outdoor rock gardens, provided the soil in which they are planted drains freely. Alternatively, grow them in troughs.

▼ **406** *Concrete troughs provide a perfect environment in which to introduce different plants into the garden.*

408 Which plants are suitable for growing in troughs?
Androsace
Arenaria purpurascens
Centaurium scilloides
Dianthus alpinus
Dryas octopetala 'Minor'
Gentiana
Morisia monanthos
Oxalis enneaphylla
Paraquilegia anemonoides
Phlox subulata
Primula farinosa
Saxifraga
Sedum cauticola
Thymus serpyllum
Vitaliana primuliflora

409 Can I use a cold frame for growing alpines?
The problem with cold frames is that the plants are at ground level, so light levels may not be sufficiently high for them to flourish. The plants need to be in full light. Cold frames can be used to grow on bulbs until they are ready to flower. Cold frames are usually sited to harden off tender young plants from the greenhouse before they are planted out, or to protect tender plants over the winter, and as such are not usually sited in a position that will draw maximum attention to a feature area such as an alpine garden.

CARE AND MAINTENANCE

Whatever the garden design, most of the plants in your garden will require some level of care and attention on a regular basis to keep them in top condition, including watering, feeding, deadheading and staking, as well as the overwintering of tender plants.

410 How can I use water sensibly when caring for my plants?

Good watering techniques are vital to avoid waste. It is best to water thoroughly, preferably in the morning or evening when temperatures are lower in order to reduce evaporation. Mulching the soil surface with composted bark or well-rotted garden compost minimizes evaporation, but make sure that the soil is already moist before mulching or rain may not reach the plant roots. In areas with seasonal water shortages consider growing drought-tolerant plants.

411 What are the different methods of watering?

Plants can be watered in many ways, but all methods generally fall into two categories: hand watering or automatic systems. For hand watering, you can use either a watering can or a garden hose. Garden hoses can also be used with various nozzle attachments to deliver a shower, rather than a jet, of water. If you opt for an automatic system, you will find that there is an array of devices to choose from, some of which can deliver doses of water at set times of the day or week. Even the most complex of these use relatively simple water-delivery methods such as seep or drip hoses and sprinklers.

412 Do I have to feed my plants in order to keep them healthy?

Additional feeding should not be necessary for most plants growing in a bed of reasonably well-prepared garden soil. Most plants extract vital nutrients, including the major ones such as nitrogen (N), phosphorus (P) and potassium (K), as well as the trace elements such as calcium, magnesium and sulphur, that they need from the soil. However, many gardeners like to give their plants some form of supplementary feeding at some stage.

▲ 411 *A garden hose punctured with holes can be a permanent feature of beds and borders.*

413 What are the different types of inorganic fertilizer?

You can buy general-purpose granular fertilizers that are applied as a base dressing before cultivating new plants, as well as to established plants at the start of the growing season (perhaps in early spring). Soluble fertilizers are also available, which take effect more quickly than the granular ones. But they need to be applied at regular

▲ 412 *Shrubs that are newly planted will benefit from a handful of fertilizer being sprinkled in the planting hole.*

intervals during the growing season. If you do not have enough time for such a feeding regime, then you could try slow-release fertilizers that, as the name suggests, are released when the soil is damp and warm enough for plant growth. You can also purchase fertilizers for specific purposes such as for roses, lawns and tomatoes. Always follow the manufacturer's directions when using any chemical products in the garden.

414 Are there any organic fertilizers that I can use?

A wide variety of organic substances can be used to boost nutrient levels. They should be used in addition to garden composts and manures. Fish, blood and bone is a balanced general-purpose fertilizer that is normally applied in spring to promote root and shoot growth. Another balanced organic fertilizer is pelleted chicken manure. Hoof and horn can be used to give a slow release of nitrogen where strong growth is needed and is applied in spring or

◀ 417 *Nettle tea can be diluted to feed all garden plants.*

early summer. Bonemeal promotes strong root growth and can be applied as a base dressing prior to planting. (Remember to use gloves and wear a mask when handling bonemeal, and choose a still day.)

415 What is foliar feeding?

Plants in need of a fast-acting treatment, perhaps due to a lengthy dry spell that is affecting the plants' roots or to an attack by a pest or disease, should be foliar fed. Simply spray the leaves with a dilute solution of the chosen fertilizer early in the morning or evening.

416 Do I have to feed all the plants in an ornamental garden?

Trees and shrubs do not generally need regular feeding, although there are some exceptions. A newly planted tree or shrub, for example, should be treated to a slow-release fertilizer such as bonemeal. Also, shrubs with large flowers such as hydrangeas, or a lengthy flowering season, should be fed each year. Border perennials can be treated with a general-purpose fertilizer in spring, while bulbs will also benefit from regular feeding. As they do not have to develop a

storage root system to help them survive the winter, annuals need much less feeding, as do alpines.

417 What is a liquid tea and how do I make it?

Organic liquid teas, often made from comfrey or stinging nettles, are easy to make. You can also use sheep or goat manure, or finely sifted garden compost. Simply fill an old pillowcase with your chosen material and sink it in a large bucket of water. Cover the bucket and let it steep for a few days. Remember, the longer you steep the mixture for, the stronger the resulting tea will be. You can use the final 'solution' as a light liquid feed. It can also be used as a foliar feed (which means that is sprayed directly on to the plant), as long as it is well diluted. The residue in the pillowcase can be used as a mulch.

418 Why is it a good idea to deadhead flowers?

Deadheading is the removal of flowerheads from a plant as they fade so that the plant does not set seed. It is usually recommended in order to enable the plant to concentrate its energies on producing more flowers.

Particularly useful with roses and sweet peas (*Lathyrus odoratus*), the technique does not work for all plants. Poppies (*Papaver*), for example, do not produce more flowers after deadheading. Do not deadhead if the seedpods or fruits are required for ornamental effect, as is the case with honesty (*Lunaria*), for instance.

419 Why is staking important?

Stakes, canes, wire meshes, pea sticks and other means of support are vital for plants with weak stems or those with large flowers that are liable to topple over in an ungainly fashion. The stakes for some plants, such as chrysanthemums and dahlias, are inserted into the ground at the same time as planting, while other plants can be supported while they are quite small, which means that the stems can grow over and disguise the support.

420 Why do I have to overwinter some plants?

Tender plants such as dahlias and chrysanthemums, as well as many bedding plants such as pelargoniums and fuchsias, must either be taken under cover for the winter or be given adequate protection outside.

▼ **418** *Remove faded flowers to encourage the plant to produce more.*

▼ **419** *Use twigs bound together to create a mesh through which plants grow.*

▼ **419** *This wire mesh will quickly be covered by the growing plants.*

GROWING IN CONTAINERS

Container growing is one of the most rewarding branches of gardening, allowing you to grow a much wider range of plants, including exotics. Hanging baskets and window boxes will bring colour right up to the house walls.

421 Which are best – terracotta or plastic containers?

Plastic containers are lightweight, so are relatively easy to move, cheap and easy to keep clean. Available in a wide range of sizes, they can be used for raising and growing on seedlings, striking cuttings, as well as for more permanent plantings. The usual objection made to them is that they are not particularly attractive, though nowadays there are many plastic containers with strong aesthetic appeal. Terracotta is heavier, so is best for large-scale plantings of permanent trees or summer bedding – use plastic and you can end up with a top-heavy container that blows over easily. Many gardeners find that terracotta ages sympathetically, with chips acquired through usage, adding to its charm. But the material is easily broken and can split in hard frosts.

422 What are John Innes potting mix composts?

Potting mix composts based on sterilized soil (sometimes also called loam-based composts) are usually formulated according to formulas laid down by the John Innes Institute.

'John Innes' is not a trade name, and any horticultural company can sell potting mixes that bear this name. John Innes potting mixes come in three grades, each suitable for a different purpose.

423 What is the difference between the various John Innes potting mixes that are available?

John Innes No.1 is used for pricking out seedlings. John Innes No.2 can be used for potting on and is suitable for other plants grown in containers as well as for most houseplants. John Innes No.3 is the potting mix of choice for shrubs and trees that will be in their containers long term. John Innes seed potting mix can be used for germinating seeds, while John Innes cuttings potting mix is low in nutrients, specifically suited for rooting cuttings.

◀ *421 Terracotta pots always look attractive in the garden. Large pots are heavy, however, when full of potting mix and plants, making them difficult to move once fully planted.*

▲ *422 Always use a proprietary potting mix in containers – not garden compost or soil.*

424 What are the advantages/ disadvantages of each potting mix?

Multi-purpose potting mixes are cheap and widely available. They are lightweight and pleasant to handle. However, they do not give such reliable results as soil-based types that are formulated for specific purposes. In use, it is easy to overwet them when watering – conversely, if allowed to dry out, they can be difficult to wet. Some gardeners object to the use of peat, since it is not a renewable resource. Soil-based potting mixes are more expensive and heavier.

425 What is an ericaceous potting mix?

Most potting mixes are alkaline, so are unsuitable for growing camellias, rhododendrons, blueberries and other acid-loving plants. For these, an acidic, ericaceous potting mix should be substituted. Many are based on peat, though, increasingly, soil-based ones are available. For plants that need only slightly acidic conditions, such as citrus, ericaeous potting mix can be mixed with a John Innes type.

426 What is hanging basket potting mix?

It is important to restrict the weight of a hanging basket, so that strain is not put on the fixing. Most potting mixes for hanging baskets, therefore, contain perlite and/or vermiculite to reduce the weight and should have enough fertilizer to keep the plants healthy. Most also contain water-retaining gels. These swell up when you water the basket and reduce the need for regular watering – though this is still important. You can make your own potting mix for use in hanging baskets by adding perlite or vermiculite, fertilizer and gel to multi-purpose potting mix. Plants will still need feeding, however.

427 What is bulb fibre?

Bulb fibre is an open potting mix, often based on peat, that contains charcoal or other material that keeps it 'sweet' – so it can be used in decorative bowls that do not have drainage holes. It is usually used for indoor hyacinths and other bulbs such as freesias that are often grown for

▼ **428** *Potting mix with added grit is good for spring and autumn bulbs.*

interior decoration. Bulb fibre is low in nutrients and should be used for short-term plantings only.

428 What other types of potting mix are there?

Some groups of plants have very specific requirements and for these, it is best to use a special potting mix. Orchid potting mixes are free-draining and nutrient low. Cactus potting mixes are also swift-draining but mineral-rich.

429 How often do I need to water containers?

Potting mix should not be allowed to dry out completely when plants are growing strongly in spring and

◄ **426** *Plants in containers grouped below a hanging basket waste least water.*

summer. Water every day during warm weather. Pay particular attention to trees and shrubs in containers if their canopy extends beyond the container edge. Even during a downpour, the spread of leaves will prevent moisture reaching the compost – they will still need watering.

430 What is the best time of day for watering?

If possible, water in the evening during hot spells – temperatures are lower at night, so the water will evaporate more slowly. Avoid watering during the hottest part of the day. If the plants are in full sun, water on the leaves can scorch them.

431 What should I do if the potting mix has dried out completely?

Potting mixes can become dust-like if they are left unwatered for a while, and it can be difficult to rewet them, particularly in hot weather. Peat-based potting mixes are particularly prone to this problem. It can help if you add a drop of washing-up liquid to the water to help water take-up.

▼ **428** *Bedding plants need nutrient-rich potting mix to flower prolifically.*

432 How do I protect plants in containers from frost?

Plants in containers are much more vulnerable to cold than those grown in the open ground. During very cold weather, the roots can even freeze, especially if the potting mix is wet. To guard against winter losses, plants need some protection during cold snaps. Just bringing them under the cover of an open carport or moving them close to the house wall can be sufficient, but if the plants are too heavy to move, simply wrap a length of hessian (burlap) or plastic bubble wrap around the container, loosely tied in position with garden string.

433 How do I protect the topgrowth?

If you need to keep frost off the buds of early-flowering camellias or the young foliage of a Japanese maple (*Acer palmatum, A. japonicum*), lightly tent the plant with a length of horticultural fleece (or an old net curtain or even sheets of newspaper stapled together). You can also buy special fleece bags designed to fit over the topgrowth and available in different sizes. Whatever you use, the covering should be removed during the day, to allow the leaves to 'breathe'.

▼ **434** *Hanging baskets filled with summer bedding plants flower prolifically if they are nurtured and fed.*

▲ **436** *Fertilizers are formulated as granules or liquids to be dissolved for watering or spraying over plants.*

434 Do my plants in containers need feeding?

Feeding is often overlooked – but the nutrients in potting mix are rapidly used up by the plants, so supplementary feeding is necessary. Feed plants when they are growing strongly in spring and summer, stopping when they go dormant.

435 What do I feed them with?

Trees and shrubs in containers can be fed with an all-purpose garden fertilizer. Roses, rhododendrons, fuchsias and other plants grown for their flowers need a potassium-high fertilizer to improve their flowering. Plants grown for their leaves, such as ferns, hostas and grasses, will appreciate a nitrogen fertilizer such as seaweed extract. Short-term plantings of annuals can be given a tomato fertilizer until they start flowering. Feed bulbs with a general fertilizer immediately after flowering.

436 How do I apply the fertilizer?

Granular or powdered fertilizers can be forked around the base of the plant. Some are sold as pellets that are very convenient to use: they can simply be pressed into the potting mix around the base of a plant. Liquid fertilizers should be watered around the base of a plant (not directly over the leaves or flowers). There is inevitably some wastage with these, so repeated applications have to be made.

437 How do I tell when a plant needs repotting?

Plants that are staying in their containers long-term, such as trees, shrubs, roses and hostas, need repotting when they outgrow their present container. This will become obvious when the roots fill the container. Early to mid-spring is probably the best time for repotting, or, for spring-flowering shrubs, immediately after flowering.

438 I have heard that you should move a plant only into a container the next size up – why is this?

It is not good to sit a plant with a small rootball in too large a container – the large volume of potting mix around the roots will act as a sump, holding water and (potentially) fungi, bacteria and other disease-causing pathogens. Potting into the next size container allows the roots to fill the container rapidly, and they will suck up available moisture so that this problem does not occur.

439 How do I repot a plant?

Water the plant first (to consolidate the potting mix around the roots), then allow it to drain. It should be easy to slide the plant from the container, but you may need to slide a knife around the edge of the rootball. If the roots have become very congested, you may need to cut off the container (if plastic) with a knife or break it. Wash off the old compost and trim any damaged or dead-looking roots. Pot up in the new container using fresh potting mix.

440 I have a plant growing in a bulbous oriental container and the roots now fill this. How can I get the plant out of the container?

In this scenario, there is no option but to cut around the rootball using a knife with a long, sharp blade. Damaging the roots in this way is not necessarily a bad thing, provided the cuts are clean, as it encourages new, fibrous roots to be produced. You can then return the plant to the same container.

441 What is meant by topdressing?

Ideally, if a plant has to be repotted, all the existing potting mix should be removed and replaced. If the plant is very large and it is impractical to repot it, you can still refresh the potting mix. Tip the container sideways and scrape away as much of the uppermost layer of the potting mix as possible. Replace with fresh potting mix.

▲ **441** *Topdressing a plant with grit helps keep roots cool and cuts down on watering.*

442 What are the best flowering plants for hanging baskets?

Anagallis monelli
Antirrhinum
Begonia
Bidens
Diascia
Fuchsia
Impatiens
Lobelia
Mimulus aurantiacus
Pelargonium
Petunia
Verbena
Viola

▲ **443** Ajuga reptans *has attractive foliage all year around and deep blue flower spikes in spring.*

443 What are the best foliage plants for containers?

Ajuga reptans
Asparagus densiflorus
Aspidistra elatior
Chlorophytum comosum 'Vittatum'
Hedera helix
Helichrysum petiolare
Lamium maculatum
Lotus berthelotii
Lysimachia nummularia 'Aurea'

▼ **443** *A window box planted with foliage plants is a sophisticated solution for a city windowsill or step.*

CHAPTER FIVE

THE KITCHEN GARDEN

Nothing can rival the flavour of home-grown fruit and vegetables, picked fresh from the garden. With some advance planning, it is possible to have something from the vegetable plot during every season of the year, even if you have only a small plot or have to share an allotment. And a surprising number of fruit and vegetables can be grown successfully in containers. But which should you choose, and when and how to start them off?

GROWING
FRUIT

FRUIT TREES

SOFT FRUIT

GROWING
VEGETABLES

SOWING
VEGETABLE SEEDS

POTATOES

ONIONS

TOMATOES

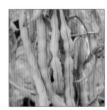

PEAS AND BEANS

MARROW AND
SQUASH

ROOT
VEGETABLES

OTHER
VEGETABLES

SALAD
VEGETABLES

GROWING
HERBS

◀ *Vegetable gardens can be beautiful as well as practical.*

GROWING FRUIT

Fruit is an appealing crop to grow, especially in summer when an abundance of soft fruiting berries are available and can be picked and eaten fresh from the plant. If you have space to spare you could plant different varieties to have fruit all year around.

444 Why would I grow my own fruit when such a wide range is available in supermarkets?

There are many good reasons for growing your own fruits. Commercial fruit growers concentrate their efforts on varieties that produce uniform crops that will travel well and have a long shelf-life. But many varieties do not store well and need to be eaten straight from the plant, making them ideal for home growing. Additionally, much fruit sold in supermarkets is imported and has travelled hundreds, even thousands, of miles. Any gardener concerned with their carbon footprint is likely to prefer locally grown produce. Home grown has the best flavour of all.

445 Which are the best fruits for a sunny, sheltered garden?

If your garden is sheltered, it is well worth trying to grow fruits such as peaches, apricots, figs and some of the pears that need considerable warmth to ripen the fruits adequately. You may still need to protect the blossom, which opens early in the year, often coinciding with hard frosts.

▲ *444 Fruit picked straight from the plant, with the warmth of the sun still on it, is one of the garden's finest offerings.*

446 Which fruits can I grow in a cool garden?

Certain fruits appreciate cool conditions. Blackberries and the hybrid berries (for example, loganberries and tayberries) do well in damp climates. The morello cherry can be trained against a cool wall. Alpine strawberries do well in shade. All fruit need some sun to ripen fully.

447 Do any fruits need special soil conditions?

A well-drained, fertile soil suits the majority of fruiting plants. Blueberries, however, must have acid soil. If you garden on alkaline soil, they can be grown successfully in containers filled with an ericaceous (acid) potting mix such as is used for rhododendrons, camellias and other acid-loving plants.

◄ *445 Apricots need protection from frost and cold weather. They prefer a sunny spot in the garden.*

▲ *445 Pear trees fruit best if they can be trained against a wall or fence, so their fruits can ripen fully.*

Cranberries grow wild in acidic bogs, which are difficult conditions to replicate in most domestic gardens.

448 Should I water my fruit plants?

All new plantings should be kept well watered during their first growing season to make sure they establish properly. Thereafter, supplementary watering is necessary only during periods of drought in the summer.

449 Should I feed fruiting plants?

Regular applications of garden fertilizers are beneficial. Most products recommended for fruiting plants are high in potassium (K), as this ensures good flowering and fruiting. Fork fertilizer around the base of plants in mid-spring, with a second dose in mid-summer. A third application in late summer can help firm woody growth, improving the plant's hardiness. Mature trees such as apples can crop well without extra feeding.

FRUIT TREES

The development of different rootstocks in recent times has given the gardener greater control over the size and shape of fruit trees such as apples, pears, cherries and plums. They can be grown as free-standing trees, trained against walls or fences, or even planted in pots.

450 What is a fruit tree's rootstock?

The vast majority of fruit trees are not growing on their own roots, but have been grafted on to the root system of a related plant. Grafting is a commercial procedure that allows professional nurserymen to produce saleable plants that are large enough for sale very quickly. The most commonly used are:

Apple	M27, M9, M26, MM106, MM111
Apricot	St Julian A, seedling peach or apricot
Cherry	Colt, Malling F12/1
Citrus	sweet orange, rough lemon, trifoliate orange
Peach/nectarine	Seedling peach
Pear	Quince C, Quince A
Plum	Pixy, St Julian A, Brompton, Myrobalan B

451 Why is it important to know which rootstock has been used?

Rootstocks influence a tree's growth habit. Some very useful rootstocks have a dwarfing effect, so that what would otherwise grow into a large tree develops a much more compact habit. This knowledge is useful if you have limited space for fruit trees. Dwarfing rootstocks allow growers to plant the maximum number of trees in the smallest area of ground, and ladders are not needed to harvest the fruit. Other rootstocks can have a significant influence on a plant's hardiness, adaptability to differing climatic conditions and resistance to disease.

452 What is a pollinator?

A pollinator is another tree whose flowers open at the same time as those on the fruit tree and which are known to be compatible. Pollinators should be grown within 10m (30ft) or less to the fruiting tree. One pollinator can service up to five other trees.

453 What is an apple family tree?

A family tree comprises two or more varieties grafted on to a single main stem. They are useful for gardeners who have limited space and want small crops of a number of different varieties. No pollinator is required as the grafted varieties are chosen for their compatibility.

454 How do I hand pollinate a fruit tree?

Hand pollination was traditionally done with a goose feather, though an artist's paintbrush is just as effective. Lightly brush the anthers of one open flower to collect the pollen grains, then transfer these to the stigmas of another open flower. Do the job on a warm, dry day, when the flowers are fully open.

455 Which fruit trees do not need pollinators?

Trees described as self-fertile do not need pollinators. Some apples are self-fertile. Most pears need a pollinator. However, even self-fertile trees usually crop better if there is a pollinator.

◀ *457 Free-standing trees can also be trained – here as an inverted goblet.*

456 What is the chilling requirement of a fruit?

For successful cropping, some fruit trees need a period of cold in winter – known as the chilling requirement – to trigger flowering in spring. This is why it is important to restrict your choice to varieties known to perform well in your area. A reputable nursery should be able to give advice on this.

457 What is the purpose of pruning and training fruit trees?

The aim of pruning and training fruit trees and shrubs is to encourage the plant to produce the largest possible crop without exhausting it. Keeping the plants within a height of about 2m (6ft) or even less, also makes harvesting much easier – ideally the fruit should be produced around eye level so that ladders are not needed. Trained fruit trees make beautiful additions to the kitchen garden.

▼ *457 It is possible to create free-standing fans – garden wall optional.*

▲ **459** *A ballerina crab apple tree is perfect for growing in a container or small space.*

458 Can any fruit trees be grown without special training?

While many fruit trees crop best with a regular pruning regime, some need no pruning at all. Mulberries, walnuts and chestnuts can be grown without pruning but will eventually make very large trees making harvesting the fruit difficult. Smaller fruit trees that need minimal pruning are quinces and medlars. Crab apples grown as pollinators in an apple orchard can be grown with minimal pruning.

459 What is a ballerina tree?

A ballerina apple tree is a compact, columnar tree, which only grows to about 3.5m (12ft) tall by 60cm (2ft) wide. It is perfect for small spaces or growing in pots. This tree requires little or no pruning and many varieties are available. A ballerina tree produces a large crop of medium- to large-sized, excellent-flavoured fruit. Pairs of trees can be bent over and joined at the top to form arches.

▶ **461** *Plums crop so heavily that branches can break if not supported. Thin fruits out when they are small and ensure the branches are tied to the support.*

460 What are the various methods of training fruit trees?

Fruit trees can be grown as standards or half standards – on a single trunk with a spreading crown. Apples and pears are often grown with shorter trunks as bushes or pyramids. Cordons are single trunks that are trained at an angle and tied to a system of wires, either free-standing or against a wall. These allow you to grow a lot of plants in a limited space. To produce a fan, stems radiate out

▲ **460** *A fan-trained fruit tree is a spectacular thing to look at – and also highly productive.*

from a low trunk and are tied to wires, usually stretched across a wall. On an espalier, the stems are pulled strictly to the horizontal. If you garden in a cold area, wall training allows you to grow fruit that needs a long warm period to ripen the fruits. Many pear varieties produce better crops if the trees are trained against a warm wall.

461 What is fruit thinning?

Many fruit trees and shrubs bear heavy crops, and, contrary to expectation, this can be bad news both for you and for the plant. If there are many fruits on a branch, they can crowd each other out. They may not reach full size and will probably not ripen evenly. The weight of a large crop can pull branches down and even cause them to break – a common problem on plums. Finally, bearing a large crop can wear a tree out, meaning it may well not crop well the following year. Reducing the number of fruits produces a better crop in many cases.

462 When and how should fruit thinning be done?

In early summer, cut out the central fruit of a cluster, then remove any damaged fruits. A few weeks later, thin the crop again so that individual fruits are not rubbing against or shading each other – this may mean retaining only one fruit per cluster. For plants that produce single fruits (rather than in clusters) thin them in early summer so that they are evenly spaced along the branches and have room to grow.

463 How should I mulch a fruit tree or bush?

Spread organic matter in a doughnut-like ring around the plants in spring or autumn, making sure the material is not in contact with the bark if it is wet – this could lead to rotting. The mulch will feed the plant as it breaks down, suppress weeds and maintain soil moisture.

464 I have an olive tree. Can I expect it to bear fruit?

Olive trees are borderline hardy and are increasingly popular as ornamentals, especially in containers. But they only fruit reliably in a Mediterranean climate where long, hot summers are the norm. In cooler areas, they sometimes flower and produce small fruits – but without adequate heat and light these cannot ripen fully.

▲ **463** *A mulch will benefit fruit trees. Spread liberally around the trunk area to discourage weeds.*

465 Can I grow lemons and other citrus outside?

Many citrus are grown outdoors in warm parts of the world – Florida, parts of Australia and Mediterranean regions among others. The fruits can take up to nine months to ripen. Though they can be grown successfully as ornamentals in colder areas – they can spend the summer outdoors and overwinter under glass – they are unlikely to fruit heavily.

▼ **465** *Citrus trees do well in containers in a sheltered, sunny part of the garden.*

▲ **464** *Olive trees need protection in cold climates. The fruit they produce are unlikely to be edible.*

466 Can I grow fruit trees in containers?

Fruit trees can be grown successfully in containers provided they have been grafted on to dwarfing rootstocks. Use a soil-based potting mix (John Innes No.3) and feed and water the plants well. Figs do particularly well in containers. They are vigorous plants – restricting the roots in a container diverts their energies into fruit production.

▼ **466** *Fig trees will still fruit if grown in containers.*

SOFT FRUIT

Soft fruits such as raspberries, blackberries and gooseberries have always been one of the mainstays of the kitchen garden. They are relatively easy to look after, as long as pruning takes place regularly and you guard against weeds and marauding birds.

467 How can I grow a good crop of raspberries?

Raspberries should be planted out in late autumn or early winter, a little deeper than they were in their original pot. Cut the canes to 15cm (6in) above ground and water thoroughly. Winter-planted specimens will start into growth the following spring and produce tall canes. Raspberries need little or no feeding once planted. A mulch applied in spring will usually supply their nutrient needs. Raspberries bear their fruit in either autumn or summer, depending on the pruning methods used.

468 Do I need a large garden to grow blackberries?

Blackberries and hybrid berries, such as tayberries and loganberries, all take up a considerable amount of space. They grow on canes (like raspberries) which can be trained on either a sturdy post-and-wire system or against a fence. The previous year's canes (on which the fruit will be carried) are

▼ **467** *There are both summer- and autumn-fruiting raspberries.*

tied singly along the horizontal wires, while the current year's new canes are kept separate until next year, and temporarily tied in vertically along the top wire. After fruiting, all the fruited wood is cut out and the current year's wood tied in to replace it.

469 What is the best way to grow blackcurrants?

Blackcurrants are a popular garden fruit because of their high vitamin C content. They are grown as neat bushes, which will need netting to prevent birds stealing the fruit. One or two bushes can be individually netted, but it is more practical to grow blackcurrants in a fruit cage.

470 Should I grow redcurrants in the same way as blackcurrants?

Redcurrants can be trained as cordons, espaliers, fans and standards, as well as fruit bushes. These forms will need training, using wires against a wall or fence or stretched between posts. Standards will need a stake.

▼ **475** *Strawberries grow best when kept off the ground.*

471 Are there any particular growing methods for gooseberries?

Gooseberries are traditionally grown as a goblet-shaped bush, but modern techniques include growing them as single, double or triple cordons, which can take up very little growing space, making them ideal for a small garden. Freestanding bushes need no support. Cordons require wires, either attached to the fence or to posts. Gooseberries are grown on a 'leg' or stem, so cut back all the side shoots before planting.

472 Do gooseberries require any special treatment?

Gooseberries need high levels of potassium and feeding with a general-purpose fertilizer in spring, as well as mulching with well-rotted manure or garden compost. If growth is poor, feed again in summer. Browning of the leaves indicates a potash deficiency; apply a liquid foliar feed of seaweed extract.

473 How do I stop my strawberries from spreading?

Strawberries increase by putting out runners – long flexible stems. These produce plantlets at their tips which root where they touch the ground. Left to their own devices, they will soon form impenetrable mats that do not crop well. Pinch out runners as they appear.

474 How do I keep the strawberry fruits clean?

As the berries start to ripen, spread straw around the plants.

475 Can I grow strawberries in containers?

It's most practical to grow strawberries in special pots (sometimes called strawberry towers). These are tall jars with pockets in the sides.

GROWING VEGETABLES

Vegetables are a large group of edible plants that provide leaves, stems and roots for eating either raw or cooked. While most taste best when freshly harvested, many root crops can be stored successfully. Growing your own vegetables is a satisfying pastime.

476 What are the ideal conditions for a vegetable garden?

Vegetable gardens should be sited in full sun. The soil should be fertile and well-drained. In a large area you can grow a wide range of vegetable plants. If there is room for a greenhouse, you can add some tender crops such as tomatoes, cucumbers and chillies.

477 Are any vegetables permanent in the kitchen garden?

Asparagus, globe artichokes and Jerusalem artichokes are perennials that will produce every year. Rhubarb (actually a vegetable though used in desserts) and herbs can also be grown in a permanent bed. Such plantings are, however, wasteful of space, as the ground is unproductive for most of the year, so set aside a specific area that you will not need for annual plants. How much space you devote to a permanent bed depends on how much you enjoy the produce.

478 What is crop rotation?

Some crops are prone to certain soil-borne diseases. Growing the same type of vegetable in the same soil each year can lead to a build-up of disease in that particular patch. Growing

▲ **476** *In a large vegetable garden you can grow both hardy and tender crops.*

different crops is believed to minimize the chance of disease. It is usual to apply a four-year cycle.

Four-year crop rotation

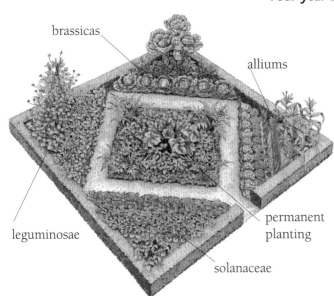

brassicas

alliums

permanent planting

leguminosae

solanaceae

▲ **478** *A formal layout can make the vegetable garden an attractive as well as productive space.*

1 Leguminosae
Peas
Broad (fava) beans
French (green) beans
Mange touts (snow peas)
Runner beans
Sugar snap peas

2 Brassicas and crucifers
Broccoli
Brussels sprouts
Cabbages
Calabrese (Italian sprouting broccoli)
Cauliflowers
Kohl rabi
Radishes
Swedes (rutabagas)
Turnips

3 Alliums and others
Garlic
Leeks
Lettuces
Onions and shallots
Corn
Marrows, squashes, courgettes (zucchini) and pumpkins

4 Solanaceae and others
Beetroot (beets)
Carrots
Celeriac and celery
Parsnips
Potatoes
Salsify
Scorzonera
Tomatoes

479 What are raised beds and do I need to have them to grow vegetables?

Raised beds bring certain advantages in a vegetable garden. The ground will drain more freely and it is easier to gain access to the crops when it comes to harvesting them. Also, once made, you do not need to dig the beds – simply add a 10cm (4in) layer of organic matter each year.

480 How do I make raised beds?

Simple raised beds can be made by nailing 15cm (6in) deep planks to stakes driven into the ground. Unless the planks are painted with plant-friendly wood preservative, they will need to be replaced after a few years. If they are available, you could also use railway sleepers, which will be longer-lasting. However, if they have been treated with a preservative, nail sheets of tough polyethylene to them on the inside to prevent this leaching into the soil. If you are using planks, sink them slightly into the ground to stop the soil from leaching out at the bottom. Dig over the soil at the base of the bed, forking in grit if the soil is heavy,

before filling the framework with topsoil mixed with garden compost. You may need to top up the level.

481 How can I protect my crops?

A physical barrier or horticultural fleece is usually the best way of protecting crops from such general garden problems as pests or even hard frosts. This can take the form of a floating mulch or fleece when the plants are young (and often at their most tempting to insects and other pests). Place the fleece lightly over the crops. Hold the material down at the edges with stones or bricks, allowing a little excess over the plants.

482 What is companion planting?

Companion planting is a method of pest control. Some plants deter pests and if these are interplanted with vulnerable crops, other forms of pest control may not be necessary. Strong-smelling herbs, such as rosemary, and alliums will deter some pests.

483 What make good companion plants to common crops?

Grow cabbage with rosemary, chamomile and dill. Grow carrots with lettuce, sage and chives. Grow potatoes with nasturtium, marigolds and foxgloves. Grow tomatoes with parsley, basil and foxgloves.

484 What is intercropping?

Intercropping is a means of making the best use of limited space. Plants that need a long growing season, such as onions and Brussels sprouts, are alternated in rows with faster-growing crops such as radishes, spinach and other leafy vegetables. Once you have harvested the latter, the slower-growers will grow into the space left.

485 Can I grow vegetables in containers?

Yes, provided you keep them well fed and watered. Carrots and potatoes are successful as container-grown crops, as are all leafy vegetables and summer-fruiting vegetables such as tomatoes, aubergines (eggplants), cucumbers and (bell) peppers.

486 What can I cultivate in growing bags?

Growing bags were developed for tomatoes, but aubergines, cucumbers and chillies also crop well in them.

487 Can I use growing bags more than once?

No. The nutrients in the potting mix will be exhausted by the end of the

▼ **479** *Raised beds are neat and tidy as well as productive. They can be a great help to people with back problems.*

▼ **481** *Use horticultural fleece to protect young and/or vulnerable crops from frost and certain pests.*

Making a raised bed

1 To make a raised bed 2.4m x 1.2m x 0.5m high (8 x 4 x 1½ft), using tanalized timber, cut four 10 x 10cm (4 x 4in) corner posts each 60cm (2ft) long. Using 15 x 5cm (6 x 2in) timber, cut six 2.4m (8ft) lengths and six lengths 1.2m (4ft).

2 Work on a flat surface. This raised bed is assembled upside down. Place a corner post at one end of one short plank, align the edges and secure in place using two 9cm (3½in) screws. Secure a corner post to the same side at the other end.

3 Repeat with the other corner posts and another short plank. Join the short sides with long planks to form the framework. The frame is three planks high and the planks should sit on top of each other without a gap.

4 Decide on the position of the raised bed and dig four post holes at appropriate points. Turn the raised bed (you will need assistance) and fit the posts in the post holes. Fill with topsoil mixed with garden compost.

▲ **485** *If you have limited soil space, grow vegetables and herbs in containers.*

evenly and soil can slide down the slope. Terracing can offer a solution. Use planks to retain the soil in a series of steps. Remember that the soil will be damper at the bottom of the slope.

491 Will growing vegetables every year exhaust the soil?

Crops use up nutrients in the soil, so these should be replaced if you want to carry on growing vegetables. Spread an 8–10cm (3–4in) layer of organic matter (garden compost and/or well-rotted animal manure) over the soil annually in spring or autumn. If you need to plant immediately, fork this well into the soil. Otherwise, simply leave it on the soil surface and allow it to break down. Many gardeners treat this as an annual autumn task and spread the material over soil that would otherwise be bare over winter.

You could grow green manure in a bed that has ceased to be productive at a particular time of year. Green manures benefit the soil, fixing nitrogen into it with their roots, or bringing other nutrients to the surface for the benefit of the plantings that follow. They can be sown at different times of the year according to type, and according to soil type. They take varying amounts of time to crop.

growing season. Instead, add it to the compost heap or use it as a mulch around other plants.

488 My garden is exposed and windy – can I still grow vegetables?

Vegetables do not flourish in windy conditions, but can be sheltered by a windbreak. Stretch windbreak netting between stout upright posts up to 1.8m (6ft) high and spaced 1.8m (6ft) apart. The netting filters the wind without cutting down the light levels.

489 What can I grow in shade?

Most fruit and vegetables need full sun, but some tolerate shade. Lettuces and rocket (arugula) do well, and for a herb, try mint. Blackberries, raspberries and alpine strawberries grow in light shade. The morello cherry can be trained against a north-facing wall.

490 Can I grow vegetables on a sloping site?

Sloping sites present certain difficulties. Crops may not grow

SOWING VEGETABLE SEEDS

Rather than buying little plants from the garden centre, it is worth growing your own from seed. Most germinate easily, and the aftercare is not too arduous. In addition you will have a wider choice of varieties including many heritage vegetables.

492 I have some vegetable seeds left over from last year. Is it still worth sowing them?

All seeds are dormant until favourable conditions arise that encourage them to germinate. Some are capable of surviving for many years – even centuries – in the dormant state. Vegetables are short-lived plants, however, so seed is best sown fresh. Most seed packets are stamped with a 'sow by' date. However, if you have any seed unsown in the packet from earlier years, it is always worth sowing it, but do not expect such a high proportion to germinate. The seed that does germinate should still produce excellent plants.

493 Do I need a propagator?

No. Seeds germinate at different temperatures, and these occur naturally in the garden. A propagator gives you more control, enabling you to achieve the appropriate temperature artificially. Seedlings raised in propagators need hardening off before planting outdoors.

494 What is sowing *in situ*?

Sowing *in situ* means sowing seed where you actually want them to grow – usually in a vegetable garden,

▼ **494** *If you are sowing seeds in open ground, use taut string to maintain a straight line. Weeds will be easier to spot.*

▲ **493** *A propagating case with a lid will help with seeds that need a little warmth to germinate.*

though flowering annuals are also often sown where you want them to flower. This dispenses with the need to raise seedlings in containers and is often recommended for those crops that do not respond well to transplanting.

495 How do I prepare seed trays and pots?

Use a seed or multi-purpose potting mix. Fill pots or trays and water them well. Allow them to drain completely. The surface should be just moist to allow the seed to adhere to it.

496 How deep do I sow the seed?

Seed should be covered to its own depth. For instance, a large bean seed about 1cm (½in) across should be planted 1cm (½in) deep. Very fine seed can be surface sown.

Preparing seed trays

1 Fill trays or modules with seed potting mix, tamp down and water. Surface sow the seed.

2 Water carefully. Too much water can compact the compost and lead to damping off.

It is important that the soil is damp so that the seed sticks to it and is not blown away.

497 How do I sow very fine seed?

Seed that is too fine to handle individually can be sown in small pinches. Alternatively, take a pinch between finger and thumb and sow as thinly as possible in rows in seed trays.

498 What is 'thinning'?

The seeds of some annuals and vegetables are too small to be sown individually, and outdoors should be sown in rows, as thinly as possible.

◀ **495** *Label seed trays carefully as seedlings look similar when small.*

▲ **495** *Some seeds are large enough to be sown individually straight from the packet into pots, trays or modules.*

When the seedlings emerge, it is important to remove a high proportion so that the remainder have adequate space to develop fully. If this seems wasteful, many vegetable seedlings can be added to salads – they are healthy and very tasty.

499 What is 'pricking out' and how do I do it?

If you have decided to germinate your seeds in pots or trays, once the seedlings have developed the second

▼ **499** *If seed can be sown individually, try using modules – it makes transplanting later much easier.*

▲ **497** *You may find it easier to sow fine seed direct from the packet, sprinkling it carefully on the soil mix surface.*

set of leaves they will need moving into larger containers to allow them to develop fully.

Prepare fresh pots or trays of potting mix. Handling the seedlings by the leaves, gently ease them from their original potting mix with a dibber. Use the dibber to make suitably sized holes in the fresh trays and drop in the seedlings. Gently firm them in, then water them well. Further potting on may be necessary as the seedlings grow. They can be

▼ **500** *A cold frame offers protection from cold and mice, as well as saving valuable greenhouse space.*

▲ **498** *Thin seedlings as necessary to reduce overcrowding. Always hold seedlings by their leaves.*

planted out when large and sturdy enough and when conditions outdoors are suitable.

500 What is meant by hardening off?

Seedlings raised under cover need to be acclimatized to conditions outdoors before they are positioned there permanently. Remove the covers of the cold frame for part of the day – for an increasingly long period – over one or two weeks. The seedlings can then be placed outdoors in daylight hours, but in a sheltered position out of direct sunlight, again for increasingly long periods. Protect them overnight either indoors or in a cold frame.

POTATOES

Potatoes are an important crop, as some people like to eat them virtually every day of the year. It is always worth trying new varieties annually, as well as old favourites, because flavour and disease-resistance varies. Potatoes are a good first crop for a plot.

501 What are seed potatoes?

Seed potatoes is the name given to the small tubers that are planted in late winter to early spring in order to produce potato crops. They grow best if they are allowed to sprout before planting.

502 What is 'chitting'?

Chitting the tubers means encouraging them to produce short shoots before planting. This results in earlier crops, as the tubers are effectively already in growth when you plant them. To chit the tubers, place them in a shallow tray and keep them indoors in an evenly lit, cool, but frost-free place. Make sure that any buds (or 'eyes') are facing upwards. Plant them out six weeks later or when the sprouts are about 2cm (¾in) long.

503 When should I plant out the tubers and how deep should I plant them?

Potatoes as a crop are susceptible to cold, so should not be planted out until all risk of heavy frost is gone and the soil has reached a temperature of 7°C (45°F). Dig individual holes for the tubers about 8–15cm (3–6in) deep. Plant a tuber at the base of each

hole, then draw the soil over. Leave 30cm (12in) between each tuber and 45cm (18in) between the rows. Every tuber should be covered with at least a 2.5cm (1in) layer of soil.

504 I live in a cold area. How can I get an early crop?

To raise the soil temperature, cover it with horticultural fleece. When the shoots appear, cut holes in the material and ease them through. Or, place cloches over the plants to keep the cold off them. Potato plants can collapse in the cold, but will recover.

▼ **502** *These tubers are chitting nicely in trays that are usually used for transporting and selling fruit.*

▼ **505** *Potatoes are vulnerable to frosts. Plants can be protected with individual cloches.*

▲ **503** *When planting the tubers, space them correctly so that the crops have adequate space to develop underground.*

505 My potatoes are growing well but I am concerned there may be a late frost. How can I protect them?

Although topgrowth can collapse after a frosty night, the plants usually recover if the frost is not too severe. You can protect plants from the worst of the weather by placing straw around them whenever frost is forecast or by placing a sheet of horticultural fleece over them.

▼ **506** *Draw the surrounding earth up around the stems of potatoes as they grow with a hoeing implement.*

▲ **509** *Store any excess potatoes in paper sacks in cool, dark, damp-free places.*

about 5cm (2in) above the ground, but do not dig up the crop for about another two weeks. This helps firm up the skins so they will store better.

509 How do I store maincrop potatoes?
Dig up the potatoes on a warm, sunny day, then leave them to dry outdoors for a couple of hours. Store them in sturdy paper sacks in a cool, dark place.

510 Is it possible to produce a crop of new potatoes in the winter?
Yes, but the plants will need protection from frost. Plant the tubers in summer, then cover with a cloche in autumn to keep off the worst of the weather. Dig up the tubers in winter.

506 What is meant by earthing up?
Mounding up the soil around the growing plants prevents the tubers underground from turning green – and hence inedible. When the plants are around 23cm (9in) tall, mound up the soil to a depth of around 13cm (5in).

507 How and when do I harvest early potatoes?
Lift the pototoes when or just before the plants flower. For the best flavour, they are best eaten as soon after harvesting as possible, so dig them up only as you need them.

▼ **508** *Fork up potato crops carefully so as not to damage individual tubers.*

▲ **510** *New and maincrop potatoes can be harvested in the winter.*

508 How and when do I harvest maincrop potatoes?
Leave maincrop potatoes in the soil for as long as possible. In summer to autumn, cut back the topgrowth to

▼ **509** *Allow freshly dug main crop potatoes to dry for a while before storage.*

ONIONS

Onions are an important crop, helping to form the base of a whole range of soups, stews and sauces. Some types are mild enough to eat raw, while others have a much stronger flavour and have to be cooked.

511 What are onion sets?

Although onions are annuals and it is easy to raise them from seed, as they need a long growing season, you may get a better result by using sets. These are onions that have been specially grown the previous year and harvested while the bulbs are still very small. They can be planted in spring. However, you have a wider choice of varieties if you opt for seed.

512 How do I grow onions successfully from seed?

To make sure the onions grow for as long as possible, start them off early, in late winter to early spring, in trays or modules. The seeds germinate at a temperature of 10–15°C (50–59°F).

513 What are Japanese onions?

Japanese onions are hardier than other types, so it is possible to sow seed in late summer – the seedlings survive the winter and grow on the following year. Some other varieties are hardy enough to overwinter.

▼ **516** *Dry onions before storing them.*

▲ **511** *Many gardeners prefer planting onion sets to growing from seed.*

514 What are shallots?

Shallots are very small, strongly flavoured onions that are often used for pickling. They are hardier than ordinary onions, so the sets can be planted out in late winter to early spring. Protect them with a covering or birds may pull them out of the ground.

▲ **515** *Spring onions are harvested before the underground bulbs have swollen.*

515 How do I grow spring onions (scallions)?

Spring onions are grown from seed. For continuous cropping, sow thinly in rows at three-weekly intervals over summer. Thin the seedlings as necessary (they can be used in salads). The remainder can be pulled around two months after sowing. Late-summer sowings can be overwintered if protected for harvesting in spring.

516 How do I store onions?

Wait until the topgrowth has died back, then dig up the onions with a fork, taking care not to damage them. Wipe off any soil, then leave them to dry, either on trays or in nets. If the weather is dry and sunny, dry them outdoors – otherwise put them in a well-ventilated greenhouse. After about ten days, they should be thoroughly dry. They can be stored in trays kept in a cool, frost-free place such as a garage or, if there is enough of the topgrowth still attached, they can be plaited together. Onion plaits need to be kept in dry conditions – humid kitchens encourage rotting.

TOMATOES

Tomatoes are technically a fruit, though hardly ever used in anything but salads or in cooked savoury dishes. They vary in size from cherry tomatoes that can be eaten whole to larger 'beef' tomatoes that are good for slicing.

517 Is it true that tomatoes are really fruits?

Yes, tomatoes are fruits – as are cucumbers, aubergines (eggplants), (bell) peppers and chillies. But, because they are annuals and only used in savoury dishes, they are generally grown alongside vegetables.

518 Why are tomatoes grown in containers or growing bags?

Tomatoes are prone to soil-borne diseases, so have to be grown in fresh soil each year. It is easiest to achieve this by using growing bags or potting mix-filled containers that can be discarded after you have harvested the crops. Alternatively, you can grow tomatoes in large pots.

519 How do I grow tomatoes?

For the best crops, most tomato varieties are grown as cordons. Either tie the plants to tall canes inserted into the growing medium or on

▲ **518** *Tomato plants develop long roots so need to grow in plenty of earth. Keep them well watered.*

▲ **519** *Tomatoes need to be grown in fresh soil, so gardeners often use large containers or growing bags.*

▼ **519** *Training tomato plants on canes keeps the stems upright and ensures a good crop.*

vertical wires or strings next to the main stems. Bush and dwarf varieties do not need tying in to a support but can be allowed to sprawl on the ground. Trailing cherry tomatoes are suitable for growing in hanging baskets. Water the plants well and feed with a tomato fertilizer.

520 How do I train the plants as cordons?

Tie in the plant's main stem to the cane, wire or string as it grows. Pinch out all the side shoots that form in the leaf axils, when they are 2.5cm (1in) long. In late summer or when the plant has reached the desired height, by which time it should be flowering and fruiting, pinch back the main stem, counting two leaves above the topmost flower or fruit truss.

521 Can I use the green tomatoes that have not ripened by the end of summer?

Green tomatoes are inedible raw – indeed they can be poisonous – but can be used cooked and made into chutneys. Alternatively, place the green tomatoes in a paper bag. They should carry on ripening in the bag. You can also try ripening the green tomatoes on the plant. Untie it from its support, bend over the stem, then cover with a cloche that will raise the ambient temperature around the tomatoes.

PEAS AND BEANS

Peas and beans (including runner beans, French beans and broad beans) grown at home will be far superior in taste and flavour to any that can be bought in the supermarket. They are worth the time and effort it takes to grow them.

522 How do I grow runner (green) beans?

Runner beans, with their bright red flowers and long, green pods, can be grown up decorative supports in the ornamental garden. They prefer a sunny, sheltered position and a rich, moisture-retentive soil. Sow directly outside in late spring or grow from seed under glass in early spring for planting out in early summer. Build a support for the beans before sowing, which is traditionally made up of a double row of canes tied at the top.

523 How do I know when to harvest runner beans?

Pick the pods when they have reached 20–30cm (8–10in) in length and before they become stringy and hard. It is important to pick regularly or the plants will stop flowering. Surplus beans can be frozen.

524 How do I grow French (green) beans?

French beans can be either dwarf or climbing. The dwarf varieties are the most popular because they take up

▼ **524** *French beans need supporting as they grow.*

little room. Both types are frost tender and need to be sown or planted out after all risk of frost has passed. You can also buy coloured varieties in yellows and purples to add interest to the vegetable plot. French beans require an open, sunny site and fertile, free-draining soil. Sow outdoors in early summer in a single or double row. Climbing French beans will need some form of support.

525 How do I know when to harvest French beans?

Harvest French beans when the seeds are still immature on the plant. Pick regularly to encourage new pods to form. French beans are best eaten fresh, but they can also be frozen. However, they can be dried and stored.

526 How do I grow peas?

Peas need an open, sunny site, but can tolerate light shade. Grow in a fertile, moisture-retentive soil (do not grow in a soil that is liable to become waterlogged). Varieties are categorized as first earlies, second earlies and

▼ **526** *Peas grow up a wigwam of bamboo canes.*

maincrop. Sow first earlies outside in mid- to late autumn and overwinter under cloches. For a slightly later crop, sow second earlies in late winter to early spring, starting them off under cloches. Maincrop varieties are sown at regular intervals from early spring to mid-summer without protection. Protect the crops from birds immediately after sowing. Provide some means of support, such as pea sticks, or plastic or wire netting.

527 How do I grow broad (fava) beans?

These are the hardiest and earliest of all the beans grown. There are green, white or red varieties available. Broad beans need an open, sunny site that is sheltered from strong winds and a well-manured heavy soil with good drainage. Sow overwintering types in late autumn. Other varieties are sown from late winter to late spring. Sow in double rows in a shallow trench. The crop can also be started off under glass in late winter and planted out in spring. Provide plenty of water during any dry spells and some form of support for taller varieties.

528 How do I know when to harvest broad beans?

Pick the pods when they are swollen. Do not allow them to become tough and leathery. Continous harvesting will extend the growing season. Although broad beans are best eaten fresh, they can also be frozen or dried.

529 How do I know when to harvest peas?

Harvest when the pods are plump, but not yet fully grown, starting from the bottom of the plant and working your way up. Keep picking the pods to encourage further production.

MARROW AND SQUASH

Pumpkins, squashes, and marrows and courgettes are popular vegetables with young children who are attracted by their bright colours and interesting shapes. They all make an exciting visual contribution to the kitchen garden.

530 How do I grow marrows and courgettes (zucchini)?

Although these vegetable fruits are largely grown for their juicy fruits, the male flowers can also be eaten raw in salads or cooked. They require an open, sunny site. Sow under glass in late spring. Soak the seeds in water overnight because this speeds up germination. Harden off the seedlings and plant out in early summer. You can also sow outside directly in early summer. Water regularly throughout the growing season. Trim trailing varieties to keep them contained. Marrows need to be kept off the ground with some level of support.

531 How do I harvest marrows and courgettes?

Harvest courgettes when they are about 10cm (4in) long. If left much longer, they are classified as marrows. Use a sharp garden knife to cut them from the plant leaving only a small amount of stalk with the courgette.

532 How do I grow squashes?

Squashes are available in a wide range of shapes, sizes and colours, ranging from white to deep orange. Squashes need an open, sunny site that is sheltered from strong winds. Grow them in a soil rich in organic matter. Sow under glass in early spring, then harden off and plant outdoors in early summer. They need a lot of room to grow, so leave 1.8m (6ft) between plants. Alternatively, they can be sown directly outside in early summer. Keep well watered during the growing season. Train the trailing stems around the plant in a spiral to save on space.

533 When should I harvest squashes?

Harvest summer squashes when they are large enough, cutting off the fruits and leaving 5cm (2in) of stem. Cut

winter squashes in the same way if they are to be eaten fresh; otherwise, leave them on the plant and harvest just before the first frosts. Leave in a sunny position to harden the skins before storing.

534 How do I grow pumpkins?

Pumpkins require a sunny position, sheltered from strong winds, and a fertile soil that is rich in organic matter. Sow under glass in late spring, soaking the seeds overnight to speed up germination. Plant out in early summer. Alternatively, sow in situ in early summer allowing 1.8m (6ft) between plants. To keep the vigorous growth in check, pin the stems to the ground with wire pegs. Protect the underside of the pumpkins with a layer of straw. Water continually and feed every two weeks during this period. Stop watering and feeding once the fruits are mature.

535 How do I produce a giant pumpkin?

For larger pumpkins, perhaps for show or exhibition purposes, choose one to three good fruits when they are small and remove the rest. Giant pumpkins are grown from giant seed.

▲ **530** *Net marrows to support them.*

536 How should I harvest pumpkins?

Allow the fruits to mature on the plant. Harvest the entire crop before the first frosts, leaving a stem on the fruit of about 5cm (2in) in length. Leave in a sunny position for about a week for the skins to harden. Orange-skinned pumpkins will store well for several weeks, while blue-skinned ones will last for up to three months.

▼ **534** *Protect pumpkins on a straw bed to stop the underside rotting.*

ROOT VEGETABLES

Root vegetables are a traditional crop for winter, much valued for use in casseroles. Most can be stored for several weeks, even months, and come to no harm. Cold even seems to improve the flavour in some cases. Remove all stones to stop the crops from distorting.

537 What are root vegetables?

A number of plants are grown for their edible roots. Apart from potatoes, the most common are carrots, turnips, parsnips and radishes. Jerusalem artichokes and celeriac are less popular because they are difficult to peel. Sweet potatoes (yams) are tender and can only be grown in tropical and subtropical regions.

538 Can I eat other parts of the plants besides the roots?

Young leaves of turnips and beetroot (beets) can be used lightly blanched as a vegetable or raw in salads. When thinning beetroot seedlings, the discards can be used whole in salads, provided you wash them well first.

539 What is the best soil type for root vegetables?

Root vegetables do best in a fertile but light, free-draining soil. Large stones in the soil can lead to distorted growth, so remove any when digging over the soil prior to sowing/planting. Wet soils can lead to rotting.

▲ **537** *Radishes are a fast-maturing crop that can be harvested at any size.*

540 Can I grow root vegetables in containers?

Many root vegetables need a long growing period and have high nutrient requirements, so most are

▼ **537** *Root vegetables are a large group, providing plenty of ingredients for winter stews.*

▲ **537** *Carrots are a root vegetable that are available all year round.*

unsuitable for containers. Radishes and beetroot, however, are quick to mature and can do well in deep containers, provided they are kept well-watered.

▼ **538** *Beetroot is one of the easiest crops to grow, and its leaves and root can all be eaten.*

541 How do I sow carrots?

Seedling carrots do not transplant easily, so should be sown in rows where they are to crop, then thinned. Alternatively, seeds can be sown individually in modules, then transplanted when the roots fill the modules.

542 What are round-rooted carrots?

While most carrot varieties produce long, tapering roots, some are rounded. These can be grown in small clumps rather than being thinned individually, so it is possible to grow more in a smaller area – though the roots themselves are much shorter. If you are starting the plants off in modules, the seed can be sown in small pinches rather than singly, then the clump can be planted out without separating out the seedlings.

543 How do I grow Jerusalem artichokes?

Jerusalem artichokes are perennials. They are not grown from seed – instead, plant small tubers in spring. Cut off any flowers that form, then lift the tubers when the foliage starts to die back for storing over the winter.

▲ **541** *Carrots are best sown directly in rows, as they do not transplant well. The seeds do not store well.*

544 Can I cut the Jerusalem artichokes I bought into smaller pieces to get a bigger crop?

Large tubers can be cut into pieces before planting out, provided each section has several eyes or growth buds. Use a sharp knife and allow the cuts to dry out before planting.

545 How do I grow parsnips?

Parsnips need a long growing period, so should be sown as soon as the soil warms up in spring. They can be sown in modules under

▲ **543** *Jerusalem artichoke tubers are knobbly like ginger roots, and can grow like weeds.*

cover, then transplanted when conditions outdoors have improved. Freezing temperatures seem to improve the taste of parsnips, so they can be left in the ground over winter even after the topgrowth has died back. During very cold periods, cover the soil with a 15cm (6in) layer of straw so that it stays workable and the roots can be lifted easily.

▼ **540** *Grow potatoes close to the kitchen in containers if necessary, to make harvesting easy.*

▼ **545** *Parsnips are harvested after the first frosts for best taste. Store them for several months.*

▲ **546** *Radishes are hot and peppery in taste. Grow them between other crops for fast harvesting.*

▲ **548** *The turnips most commonly grown are white-skinned. They are fast growing and require high soil fertility.*

▲ **549** *Keep swedes weed-free as they grow, and water them in dry weather to produce a healthy root crop.*

546 Are there any root crops that can be grown year round?

Radishes are an easy crop with a large number of varieties available. Seed can be sown throughout the growing season – and this period can be extended either side if you have a cloche or polytunnel, using types developed for growing under cover. In summer, you can sow overwintering radishes. It is usually safe to leave these in the open ground for harvesting during the winter as required, though it may be necessary to lift them for storing in a clamp if the weather is very severe.

547 Why have my radishes gone woody?

Small radish varieties can deteriorate in texture if they are left in the ground too long, losing their crispness and bite. They are always best harvested young, so it is best to sow a few seeds every other week to maintain a supply. Only the overwintering types can safely be left for prolonged periods.

548 How do I grow turnips?

Sow turnips outdoors as soon as the ground is workable in spring (or earlier, under cover). To provide roots over an extended period, make three-weekly sowings. Late crops should be lifted before the first frosts, then stored in a clamp.

549 How do I grow swedes (rutabagas)?

Swedes need a very long growing season – up to six months. Sow the seed *in situ* in spring. Lift them at the end of the year for immediate use or to store over winter. They can also be left in the ground, with a layer or straw as protection from hard frosts, but this can cause woodiness.

550 How do I prevent my rootcrops from bolting?

Bolting – when the plants put out flowers and form seeds – can be put down to stress, usually a result of the plants drying out. Keep plants well watered during the growing season so that the soil around the roots stays moist (but not wet). Plants that have bolted should be put on the compost heap.

551 What is celeriac and how do I grow it?

Celeriac is related to celery. The flesh of the root is similar in texture to a potato, but with a distinct celery taste. Ideally, apply any fertilizer or organic matter to the site during the season before planting – too much nitrogen will encourage leafy growth at the expense of root development. Celeriac will tolerate any well-drained soil, preferably in sun. Sow *in situ* in early spring, thinning the seedlings to 30cm (12in) apart. In cold areas, start the plants off in a greenhouse or cold frame, then transplant in late spring. Harvest from late summer or, for a better flavour, harvest over winter.

▼ **551** *Celeriac is a winter-grown vegetable. It has the texture of potato and tastes of celery.*

OTHER VEGETABLES

Certain vegetables do not fit easily into the earlier categories or have special growing requirements if they are to crop successfully. In some cases, specific gardening procedures can enhance the flavour or appearance of the crop.

552 How can I protect my cauliflowers from frost?

Some cauliflower varieties can be sown in summer for cropping in winter, but the heads (or 'curds') are prone to frost damage as they mature. To protect them, simply wrap the leaves loosely around the head, tying them in position with garden string.

553 Can I get a second crop of leaves from my spring greens (collards) ?

If you want your spring greens to produce a second crop of leaves, cut the leaves just at their base to leave a stump, when harvesting. When you have cut all the leaves, cut a cross in the top of the stalk. New leaves should grow from the stalk.

554 Why are corn plants grown in blocks rather than rows?

Growing corn in blocks – at least four plants each way – is essential if good pollination is to occur, otherwise there

▲ **553** *Spring greens will produce new growth from the stem after the first vegetable has been harvested.*

▲ **554** *Corn plants are usually grown in blocks rather than rows to ensure successful pollination.*

555 How do I force chicory?

Chicory plants can be forced to produce soft, pale green leaves – chicons – for eating lightly cooked or raw in salads. Sow seed in spring or early summer and crop from the leaves as needed. Around late autumn, lift the plants from the ground, then trim back the leaves to 2.5cm (1in). Also trim the base of the root and remove any side roots. Pot up the roots in potting mix, so that the crowns are exposed. Invert a second pot over each pot, and cover the drainage holes to keep out all light. Keep the chicory at about 10–18°C (50–64°F). You can harvest the chicons around three to four weeks later.

▼ **552** *The heads – or curds – of cauliflowers can be protected simply by folding the outer leaves over them.*

will be no cobs on the plants. Since the flowers are pollinated by the wind, growing plants in rows can lead to uneven or no pollination. Blocks of strongly growing plants ensure even cropping.

◄ **555** *Chicory likes to be positioned in a sunny spot in well-drained soil. Seed should be sown in mid-summer in earth that has been sprinkled with bonemeal. Harvest in autumn and winter.*

▲ **556** *Shielding celery stems from light, with a sturdy cardboard or plastic sheet, makes them white and tender rather than green and tough. You can also earth up soil around the stems to have the same effect. Keep the soil weed-free.*

556 What is meant by blanching celery?

White stems on celery are more tender and tasty than green stems, which can be coarse. Excluding light encourages a plant to produce white stems. Two or three weeks before you want to harvest the plants, wrap brown paper or newspaper (or a plastic sleeve) around the plants, and tie it in position with string. Alternatively, grow the celery in the

▲ **557** *From planting to harvesting, rhubarb will need approximately 18 months to mature. It can be harvested in late spring to the end of summer of its second growing season. Pull and twist the stems to harvest them.*

base of a trench and as the celery grows, back fill the trench part way up the stems. Some varieties are self-blanching – they naturally produce tender stems.

557 How do I force rhubarb?

Rhubarb – almost exclusively used in sweet dishes – is actually a vegetable, a perennial plant that will crop every year when well established. Young, slender, pink stems are much tastier than thick, old, green ones, which can be poisonous. To ensure a good quantity of material for cooking, cover emerging stems with a layer of straw in late winter, then place over them a special rhubarb forcer or an inverted dustbin or large bucket that will exclude light. Harvest the stems four to six weeks later. Newly planted crowns should not be forced, but allowed to establish for a year or two as this process weakens the plant.

◀ **557** *Rhubarb forcers, placed over the plant, encourage long, slim, pink stems that have a very sweet flavour. Early crops are forced to extend the growing season, but a different plant should be chosen to be forced each year.*

If you have several rhubarb plants, force only a number of them each year, giving the others a rest.

558 Can I grow asparagus from seed?

Asparagus is a perennial vegetable that has to be grown in a dedicated bed. Seed gives variable results, so, for a reliable crop, plant one-year-old crowns in spring. If you have the patience you could try growing some asparagus plants from seed and at the same time, plant some one-year-old crowns to ensure a steady supply over the following years. It will take two years to produce a good crop from crowns and three years from seed.

559 I have heard there are male and female varieties of asparagus – which are best?

Male asparagus plants produce the best spears. Females need to divert some of their energies into berry production, so the males tend to be more productive. However, the female plants are said to produce longer spears.

▼ **558** *Asparagus is a long-term investment of time and can take up to three years to produce a crop, or up to two years if grown from a one-year-old crown. Each crown produces 20 or so spears per crown for up to 20 years.*

SALAD VEGETABLES

Salad vegetables, which are eaten raw, are quick to grow because they have to be harvested while they are still young. It is usually possible to grow several crops in each season, so experiment with different varieties.

560 What are cut-and-come-again crops?

Some leafy vegetables can be cropped when they are still at the seedling stage – the young leaves are highly nutritious and the plant will sprout again. You can carry on cutting the leaves at intervals until the plant is exhausted. If you keep sowing seeds, you can produce a supply of replacement plants for when this happens. Rocket (arugula), cress, some lettuces and other salad crops can be treated this way. You can cut leaves from endives, chicory and Swiss chard regularly once the plants are growing well.

561 What is bolting?

When applied to leafy vegetables, 'bolting' means flowering and setting seed. This happens when plants are under stress, usually during hot, dry periods in summer. At the same time, the leaves toughen and lose flavour. Put bolted crops on the compost heap.

▼ **562** *As a response to drought, lettuces will produce tough stems, which then flower and set seed.*

▲ **560** *Sow rocket successionally, and remove leaves as needed. Flowers can be eaten and make a pretty salad garnish.*

562 How do I stop my lettuces from bolting?

Choose bolt-resistant varieties and either avoid planting them in full sun, or plant them where they will be shaded during the hottest part of the day in summer. Keep plants well watered during hot weather to keep them cool.

563 What types of lettuce are there?

There are plenty of varieties of lettuce. Cos or romaine lettuces have long leaves; round (butterhead) lettuces have smooth, soft leaves forming a heart; icebergs have very crisp leaves; loose-leaf or salad-bowl types do not form hearts and are slow to bolt. These can have smooth or curly leaves and can be grown as cut-and-come-again crops.

564 Can I grow watercress at home?

Watercress grows naturally in fresh running streams – conditions that are difficult to replicate in most gardens. You can try growing it in pots of potting mix stood in water. Change

▲ **563** *Curly-leaved lettuce varieties are pretty enough to grow in flower borders, as well as having an excellent texture.*

the water daily. You can raise the plants from seed or cuttings. If you buy bags of watercress from the supermarket, you can root some of the stems – which may already show signs of rooting – in jars of water.

▼ **564** *Watercress should be harvested when young. The flavour is strong and peppery, perfect for soups and salads.*

GROWING HERBS

Herb gardens are always a delight, rich in scent and historical associations and always an appealing refuge for whiling away an hour or two in summer. And the plants themselves provide leaves for flavouring many dishes.

565 What is a herb?

Certain plants have been traditionally valued for their medicinal or health-promoting qualities. They include not only culinary herbs that are used to add flavour to cooked dishes and salads, but others that deter mice and vermin, produce oils for use in cosmetics and perfumery, or can be used to control the symptoms of – or even cure – a wide range of diseases and ailments.

566 Is it worth growing my own herbs?

Although herbs – even as growing plants – are available in most supermarkets, you will find that plants you have grown yourself have much better flavour. Once cut, the leaves rapidly lose freshness and flavour. If you use herbs in cooking it makes sense economically to grow your own and have a ready supply to hand.

▶ *566 Bay* (Laurus nobilis) *is an evergreen tree or shrub, so fresh leaves are available throughout the year. Grow it in a sheltered position.*

567 What conditions suit herbs?

Unlike vegetables, most herbs do not need highly fertile soil – but the soil must be well drained, especially for Mediterranean herbs such as bay (*Laurus nobilis*), rosemary (*Rosmarinus*) and sage (*Salvia officinalis*). The site should also be in full sun. Mint is unusual among herbs in that it prefers a shady position in reliably moist soil.

◀ *568 In this traditional herb garden, the beds are edged with box that has been clipped formally to shape.*

568 Can I grow herbs among other shrubs in the flower garden or do I need to keep herbs separate?

Many herbs are ornamental and can be included in flower borders. Lavender, rosemary, bay and sage, among others, are all attractive plants in their own right.

569 Which are the best herbs for herb teas?

A soothing after-dinner drink can be made with mint (*Mentha*) or lemon balm (*Melissa officinalis*). Cut a handful of leaves and lightly crush them. Pour over boiling water and allow to infuse. Strain and serve.

570 Can I plant garlic bulbs bought from the supermarket?

Yes, but you will get better results from buying cropping bulbs from a garden centre or nursery. Plant the individual cloves deep.

▼ *569 Lemon balm* (Melissa officinalis) *leaves emit a delicious citrus tang.*

Planting garlic

1 Take a head of garlic and snap off the individual cloves. Plant in fertile but well-drained garden soil.

2 Plant the cloves to twice their own depth, then draw the surrounding soil around them. Harvest the crop in summer.

571 When should I plant garlic?

To produce the fattest bulbs, garlic needs a long growing period. Although you can plant the cloves in spring for cropping later in the summer, you will get better results by planting in autumn. As a rule of thumb, plant around the shortest day in the year, then think about harvesting around the longest day when the foliage has died down. Dry off the bulbs for storage in a warm, dry, well-aired place.

572 Which herbs can I grow from seed?

Many annual herbs are easily grown from seed – the most popular are parsley (*Petroselinum crispum*),

coriander (cilantro), (*Coriandrum sativum*) and basil (*Ocimum basilicum*). Perennial and shrubby herbs such as mint, thyme (*Thymus*), lavender, rosemary and sage are more easily raised from divisions or cuttings.

573 Can I grow herbs in containers?

With ease – most herbs thrive in containers. Additionally, regular harvesting of the leaves keeps the plants compact. Bay, rosemary, lavender, sage, thyme, parsley and basil are all suitable.

574 Do any plants have edible flowers?

Many herbs – and other ornamental plants – have flowers that can be added fresh as an attractive garnish to salads. Pick them at the last minute and scatter over the salad leaves after you have added any dressing to the leaves. The following all have edible flowers:

Chives (*Allium schoenoprasum*)
Borage (*Borago officinalis*)
Pot marigold (*Calendula officinalis*)
Sweet rocket (*Hesperis matronalis*)
Lavender (*Lavandula*)
Musk mallow (*Malva moschata*)
Lemon basil (*Ocimum* x *citriodorum*)
Oregano (*Origanum laevigatum*)
Rosemary (*Rosmarinus*)
Nasturtium (*Tropaeolum majus*)
Violet (*Viola*)

▲ **574** *Chives have fluffy, mauve flowers that are attractive to bees, but the flavour of the stems deteriorates after flowering.*

575 How do I stop mint from spreading?

Grow it in a container, and water it frequently as it prefers damp soil. To restrict its spread in the garden, grow it in a container – even an old washing-up bowl with a few holes punched in the base for drainage – sunk in the ground. Keep a look out for runners that appear around the perimeter of the container.

▼ **575** *To restrict the spread of mint, grow it in containers sunk in the ground.*

CHAPTER SIX

THE WATER GARDEN

Water brings a fresh element into the garden that can be either soothing or dynamic, depending on whether you opt for a tranquil stretch of still water or a more dramatic feature where the water tumbles over rocks or down through a sequence of linked pools. Water seems to pull light down into the garden and offers beguiling reflections, as well as being a cooling presence in hot summers. It also attracts a wide range of wildlife, including birds, insects, frogs and toads, an important consideration if you are concerned about the ecology of the space. But can all gardens accommodate a water feature? And which plants grow in – or near – water? Also, once you have decided to introduce water into the garden, how do you decide where to put the water feature, and how do you create and maintain it as well as keep children safe from it?

PLANNING
A POND

FLEXIBLE
LINERS

PREFORMED
LINERS

POND
FEATURES

WATER
LILIES

OTHER POND
PLANTS

ROUTINE POND
MAINTENANCE

BOG
GARDENS

◀ *Water adds a sense of tranquillity to the garden.*

PLANNING A POND

There are a number of considerations to bear in mind when planning a pond or natural pool, including whether it is to be dedicated to wildlife or purely ornamental, that will ensure you get the best use out of it.

▲ **576** *Garden ponds act like magnets for wildlife. Even a new pond will soon have plenty of insects and frogs appearing, which will benefit the whole garden.*

576 What are the advantages of water in the garden?

The benefits of creating a pond in the garden are immense. Water encourages a host of wildlife into the garden. In itself, it supports its own invertebrate population, which in turn attracts birds. Frogs that breed in the water will feed on slugs and other garden pests.

On an aesthetic level, the sight of light glinting on the surface of the water, as well as of intriguing reflections, can be fascinating.

If you are able to incorporate a small fountain or waterfall, the sound of splashing water will bring an extra dimension to the garden.

▶ **577** *A grille placed across the top of a water feature makes it safer.*

577 Are there any dangers associated with water in the garden?

While domestic ponds are usually fairly shallow, there is still a risk of drowning, especially where small children are involved. If you have small children, it is advisable not to have a pond at all – if there is already one in the garden, drain it and fill it in. If families with children are to visit your garden and you have a pond, either make sure the children are supervised at all times while out in the garden or fence off the pond to keep it out of bounds. Dogs and cats that drink from the pond rarely suffer any ill effects.

578 How do I choose the site for a pond?

To attract wildlife, and to maintain good clear water, a pool should be sited in full sun.

579 Are there any situations that are unsuitable for a pond?

If there is a high water table, you will struggle to make a deep pond. As the ground water rises, it will lift the pond lining. It is also best to avoid digging a pool too near to a deciduous tree. Not only will the tree shade the pool in summer, but leaves that fall into the water in autumn will need clearing regularly or will decay and release noxious gases.

▲ **583** *Use tap water and a garden hose to fill a new garden pond.*

580 What materials do I need to build a pond?

If you garden on heavy clay and there is a high water table, you can make a natural pond simply by digging a hollow and allowing it to fill with ground water. Ponds can also be made with concrete, and painted inside with a waterproofing paint. This method is expensive and requires the skills of a qualified contractor.

The most popular, and easiest, option is to use a flexible butyl liner. The materials are relatively cheap and you can alter the shape of the pond (within reason) as you make it. Butyl liners, sold on the roll or in pre-cut lengths, can be used to line holes dug in the ground. Self-healing liners are made of clay supported on a plastic mesh. These are used like butyl liners and form a waterproof seal once the pond is filled with water.

Manufacturers of flexible pond liners usually guarantee their products for up to ten years. However, most will last well beyond this period, so a pond made with such a liner can be considered a long-term proposition.

Much cheaper are ready-made pools, but here you have little control over the shape, size and depth. Many are actually too small to make a successful long-term water feature, though will attract wildlife. Ready-made ponds are usually made of fibreglass or toughened plastic.

581 When is the best time to make a new pond?

Spring is the best period for creating a new pond. Plant growth is just beginning to speed up at this time, and a new pond created now will mature more rapidly and present fewer problems than if it were made at other times of the year. If convenient, you could dig the pond the previous autumn and winter, but delay positioning the liner, filling with water and planting until spring.

582 What is a dew pond?

A dew pond is difficult to replicate in the garden but occasionally occurs naturally. Dew collects in hollows in the ground. If the soil is compacted and the microclimate is cool, the dew will not drain away or evaporate, as is usual. In time, enough dew collects to form a pond.

583 Is tap water suitable for filling a pool?

Yes, tap water is fine. Initially it will look murky, then turn clear after a day or so as the soil settles into mud at the bottom of the pool. Within about ten days, the water will 'mature' as invertebrate life (including microbes) begins to colonize the water.

584 Are there any problems associated with a raised pond?

A raised pond must be waterproofed and sufficiently strong to retain the weight of the water. Construction is expensive. The water in a raised pond is more likely to freeze in winter and overheat in summer than is the case with a normal pool.

▼ **584** *Raised ponds can be large features that need to be built in materials that are sympathetic to their setting.*

▲ 585 *A small pond such as this will attract wildlife to your garden. If it is not very deep, do not put any fish in it.*

585 My garden is small – can I still make a pond?

In a restricted space, you can use a half-barrel to create a water garden. You will need to waterproof it first, either by painting it with a waterproofing material or lining it with butyl. Plant up with a miniature water lily and small marginals stood on bricks within the barrel to bring them up to the required level. It may be necessary to refresh the water every year or so if it turns green.

▼ 585 *A water feature created in a special garden planter will need topping up on a regular basis.*

586 How big should a pool be to attract wildlife to the garden?

To attract the widest range of wildlife possible, make the pool large. Water in pools smaller than 1m (3ft) across is likely to become green and stagnant. A depth of 45cm (18in) at the deepest point is desirable.

587 How do I make sure small mammals do not fall in?

Make sure that one side of the pool has a gentle slope to it so that any hedgehog, mouse or other small mammal that falls in can escape easily. A shallow area, possibly including a pebble beach, will also attract birds to bathe.

588 How do I encourage frogs into the pool?

Frogs will often appear of their own accord, especially if there are wildlife pools in neigbouring gardens that are already home to frogs. It is illegal to remove frog spawn from the wild, but acceptable to remove some from a fellow gardener's pool. A pool will support only a limited number of frogs, and only a small proportion of the emerging tadpoles will make it to adulthood. Birds feed on them, and they also cannibalize each other during a certain stage of their development.

589 Is every pond suitable for keeping fish?

If you want to attract wildlife into your garden, then do not put fish in the pond because they will upset the biological balance. If you want to keep fish, create a dedicated pond for them. Fish are often better housed in a raised pond. The choice of species and size of fish is determined by the size of the pond: a local supplier will be able to advise on what will survive in your area and your type of pond.

590 How can I protect fish from freezing conditions in winter?

Fish go dormant during the cold months and gravitate towards the bottom of the pool. If the surface freezes over, the necessary oxygen supply is cut off. To make holes in the ice, fill a pan with hot water and hold it on the ice until a circle has melted. Do not smash the ice because the shock waves can disturb and even kill the fish.

591 How do I provide shelter for frogs over winter?

Frogs can hibernate in water, provided it is at least 60cm (2ft) deep (deeper than most garden ponds). Melt any surface ice that forms with hot water. Piles of logs or stones near the pond will provide a suitable alternative place for hibernation.

▼ 587 *Many small mammals can swim but should they fall into a pond, they will need an easy access escape route.*

FLEXIBLE LINERS

A flexible liner is many people's choice for creating a pool with an informal shape. Not only is the material itself flexible, but so are the shapes you can mould it into, whether you want a circular, oval or rough kidney-shape pond.

592 How do I start to make a pond with a flexible liner?

Mark out the shape of the pool with a length of garden hose or thick pipe. If necessary, hold this in position with short stakes driven into the ground or pin it to the soil with bent sections of stout wire. In most situations, a rough oval or kidney shape works best. The site must be level. Water always finds its own level, and if one side of the pond is higher than the other, bare liner will show when you fill the pond. Check the level both at the outset and as you excavate the hole.

Making a pond with a flexible liner

1 Mark out the site of the pond on level ground and dig out the soil to the required depth. Allow for marginal shelves.

2 Line the entire pond area with a thick layer of builder's sand, so that any rocks that may penetrate the liner are covered.

3 Unroll the liner, allowing generous creases. Hold in place around the edge with heavy weights, then start to fill the pond using a garden hose.

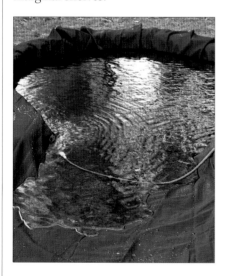

4 Fill the pond. It may take some time if the pond is large. Allow the water to settle and top up as needed.

5 After 48 hours, trim the liner around the pond edge, allowing for an extra 20–30cm (8–12in) at least.

6 The liner edge can be disguised by overlapping turf over it. Eventually plants will mask the edges.

593 How do I work out how much liner to buy?

Measure the maximum length (X) and the maximum width (Y) of the proposed pool. Decide what your maximum pool depth will be (Z). The deepest point should be at least 45cm (18in). Add twice the depth to X and Y, then allow an additional 15cm (6in) all round for an overlap around the edge of the finished pool. The size of liner needed is therefore:

Length = X + (2 x Z) + 30cm (12in) x
Width Y + (2 x Z) + 30cm (12in)

594 Should I dig the sides of the pool straight down or angled?

Slope the sides at an angle of 20 to 45 degrees. The more gentle the slope, the less the likelihood of creasing the liner. Creating a shallow shelf to one side will leave you space on which to site marginal plants in pots once the pond is complete. As you dig, remove any sharp stones around the sides and at the base of the pool because they can cut into the liner once weighed down with water.

595 What should I do with the excavated soil?

If you are cutting into turf, you can use the turves to line planting holes for trees and shrubs or simply add them to the compost heap, grass side down. Topsoil can be spread around the garden. You can use the subsoil in other projects – for instance, making a mound to one side of the pool to create a cascade. Otherwise, you may need to hire a skip and barrow the subsoil into it.

596 Do I need to line the hole before putting in the butyl liner?

Most manufacturers recommend the use of an additional liner – usually a fleece-like material – to protect and prolong the life of the butyl liner itself. In any case, lining the base of the pond with builder's sand allows you to make sure that this is level. Instead of the fleece, you could put down a thick layer of wetted newspaper or old carpet on top of the sand. The additional lining should extend up the sides.

597 How do I hold the liner in position?

Ease the liner into the hole without stretching it unduly. Some creasing is inevitable, especially at points where the sides slope steeply and over any shelf. Where the sides are level try and even out the creases as far as possible. Cover the base of the pond with an 8cm (3in) layer of topsoil. This will hold the liner in position and provide a resting ground for pondlife at a later stage. Initially, the topsoil will float and make it appear muddy. Within days it will settle, leaving the water crystal clear. Begin to fill with water using a garden hose.

598 Do I need to do anything when the pond is filling?

Fill the pond only slowly. The weight of the water will ease the liner into position so that it fits the excavated hole. As the pond fills, walk round it and manipulate the liner to even out any creases that develop, particularly at the corners. Turn off the water if you need to adjust the liner.

599 What should I do when the pond is full?

Once the water has reached the top of the pond, turn off the hose and leave it to settle overnight. Trim back the excess liner to leave an overlap of about 15cm (6in) all around the edge. Either lay this flat on the ground, or dig a shallow trench around the perimeter of the pool and sink the overlap into this.

600 How do I disguise the liner at the edge of the pond?

Position paviors, cobbles, stones or even turf at the edge of the pond to disguise the liner. They should overlap the edge slightly. Assuming the pond was dug level, the water level should reach right up to the edging stones and none of the liner should be visible.

▼ **600** *Use pebbles at the pond's edge to create a naturalistic setting.*

Repairing a butyl liner

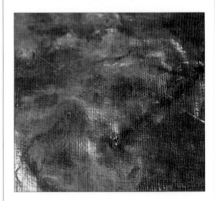

1 Butyl liners sometimes develop holes, perhaps if they are resting on a sharp rock or through accidental damage. Holes can be patched like bicycle tyres. Empty the pool and locate the hole.

2 Dry the area and seal with a patch of liner. Allow the repair to dry thoroughly before refilling.

PREFORMED LINERS

Preformed liners are usually made of lightweight fibreglass or other synthetic material and are available in a range of sizes. The advantage of using a preformed liner is that the finished shape is clear before you even start digging.

601 How do I mark out the ground to be excavated?

Decide where the pool is going to be sited and put the liner in position. Since water always finds its own level, it is important that the ground is perfectly flat, so level the site first if necessary. Drive upright canes into the ground around the pool at 1m (3ft) intervals. Run a length of garden hose or thick rope around the canes to follow the shape of the liner. Remove the liner, then cut around the hose or rope with a spade or half-moon cutter.

602 How do I dig the hole?

Begin excavating a few centimetres/ inches outside the line you have created – you need to make the hole slightly larger than the liner, so that you can position it more easily later on and make any minor adjustments that are necessary.

603 How do I dig out any marginal shelves in the pond?

Most preformed liners incorporate a marginal shelf for plants. To mark the extent of this, first excavate the hole to the depth of the shelf. Sit the liner in the hole and press down hard. This should leave the imprint of the base of the pond in the soil. You can then see the width of the shelf. Dig out the soil within the imprint, about 5cm (2in) deeper than the base of the liner.

604 How do I finish off the pond?

Put a layer of builder's sand at the base of the hole to act as a foundation – deep enough to ensure that the top of the liner is at soil level when you set it in position. Check the level. Once you are satisfied with the fit, begin to backfill with soil. Keep checking the level as you work in case you shift the liner's position. Fill with water using a garden hose. Allow to settle, then top up as necessary.

Making a pond with a preformed liner

1 On level ground mark out the position of the liner at its largest point using a garden hose or washing line and sticks.

2 Dig out the area of the pond down to the level of the first marginal shelf, checking continuously that the pond will fit the space.

3 Check the depth of the pond and dig out a hole that is slightly larger than the liner.

4 Check that the pond will sit level in the hole, then line the hole with builder's sand.

5 Position the liner and carefully backfill any gaps that might cause the liner to become misshapen.

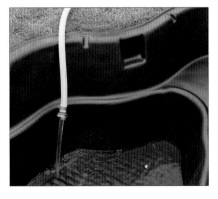

6 Fill the pond using tap water and a garden hose. Allow the pond to settle, then top up as necessary.

POND FEATURES

Although a stretch of still water has its own appeal, you may decide to add lighting or a pump that will put the water in motion, either as a fountain or cascade. Depending on available space, this can be a gentle trickle or something much more dramatic.

605 Can I have lights in the pond?

You can buy special aquatic lights that sit at the bottom of a pond and cast their light upwards. The light can be white or coloured. The wiring for these must be installed by a qualified electrician.

606 What is a watercourse?

A watercourse is a set of linked pools on sloping ground. Water spills from one to the next and collects in a final pool or reservoir, from which it is pumped back to the first, or header, pool.

607 Are there any special considerations when constructing a watercourse?

In order to be effective, the pools should accommodate a sufficiently large volume of water to maintain a consistent flow while the pump (housed in the lowest pool) is in use. In practice, it is wise to make the lowest pool, or reservoir, as large

▲ **608** *Large waterfalls require larger pumps to generate water movement.*

and deep as possible. Once the watercourse is up and running, there will inevitably be water loss through evaporation and splashing as the water cascades from pool to pool. If the reservoir is too small, you may find you need to top it up every time you want to run the water.

608 How do I know how powerful a pump to buy for the watercourse?

Once you have decided the length of the watercourse and the height the water has to be lifted, contact a specialist aquatic garden supplier. Support staff will be able to advise you how big to make the final pool. The pump must also be powerful enough to lift the water to the height of the header pool.

609 How do I make a watercourse?

Create a series of shallow pools that feed into a final, large pool. It is usually simplest to make and line the final pool separately. Line the pools

that feed into it with a single length of butyl pond liner that trails into the large pond. Trim off any excess liner. Attach the water pipe to the pump and put this in the bottom of the lowest pool. Take the pipe up to the highest pool and decide on its position. At this point, it is worth filling the pools with water, then running the pump. A watercourse always needs adjustments to create the desired even flow. You may need to lift the edges of the liner at certain points if water is being lost at the sides. You may also decide to place rocks in the water at strategic points to create eddies and currents. Once you are satisfied, turn off the pump. Disguise the pipe and the liner edges with rocks and/or plants.

610 Can I grow plants in a watercourse?

You can grow many water plants in the linked pools. Water lilies will not grow in moving water, but, provided

▼ **610** *See what plants thrive near water, then choose cultivated varieties.*

▼ **605** *Lighting can be appreciated when it is warm enough to sit out at night.*

the system is not run permanently, they can be incorporated in the lowest pool – the water in the higher pools is usually too shallow. Bear in mind that too many plants will impede the water flow.

611 I would like to have a fountain in a pond. Can I install this myself?

Yes, but the connection to the mains supply should be carried out by a qualified electrician. Usually, the connection will be made on the outside of the house, with the plug and switch concealed in a waterproof casing. You can also ask to have a switch installed inside the house. All outdoor electrical cables must be laid underground and buried as deep as necessary to comply with legal requirements. They should also be laid along the boundary, as far as possible, where there is least likelihood of them being disturbed by digging.

612 What is a bubble fountain?

A bubble fountain is one of the smallest types of water feature, and is suitable for use in a small garden. You can buy these ready-made in garden centres and DIY stores, but

▼ **611** *Fountains can be constructed to suit any size of pond.*

you can easily make one yourself. Sink a plastic bucket or large washing-up bowl in the ground to act as a reservoir. Fill it with water and place a small pump in the bottom. Lay a metal grid over the reservoir and cover with cobbles. Turn on the pump. Rearrange the cobbles so that the water falls over them evenly and the majority returns to the reservoir.

613 What is a shishi odoshi?

A shishi odoshi is a Japanese device designed to scare deer from a garden. Usually made of bamboo, it contains one or more uprights with a hollow, pivoting arm attached, into which water pours from a tube or pipe above it. When the arm gets full, the weight of the water causes it to tip over and empty. The empty arm then swings back upwards for refilling. A shishi odoshi can be used to deliver water into a watercourse, or to be the focal point of a water feature. It is very effective in an oriental-style garden.

614 Can I add an island to my pool?

An island adds interest to a large, informal pool. Although it is preferable to incorporate such a feature into the construction from the start, a small island can be added at a later date. If this is the case, drain the pool and build a retaining wall on the liner, following the outline of the island, until it is level with what will be the surface of the water. The area inside the wall can then be filled with soil, which should be graded into a gentle mound above the water level.

615 What types of rock should I use to build stepping stones?

Stepping stones can make a naturalistic feature across narrow stretches of water or streams. You will need to use flat-topped rocks or boulders for ease of passage, and preferably those with a rough hewn surface so that they don't wear smooth too quickly and be a danger to users. These rocks will be heavy, so you will

▲ **612** *Bubble fountains are perfect for small gardens or for siting near a house, where a water feature is required. They only need a small quantity of water to work effectively, but do need to be professionally connected to a power source. Kits are available.*

need help to move them into position. Suitable rocks are available from stone merchants and suppliers. A more natural effect, helping to pull the design together, is achieved by placing the same top stepping stones in the grass on either side of the water. Timber rounds can be used as an alternative to stepping stones in a bog garden.

▼ **613** *A stone basin fed from a bamboo 'pipe' makes an interesting feature.*

WATER LILIES

Water lilies (*Nymphaea*) are the queens of water plants, with their sumptuous, chalice-like flowers that sit on the water surface, but they also have a practical function as their large leaves keep the water cool in hot weather.

616 How deep does the water need to be to grow water lilies?

A water depth of at least 45cm (18in) is needed to grow most water lilies successfully. Equally important is the water surface area. Water lilies are vigorous plants and some have a spread that can only be accommodated by larger ponds. Check the ultimate spread of any variety you buy. Miniature water lilies are available that will grow in shallower water in smaller ponds.

617 What is an aquatic basket?

An aquatic basket is a plant pot used for water lilies and other deep water plants. Unlike conventional plant pots, they are usually wider than they are deep, and often square in shape, with sides sloping outwards towards the top. The sides and base are perforated. They are always made of plastic or another synthetic material that will not rot in water. The mesh is usually fine, to retain the soil.

▲ **618** *Water lilies are vigorous plants that produce their large flowers over a long period in summer.*

618 When is the best time to plant a water lily?

Water lilies die back in winter to an elongated, knobbly tuber. It is best to buy them as bare tubers in early spring when they are just beginning to put out fresh growth. This is the most practical time to handle what will be a large and unwieldy plant (if removed from the water by summer). You can also easily identify which way up to plant the tuber. Plant as soon as you can after purchase. Water lilies will not tolerate drying out, as they are adapted to permanent wet conditions.

619 Do I need a special potting mix for a water lily?

Although you can buy aquatic potting mix, ordinary garden soil is perfectly usable for growing water lilies. The soil should not be too fertile or have been recently manured – rich soil will turn the water green.

620 How do I plant a water lily?

Choose an aquatic basket that will easily accommodate the tuber with room to spare, and line it with hessian (burlap) or lawn turves (grass side outwards). Fill with garden soil, then the tuber, buds facing upwards. Add more soil around the tuber if necessary, but do not cover the top of the tuber or the buds. Place stones on top of the soil around the tuber.

621 Why do I need to put stones on top of the planting?

The stones fulfil two important functions. They help weight the basket down so that it sinks to the bottom and also prevent the soil from floating away into the water.

622 How do I get the water lily into the pond?

Actually, planting the water lily in the pond is a tricky business and may require the help of an assistant. Assuming you have room for only one water lily, it should be planted as near to the middle of the pond as possible. Working solo, this will mean stretching across the pond. It is easier to support the basket on two long canes, one in each hand, the assistant holding the other ends. Suspend the basket over the water in the desired position. Gradually lower the basket into the water, but do not submerge it

▼ **618** *Water lilies must be grown in still, not running, water in full sun.*

▲ **619** *Plant water lilies in special baskets lined with hessian (burlap), using garden soil or special aquatic potting mix.*

fully. Wait until the soil in the basket is saturated with water, then gently release is so that it drops to the floor.

623 Can I grow tropical water lilies?

Tropical water lilies are very beautiful, with a wider colour range than hardy ones. Orange and blue varieties are available, and some are scented. As permanent plantings, they need a minimum temperature of 10°C (50°F) in winter. You can grow them successfully in frost-prone areas, but need to lift the tubers annually in autumn for overwintering in

▼ **623** *Some tropical water lilies hold their flowers on stems well above the leaves.*

▲ **622** *Lower the water lily gently into the water so that the potting mix or soil does not float out of the basket.*

damp sand at a minimum temperature of 10°C (50°F). Return them to the pond in mid- to late spring once there is no longer any risk of the water freezing.

624 How do I divide a water lily?

In early to mid-spring, pull up the basket containing the water lily rhizome from the base of the pool. If very large, it may well have outgrown its basket. Wash the rhizome clean of mud under running water. Cut it into pieces, making sure each section has root and leaves (or

▼ **623** *Nymphaea 'Albert Greenberg' is a tropical water lily that requires a warm temperature, otherwise it will not flower.*

leaf buds). Return one piece to the original basket, potted up in fresh soil topped with stones, then put this back in the pond. You can grow on smaller sections in pots of ordinary garden soil topped with grit. Put these in bowls of water and keep them in a shaded place. The plant needs to be kept permanently submerged, so keep adding water as necessary so that the leaves float on the surface. They should be big enough to plant out the following year. If you intend to give some of the cuttings away, simply seal them in plastic bags to retain moisture.

Dividing a water lily

1 Lift the rhizome from the pond in early spring, but before any leaves have reached the top of the pool. Cut this into sections, each one with at least one strong growth bud.

2 Replant each section in its own basket, filled with ordinary garden soil or aquatic potting mix. Top with stones, then return the water lily to the pond.

OTHER POND PLANTS

Besides a water lily, a pond should incorporate a range of plants, both at the pond edge and in the water itself. They perform a valuable function in attracting wildlife to the pond and its surrounding area as well as helping to keep the water clear.

625 What is a deep water plant?

Deep water plants like to have their stems as well as their roots completely immersed in water. Water lilies (*Nymphaea*) are the most commonly grown. All ponds should contain at least one deep water plant. The floating leaves help keep the temperature of the water down in summer, which is beneficial for any fish that might live in the pond.

626 Are there any other deep water plants other than water lilies?

A number of desirable plants also have floating leaves and enjoy the same deep water as water lilies. *Orontium aquaticum* has smaller, more elongated leaves than a water lily and white spikes tipped with yellow

▶ **625** *This pond is well-stocked with several different types of plant, all thriving in the wet conditions.*

▼ **629** *Ceratophyllum demersum, the hornwort plant, is an oxygenator suitable for shady ponds.*

◀**629** Ranunculus aquatilis, *the water buttercup, is an excellent oxygenator. It has grass-like submerged leaves as well as floating circular leaves and buttercup-like flowers.*

flowers in summer. The water soldier (*Stratiotes aloides*) produces rosettes of spiky leaves that emerge from the water's surface in spring. In autumn, the whole plant drops to the bottom of the pool where it overwinters, resting on the mud. There is also *Alisma plantago-aquatica, Aponogeton distachyos* and *Nuphar lutea*.

627 What are submerged aquatics?

There is a group of water plants that are essential to any pond but are not in themselves of outstanding merit.

Submerged aquatics float just beneath the water's surface and fulfil the valuable function of keeping the water well oxygenated and clear – hence, they are sometimes referred to as oxygenating plants. They also provide shelter and nesting grounds for invertebrate life.

628 How do I grow oxygenating plants in the pond?

You can simply throw oxygenators into the pond tied in bunches or tie bunches to small stones that will take them to the floor of the pond.

629 Which plants function as oxygenators?

Callitriche hermaphroditica
Callitriche palustris
Ceratophyllum demersum
Egeria debsa
Fontinalis antipyretica
Hottonia palustris
Hydrocharis morsus-ranae
Lagarosiphon major
Myriophyllum aquaticum
Potamogeton crispus
Ranunculus aquatilis

630 What is a marginal aquatic plant?

Some plants, such as *Orontium aquaticum*, like to have their roots in mud, permanently wet. These are referred to as marginals. It is simplest to grow them in pots positioned on shelves at the sides of the pond.

631 Which plants are suitable for growing as marginal aquatics?

Butomus umbellatus
Calla palustris
Caltha palustris
Houttuynia cordata
Ligularia
Lobelia cardinalis
Lysichiton
Myosotis scorpioides
Orontium aquaticum
Pontederia cordata

632 What are floating aquatics?

While water lilies and some other plants with floating leaves have their roots

▲ **629** Callitriche palustris *is a marginal aquatic oxygenator.*

▲ **630** Orontium aquaticum *is easy to identify in ponds.*

▲ **631** Caltha palustris *is buttercup-like, and thrives in wet ground.*

firmly embedded in the mud at the pond bottom, others have short roots that simply trail in the water – they receive all the nutrients they need for growth from the water itself. One of the best-known is the water soldier (*Stratiotes aloides*), which has rosettes of pointed leaves that protrude from the water. In autumn the plant dies back and drops to the pond bottom, where it overwinters.

▲ **632** Stratiotes aloides *attracts a range of small insects.*

▲ **631** Calla palustris *is a poisonous bog plant.*

▲ **631** Pontederia cordata *has glorious blue flowers at the end of the season.*

633 Do I need to feed my water plants?

Emphatically not – all water plants, having a constant supply of moisture, tend to grow lushly anyway. In any garden pond, there are also plenty of plant nutrients in the form of decayed plant and animal debris. A pond is usually one of the most fertile areas of the garden.

ROUTINE POND MAINTENANCE

Like other parts of the garden, a pond needs a certain amount of maintenance. With a
constant supply of water, pond plants grow vigorously, so they have to be kept under control
in order to retain a good balance.

634 The oxygenators seem to be taking over all the space in the pond – what can I do about them?

This problem is easily dealt with. Simply pull out handfuls of the excess plant, which can then be added to the compost heap. You may like to shake them briefly in the water first to dislodge (and so return to the water) any small invertebrates and their eggs.

635 What is blanket weed?

Blanket weed is a kind of submerged aquatic that no gardener willingly introduces into a pond, but which always seems to arrive anyway. It is made of long, filament-like growths that seem to cloud the water to the detriment of the other plants. It seems to proliferate during hot summer weather.

636 What is the best way to remove blanket weed?

Hold a pointed stick in the water and twist it round. The blanket weed will cling to the stick and you will find you can carry on wrapping it round like candy floss. Pull the stick from the pond and remove the weed (which can be composted). Carry on until the pond is clear of weed.

637 What is duckweed?

As big a problem as blanket weed, duckweed is a tiny floating aquatic plant that multiplies rapidly, in severe cases covering the entire water surface. Seeds of the plant are probably brought into the pond on the feet of visiting birds.

638 How can I remove duckweed?

Use a nylon fishing net to lift the weed from the pond, then add to the compost heap.

639 How do I get rid of water snails?

You can trap water snails, which eat water plants, by floating a lettuce leaf on the water's surface. Periodically lift the leaf, and remove and dispose of any snails that cling to it.

640 How often should I clean out the pool?

Ponds are mainly self-cleaning once the eco-system it supports is in balance. But this can sometimes be upset and so it can be advisable to empty the pond completely and refill it. This job is best done in spring before the plants have put on too much growth.

641 How do I keep the water in the pond clear?

Filtration offers the means to keep the water in a pond clear, should this be necessary. A filter needs to be used in conjunction with a pump that pushes the water through the filter. A biological filter contains bacteria that breaks down the debris that enters it. Usually housed in the water itself, it will keep the water pure but not clear. Biological filters are often used in ponds that have fish in them. Ultraviolet water clarifiers are housed outside the pool and water is pumped through them by means of a pipe.

642 What maintenance does a biological filter need?

When the water temperature drops to around 50°F (10°C), the biological activity in a pond filter reduces considerably, but never dies completely. Boost your biological

▼ **634** *Oxygenators are essential in a pond if you want wildlife to thrive and the water to stay clear, but, if there are too many, they become inefficient.*

▼ **636** *Blanket weed is unsightly, and can be time-consuming to remove. Oxygen-loving plants placed in the water will help to stop it from taking over the space.*

▼ **637** *Although duckweed appears as a floating mass, it is made up of small individual plates, like scales, and is not easy to eradicate.*

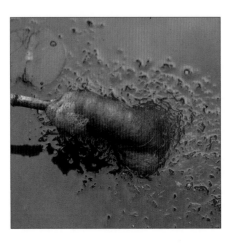

filtration with bacterial additives to replace those that are naturally lost through the winter. Regular use of a filter booster in winter will help the biological filter remain active all season long.

643 Will the pump need maintenance?

Pumps need to be overhauled or replaced during the winter months. Even with meticulous and regular maintenance there is inevitably a build-up of waste matter or sludge on the bottom of the pond. Disconnect the pump at the mains, then remove it from the water. Clean all the filters carefully before returning the pump to the pond.

644 Why is the water in my pond going green?

A certain amount of green algal growth in a pool is inevitable, especially in the first few weeks after construction. Over time, if there is a good balance of plant material and invertebrate life, the water should be self-clearing. Net the pool in autumn to prevent leaves from falling in. Oxygenate the pool in summer by agitating the water. If there is a fountain installed, turn this on for about an hour each evening. If you need to top up the pool, support the garden hose above the water's surface

so that it splashes as it delivers fresh water. Both these methods introduce oxygen into the water.

645 The water evaporates from my pond. How do I prevent this?

A certain amount of evaporation from the water's surface is inevitable, particularly during warmer, rain-free times of year. Steep fluctuations in temperature are always bad news and can result in excess algal growth. To keep the water temperature down in summer, and to prevent excessive evaporation, up to three-quarters of the surface should be covered by the leaves of a deep water aquatic plant.

▼ **643** *The pump will need clearing of blanket weed and algae, and will need cleaning regularly with clean water if it is to work efficiently.*

▲ **647** *If your pond is near trees, place a fine net over the surface to catch any falling leaves. Empty the net regularly.*

Keep topping up the water level until the plants grow sufficiently large that they arrest the evaporation.

646 The pond I made with a preformed liner is losing water – what is the solution?

Soil subsidence can cause a fibre-glass liner to crack. If this happens, you need to empty the pool completely. Remove the liner, then clean and dry it and locate the crack. Repair with a suitable product available from a specialist retailer, then return the liner to its original position and refill with water. Ensure that there are no stones or other sharp objects beneath the pond liner, which may weaken the material.

647 How do I prevent leaves falling into the water in autumn?

Site a pool away from overhanging deciduous trees that will shed their leaves into the water where they will rot and release noxious gases. This can be impractical advice, though. Cast a fine net over the pond in autumn to catch the falling leaves. Gather up the leaves regularly and either add them to the compost heap or bonfire, or turn them into leaf mould.

▼ **639** *Water snails eat oxygenating plants, algae and vegetative debris, so can be considered a beneficial addition to the pond, unless there are too many.*

BOG GARDENS

A garden that is permanently wet and never dries out even at the height of summer is known as a bog garden. Bog plants are some of the handsomest of all pond plants – vigorous and healthy, but often invasive. Gardens of this type are unusual and attractive.

648 What is a bog plant?

Bog plants are plants that have adapted to thrive in boggy conditions. These conditions are usually found around the margins of a natural pond. They will fail if the land dries out. If a man-made pond is to look natural, it should ideally have some bog plants around the edges, though the soil here may not be naturally damp. If it is dry, consider making an artificial bog garden to one side of the pond. Bog plants are always very vigorous, as they have a constant supply of moisture, and can be invasive.

649 How do I make a bog garden?

Excavate the soil to a depth of around 45cm (18in). Level the base of the area and top with a layer of builder's sand. You may wish to make your bog deeper at one end, so that you can grow deep-rooted bog plants at the deep end and moisture-loving plants at the shallow end. Lay a sheet of butyl liner in the base of the hole and pierce this all over with a garden fork. The aim is to slow down the rate at

▼ **648** *Bog plants help create a lush, almost tropical, impression in the garden.*

Making a bog garden

1 Excavate an area of soil, to a depth of 45cm (18in). Remove any large stones.

2 Spread a length of butyl liner (such as is sold for pond making) at the base of the hole.

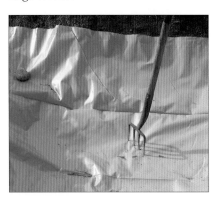

3 While the liner is intended to retain water, some drainage is necessary. Make holes through the liner with a garden fork or knife.

4 Fill with grit to a depth of 10–15cm (4–6in), then top with the excavated soil. Water the area well before planting.

which water drains through the area. Fill with soil, then plant up as desired. Even though the presence of the liner increases the water retention of the soil, it may still be necessary to water the area during periods of drought in summer.

650 Where do I site a bog garden?

A bog garden should be situated in a predominantly sunny or lightly shaded spot, ideally in a hollow or low-lying part of the garden, where rainwater will run into it.

651 Can I use ordinary tap water to water the bog?

Ideally, you should wet the soil with rainwater (collected in a water butt). If you have to use tap water, it is best to allow this to stand for a couple of days before use. This will allow any additives such as chlorine to evaporate.

652 What are the ecological benefits of a bog garden?

A bog will attract a variety of insects as well as the larger creatures that prey on them. Frogs, toads and grass snakes will also appreciate the cool, damp conditions of an established bog garden.

653 Which plants are recommended for a bog garden?

Alnus glutinosa
Aruncus
Arundo donax
Astilbe
Cornus alba
Darmera peltatum
Euphorbia palustris
Gunnera manicata
Iris ensata
Lobelia cardinalis
Lysichiton americanus
Primula florindae
Primula pulverulenta
Rheum palmatum
Salix alba
Scrophularia auriculata
Senecio smithii

654 How do I avoid walking on the soil when dealing with the plants?

Permanently wet soil is sticky – it clings to your shoes. To prevent damaging the soil structure, place a few stepping stones strategically among the plants so that you can gain access to all parts of the planting. Bog plants are lush, so will conceal the stones when they are in full growth.

▼ **653** Cornus alba *thrives in damp areas. It is grown for its attractive stems.*

▲ **653** Rheum palmatum *is an architectural plant for a large site.*

655 Do I need to feed bog plants?

Plants with a constant supply of moisture usually do not need additional fertilizers to keep them growing strongly. Nor is it necessary to apply an annual mulch, as is usual around other permanent plants.

656 How do I prevent the soil from freezing in winter?

If your garden is in a cold area, ice can form in wet soil during freezing weather. To protect plants, spread a

▼ **653** *The glossy leaves of* Lysichiton americanus *reflect light.*

▲ **653** Primula pulverulenta *flowers in late spring.*

loose mulch of bark chippings over the site in late autumn. Remove it the following spring as temperatures rise and plants start to grow.

657 Some of my bog plants have grown too large. When is the best time to deal with them?

The best time to cut back plants is early autumn, when you are least likely to disturb any wildlife. If you cut back in spring, you may expose hibernating frogs to predators.

▼ **653** Darmera peltatum *has striking flowers and leaves.*

CHAPTER SEVEN

PROPAGATION METHODS

Producing your own plants is always a rewarding business and offers a much more economical means of stocking your garden than a visit to a plant nursery or garden centre. Seeds are usually freely available, whether they are found in your own garden or given to you by a friend. There are two basic methods of propagation: with seed or by removing part of the plant and encouraging this to produce a new plant. The first is a sexual method – two parents are involved in the production of fertile seed. The second is a vegetative method that effectively produces a clone of the parent and the new plant will be genetically identical to it. The majority of propagation methods are straightforward and only the minimum of equipment is usually necessary.

COLLECTING AND
PREPARING SEED

VEGETATIVE
PROPAGATION

PROPAGATING
TREES AND SHRUBS

PROPAGATING
PERENNIALS

LAYERING

PROPAGATING
BULBS, CORMS
AND TUBERS

PROPAGATING
LILIES

◄ *Auriculas are propagated by taking offsets.*

COLLECTING AND PREPARING SEED

From summer onwards, you can start gathering seed produced by the plants in your garden.
Seed is usually produced in abundance, so there is never any shortage in the supply. The trick
is to collect it when its ripe before the plant discards it.

658 When can I collect seed?

Seed should be harvested when it is ripe, usually in late summer to autumn. Unripe seed will not germinate. If you want seed from a particular specimen, watch it closely so that you do not miss an opportunity.

659 Is seed-collecting suited to propagating particular species of plant?

Propagating by seed is an excellent method of producing sturdy, virus-free plants. You can only reproduce certain species by this method and the results are not reliable, depending on the genetic stability of the parent. For example, with the Lenten hellebore (*Helleborus orientalis*), which is worth trying, the flower colour cannot be predicted. Wisteria seedlings, on the other hand, often do not flower well.

Vegetative methods produce plants that are identical to the parent, but only limited material may be available, whereas seeds are usually available in abundance. Some plants have seeds contained in papery cases which split open when the seeds are ripe.

▼ **659** *Cut the stems just as they are starting to split and shake the seed out.*

▲ **658** *Some plants display seeds that are large and obvious. These can be collected by hand, once they have matured to a good size, but before the plant disperses them naturally.*

660 Which common garden plants are easy to grow from seed?

Acanthus
Agapanthus
Berberis
Clematis orientalis
Clematis tangutica
Cotoneaster
Helleborus orientalis

Juglans regia
Lathyrus latifolius
Lilium regale
Lunaria annua
Malus
Nigella damascena
Pyrus salicifolia
Quercus
Sorbus

661 Can I grow hybrids from seed?

Hybrids are created by crossing two different species. Complex hybrids may combine the genes from several species introduced by later crossings. Hybrids are usually very robust plants with large flowers. Some do not even produce seed, but if you collect the seed from those that do, the resultant seedlings will not resemble the parent. They will revert to one of the hybrid's ancestors, which may not be a plant that has any garden merit.

662 How do I extract the seed from fleshy berries?

Cut the berries of plants such as *Sorbus* and *Cotoneaster* in autumn when they are soft and ripe – ideally

▼ **660** *The Lenten hellebore* (Helleborus orientalis) *often seeds itself in gardens.*

▼ **660** *Acanthus seeds are held within a spiny casing.*

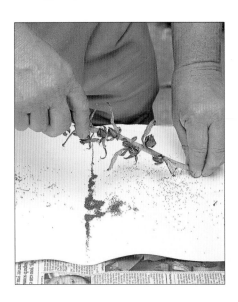

▲ **660** *It is easy to increase your stocks of agapanthus from seed. Collect the seed pods after flowering, just before they are about to distribute the seed on the wind.*

after the first frosts. Squash the berries to release the seed, then wash in a small bowl of lukewarm water. Dry the seed on kitchen paper before you sow it.

663 How do I extract the seed from hard fruits?

To extract the seeds from hard fruits such as *Malus*, cut the fruit in half with a sharp knife to expose them. Apple seeds are dark brown when ripe. Remove them with the tip of the knife, discarding any that were accidentally damaged when making the cut.

▼ **663** *Apple seeds are easily extracted from the fruits.*

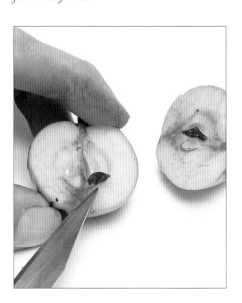

Extracting seed from fleshy berries

1 Squash the berries, which should already be soft, between finger and thumb to release the seed. Discard the flesh.

2 Wash the seed in a shallow bowl filled with lukewarm water to remove all traces of the flesh. Dry the seeds on kitchen paper.

664 How do I extract seed from the cone of a conifer?

You will often see cones on the grass around a conifer in autumn. To extract the seed, place a sheet of paper under the cone, then tap it sharply on the table. The seed should fall from the cone. If the cone is fully open, the seeds may already have been shed.

665 What should I do if the conifer cone is tightly closed?

You can encourage cones to open in one of two ways. Either place the cone

▼ **665** *Conifer cones contain seeds which are held in place until they reach maturity.*

on a sheet of paper near a gentle heat source, such as a radiator, or put it in a bowl of lukewarm water. Within 24 hours, the cone should open, and you will be able to extract the seeds.

666 Can I store seed?

Seed can be stored in a cool, dry place in paper envelopes or screwtop jars. Label with the plant name and the date of collection. Often packets of seeds will germinate long after the suggested date on the packet, and it is always worth trying.

▼ **666** *Some stored seed will remain viable for many years.*

▲ **668** *Dampen vermiculite or perlite and place it in a plastic bag. Add a few seeds, then seal the package and place it in the refrigerator. Check regularly for signs of germination.*

667 What is stratification?

The seeds of many hardy trees and shrubs have hard coats that have to be broken down before the embryo within can begin to grow into a plant. This normally occurs naturally over winter. Freezing weather softens the hard coat, so that the new plant can emerge. Take any batch of seed, however, and the temperature at which this happens will vary – some will germinate at lower temperatures than others. So, if you sow the seed outdoors, some will germinate in year one, while others will only germinate after two or three years.

▼ **669** Sorbus *produces its seed in fleshy berries – red, yellow, pink or white.*

668 Can I stratify seed artificially?

Although you can sow seed and place the containers outdoors, waiting for nature to take its course, you are gambling on suitable conditions occurring over winter that will break the seed's dormancy. To speed up the process, you can stratify the seed artificially before sowing. Mix the seed with damp perlite or vermiculite and seal in a clear plastic bag. Label the bag with the name of the plant and the date, then place in a refrigerator for three to six weeks. Then sow the seed as normal and place the containers outdoors. (Some seed may actually germinate in the refrigerator.)

▼ **669** Cotoneaster *produces small red berries in the autumn.*

▲ **670** *Lupin seeds benefit from being soaked in warm water before being sown in potting mix.*

669 Which tree and shrub seeds need stratification?

All true species that produce seed such as: *Acer*
Amelanchier
Betula
Carya
Cotoneaster
Euonymus
Fagus
Hippophäe
Sorbus
Viburnum

▼ **669** *The flowers of* Viburnum tinus *are followed by shiny, blue-black berries.*

670 What is warm stratification?

The plant family Leguminosae contains many familiar garden plants including sweet peas (*Lathyrus odoratus*), laburnums and lupins. To accelerate germination of the seeds from this family, some gardeners like to soak the seeds in warm water for up to 24 hours prior to sowing.

671 How do I deal with large seeds?

Some seeds, such as oak (*Quercus*) and horse chestnuts (*Aesculus*), have a tough outer coating that inhibits germination. It is this coating that allows seeds to remain viable in the earth for several years without germinating. This can be overcome using a process known as scarification.

672 What is scarification?

Scarification involves a physical breaching of the seed coat, either by cutting or abrasion. If you are dealing with a large seed, such as an acorn or chestnut, nick the tough outer coat with a sharp knife, taking care not to damage the tissue beneath. The abrasion allows in air and moisture, allowing the seed to germinate. You can breach the seed coats of smaller seeds such as sweet peas by rubbing gently with sandpaper or by shaking them in a small jar containing sharp sand.

▼ **673** *All seeds germinate at different temperatures and at different rates. These fuchsia seeds have been left overnight to germinate on a dampened sheet of kitchen paper.*

673 Are there any other pre-treatments for seeds?

The seed coatings of some shrubs can be softened by soaking the seed for a few hours in water – hot or cold, depending on the species. The following all benefit:
Arbutus (cold)
Camellia (cold)
Caragana (hot)
Coronilla (hot)

674 How do I deal with the seedlings?

After they have germinated, keep the seedlings growing strongly by watering and feeding them regularly. Keep them in a cold frame over the first winter. Pot them up in spring, either individually or in groups of three or five. They should be large enough to plant out in the garden after two to three years.

Sowing seed

1 Fill a pot with multi-purpose or seed compost (soil mix). Have spare plant pots to hand and some gravel and a plant label.

2 Fill each pot with compost, then water it well and allow the container to drain – the compost surface should be just moist.

3 Seed should be covered to its own depth. Very fine seed can be surface sown, then topped with a fine layer of sieved (strained) potting mix, horticultural grit or sand. For larger seeds, make suitably sized holes in the compost with a dibber, then draw the surrounding compost over.

4 Cover the compost surface with a layer of horticultural grit or sand. Place the containers outdoors in a sheltered place. After germination, protect the seedlings from slugs and snails. Place them in a cold frame on nights when hard frost is forecast; remove them again the following day.

VEGETATIVE PROPAGATION

Many plants can be propagated by cuttings – taken usually from the stems, but sometimes also from the roots or leaves. Cutting stimulates root production. Even bulbs can be increased by cutting them up.

675 Which plants can I propagate vegetatively?

All plants except annuals can be propagated by methods other than seed. Vegetative methods involve cutting a section from a plant and persuading it to produce roots.

676 Are there any benefits of choosing vegetative propagation as a method to increase stock?

Splitting perennials not only increases your stock, producing extra plants for the garden and for exchanges with friends, but can improve the health of the plant. Reducing congestion and discarding older, unproductive parts

▼ **675** *Pelargoniums for use in summer bedding and containers are easily raised from cuttings.*

of the plant keeps it growing strongly. Taking cuttings of woody plants – trees and shrubs – is a good method of creating replacement material for plants that have outgrown their allotted space or perhaps have grown out of shape. Cutting bulbs quickly produces new bulbs.

677 Can I take cuttings throughout the year?

Theoretically, yes, though autumn cuttings tend to root most readily. Spring cuttings and summer are soft and need attention to ensure they do not dry out. Winter cuttings may be slow to root but can usually be kept outdoors and need little attention. Keep taking cuttings regularly until you find a time that suits you – and the plants.

678 Do I need to put my cuttings in a specific kind of potting mix?

In order for cuttings to root, they need to be in a potting mix that is low in nutrients. Ordinary potting mix encourages the cutting to carry on producing leaves, and you want it to produce roots. A suitable mixture is equal parts of peat or coir and horticultural grit, sharp sand, perlite or vermiculite. Once rooted, the cuttings can be potted up using potting mix.

679 Do I need to use any chemicals to support and encourage the new plant's growth?

Some gardeners always treat their cuttings with a hormone-rooting compound, which takes the form of either a powder or a liquid. Other gardeners think that these compounds are not necessary. The problem with using compounds is that it is easy to use too much, which leads to the production of brittle roots that are easily damaged.

▼ **679** *Rooting powder stimulates the growth of roots, which may help to produce stronger plants. Some rooting powders contain a fungicide, which helps to prevent different types of rot. Some gardeners have success with cuttings without using any chemical aids.*

PROPAGATING TREES AND SHRUBS

Most trees and shrubs can easily be raised from cuttings, which may be taken virtually throughout the year. So, if a particular batch of cuttings fails to root, just keep taking more at regular intervals until you are successful.

680 What types of cutting can be taken to propagate trees and shrubs?

Cuttings are defined according to the degree of firmness in the growth. Softwood cuttings are taken in early summer while the new growth is still very soft. Semi-ripe cuttings, taken from mid-summer to autumn, are firmer but still flexible. Hardwood, or fully ripe cuttings, are taken in early winter when the growth is firm and woody.

681 Can I encourage a plant to produce strong material for cuttings?

If you are good at forward planning and there is a plant in your garden that you wish to propagate, prune some of the branches hard at the start of the growing season. This will encourage it to produce vigorous new growth that should provide good material for propagation later on in the growng season.

682 What are the advantages and disadvantages of each cutting type?

The softer the cuttings, the greater the percentage of them that will root, and in the shortest time. However,

▼ **682** *Soft wood bends easily when handled. It should be easy to cut.*

▲ **685** *You can root cuttings from several different plants in separate containers in a large propagator.*

subsequent aftercare requires a certain investment of time and effort. Cuttings taken later require less attention, but are slower to root and a smaller percentage will root successfully.

683 How do I know which type of cutting to take for any given plant?

Raising new plants from cuttings is a hit-and-miss affair. Take them whenever it is convenient. If the cuttings fail, take some more later on, but without sacrificing the shape of the parent plant.

684 What equipment do I need?

To maintain the humidity around softwood cuttings that is necessary for greater success, you need a closed propagating case and a heat source. This keeps the cuttings alive during the period when they are forming their roots – the damp atmosphere prevents wilting.

685 What types of propagator are there?

The simplest propagators comprise a tray with a clear plastic lid that fits tightly over it. Sometimes the lids have vents in them that enable you to moderate the humidity level. If not, you may need to lift the lid from time to time to stop the air from becoming humid, causing damage to the plants. Some models contain a cable in the base that creates a gentle warmth, like that generated by a light bulb, around the cuttings. Larger, more sophisticated versions have thermostats so that you can regulate the temperature more precisely – worth the money if you are intending to do a lot of propagating or if there is a specific plant that you are keen to propagate at a certain temperature. You can also buy mini-cloches, which are clear plastic domes that are designed to fit over single flower pots. These create a microclimate around the plant, but need lifting every so often to allow air to circulate to stop condensation damaging the plant.

Taking softwood cuttings

1 Take a cutting from new growth using a sharp knife. Put the cutting into a sealed plastic bag.

2 Trim the cutting to the required size. Fill a plant pot with potting mix and plant with cuttings.

3 Label each plant pot. Put the cuttings in a sealed plastic bag or within a propagator until well established.

686 Can I still root softwood cuttings without any of these?

You can create the appropriate conditions for rooting by tenting a flower pot with a clear plastic bag. Seal this with an elastic band around the pot or by folding the open end of the bag under the pot. If you place the pot near a radiator, you can achieve the same result. Turn the pot regularly to ensure an even heat.

687 How do I deal with softwood cuttings?

Cuttings taken in early spring are notoriously prone to wilting, which easily leads to rotting. For success, it is necessary to keep them turgid – in other words, they can never be allowed to dry out. Take the cuttings as early in the morning as possible, when they will be stiffened by overnight dews. As soon as you take the cuttings, place them in a plastic bag to retain moisture. Deal with the cuttings promptly by having all the necessary materials prepared.

688 How do I take cuttings?

First, fill pots or trays with cuttings potting mix – equal parts potting mix and horticultural grit or sand is a suitable mix – water well and allow to drain. Cut non-flowering stems from the plant, up to 15cm (6in) in length. Cut just above a leaf joint on the plant, so that it will heal quickly. Remove the lower leaves from the cutting up to about half its length. Trim the cutting at the base, just below the lowest leaf joint. There should be two or three sets of leaves remaining. Make holes in the cuttings potting mix with a dibber, then insert the cuttings so that the lower leaves are just proud of the potting mix surface. Lightly spray with a liquid fungicide, then place in a propagator.

689 Can I put more than one cutting in each pot?

It makes sense to take as many cuttings as possible because only a proportion will root successfully. You can put several in each pot or tray, but it is important that there is sufficient space between them so that they do not touch. Leaves should also not touch the lid of the propagator or the plastic tent. Where leaves are in contact with other leaves or touch the propagator or plastic, beads of moisture will collect. This moisture will tend to hold fungal spores and can lead to rotting.

690 What if the cuttings have very large leaves?

If you are dealing with cuttings of plants that have large leaves, such as hydrangeas or spotted laurels (*Aucuba japonica*), you can cut the leaves across at the widest point to halve them. This enables you to get more cuttings in the container and also reduces moisture loss from the cutting, as you have reduced the surface area of the leaves. However, you will need to keep a close eye on them, as the cut edges can be prone to rotting.

691 What aftercare do softwood cuttings need?

If you are using a closed propagator (for soft cuttings) or have tented them with a plastic bag, the humid atmosphere around the cuttings will help keep them firm. However, that humidity can be a breeding ground for fungi. Remove the covering occasionally and wipe down any excess moisture. Spray the cuttings lightly with a fungicide. Once a cutting has rooted, pot it up individually in a compost (potting mix) that is suitable for the type of plant. A rooted cutting no longer needs to be covered, but needs to be kept indoors initially. Gradually acclimatize it to conditions outdoors. A cold frame will offer suitable protection from the worst of the weather, during daylight hours. Overwinter rooted cuttings in the frame and pot them on the following spring – they may be large enough to plant out the following autumn or can be grown on in containers for a year.

Taking semi-ripe cuttings

1 Firmly grasp a side shoot and pull sharply downwards and away from the main stem.

2 This will enable you to tear a small tail of bark from the main stem at the base of the cutting.

3 Remove the leaves from the lower part of the cutting, then trim the tail of bark.

692 How long will it take for the cuttings to root?

Softwood cuttings should root quickly – within about four to six weeks. Semi-ripe cuttings take ten weeks or longer. Cuttings taken in autumn should root by the following spring. Hardwood cuttings can take up to a year to root.

693 How do I tell if the cuttings have rooted?

Give each cutting a sharp tug. If you feel resistance, the cutting has rooted and can be potted on. If you can pull the cutting from the potting mix,

check the base carefully. If you can see a callus at the base of the tissue, return it to the rooting medium – it will produce roots in time. If not, then discard the cutting. Not all cuttings will be successful, even from plants that have produced successful cuttings previously.

694 How do I take semi-ripe cuttings?

Semi-ripe cuttings are taken from summer to autumn when the growth is starting to firm up, but is still fairly pliable. Prepare them as for softwood cuttings and pot them up

in containers filled with cuttings potting mix. Place the cuttings in a propagator or cold frame, or tent the containers with clear plastic bags. Semi-ripe cuttings should put out roots within about 12 weeks.

695 How do I take hardwood cuttings?

Many trees and some shrubs can easily be propagated by hardwood cuttings taken right at the end of the season, in late autumn, when the wood is fully ripe and firm. Cut healthy stems from the plant. Remove any deciduous leaves and

▼ **686** *Sealing cuttings in a plastic bag creates a microclimate.*

▼ **691** *Spray cuttings with a fungicide spray in order to help prevent rot.*

▼ **691** *Open the vent on a progagator regularly to allow air to circulate.*

trim back the tip if this is still soft. Cut stems into 15–20cm (6–8in) lengths, trimming them straight across the bottom and with an angled cut at the top, then insert them in containers filled with cuttings potting mix. Only 2.5–5cm (1–2in) of stem should be above the compost surface. Put the containers in a cold frame. Hardwood cuttings can take up to a year to root, and only a small proportion of them will be successful.

◀ **700** *On grafted shrubs and trees, any new growth that appears below the graft will not be the plant that you want. Remove the new growth as it appears.*

Rooting hardwood cuttings outside

1 Dig a trench in a sheltered part of the garden about 15–20cm (6–8in) deep.

2 Line the base of the trench with sharp sand or horticultural grit to a depth of about 5cm (2in).

3 Place the cuttings in the trench, spacing them around 8–10cm (3–4in) apart.

4 Firm the soil around the cuttings with your hands, then water them well.

696 I have heard that hardwood cuttings can be rooted outdoors. How should I do this?
Choose an open but sheltered spot in the garden. Push a spade into the soil and move it forward and back to open up a trench. Line the base of the trench with horticultural grit or sharp sand. Place the cuttings in the trench so that only 2.5–5cm (1–2in) of stem is above ground level. However, if the cuttings are from a tree, and you want the new plants to grow with a single upright trunk, bury the cuttings so that the tips are just below ground level. They can be placed quite close together.

697 Is any aftercare required for hardwood cuttings?
Aftercare of hardwood cuttings is minimal – they do not need regular watering. However, you should check them during very cold weather. If the soil is frozen, the trench may open up. If this happens, lightly firm the soil around the cuttings with your foot.

698 Which hardwood cuttings root well outside?
Buddleja
Cornus
Forsythia
Rosa
Salix
Spiraea
Viburnum

699 What are suckers?
Some shrubs and trees naturally produce vigorous new shoots from ground level (or just below) around the base of the plant. The beauty of suckers is that they are removed with a fully formed root system so are ready for planting out straight away.

700 How do I remove the suckers?
Carefully dig up the suckers, making sure there is a fibrous root system at the base of the sucker. Sever the suckers from the parent plant with secateurs (hand pruners) or a sharp knife. Replant immediately or pot them up individually.

PROPAGATING PERENNIALS

Perennials are relatively easy to propagate. Most can simply be split into pieces in spring or autumn. But there are also some other methods of propagation that can be successful, depending on the type of plant.

701 Why would I divide perennials?

Dividing perennials is an excellent method of increasing your stocks and also refreshes the plants, providing the opportunity to discard older, woody sections of the plant that are less productive.

702 When can I divide perennials?

Divide perennials either in spring or autumn, preferably during mild, damp weather when the divisions will settle in more quickly. Most plants should be divided only every two to five years, allowing time for them to recover in between. Primulas (*Primula vulgaris*), however, should be ruthlessly divided annually immediately after flowering. You can do this throughout the growing season except during periods of drought. Be sure to keep the divisions well watered to make sure that they establish quickly.

703 How do I divide perennials?

Lift clumps with a fork or hand fork and shake the roots free of soil. You should be able to pull apart some plants, such as hardy geraniums, into smaller sections in your hands. If the plant is congested, you may find it is easier to cut the plant with a sharp knife. For larger plants, drive two garden forks, held back to back, into the centre of the plant and use them to tease it into smaller sections. Sections from around the edge of the plant are younger. Any from the centre that are straggly or woody can be discarded. You can divide the parent into several sections, but each should be well rooted.

704 Can any perennials be propagated by cuttings?

Certain perennials that do not divide easily can be increased by cuttings taken early in the season. Depending on the plant, you can take either stem-tip cuttings or basal cuttings. If in doubt, try both methods.

705 When can I take stem-tip cuttings?

You can take the cuttings any time during the growing season. Many gardeners like to take cuttings of borderline hardy plants – such as penstemons – in autumn, to act as an insurance against possible winter losses. You can overwinter the cuttings on a windowsill indoors, then harden them off the following year before planting out in mid- to late spring.

706 How do I take stem-tip cuttings?

Take cuttings around 8–12cm (3–5in) long from the tips of strongly growing shoots. They should not be flower-bearing. Trim the cutting below a node, then strip off the lower leaves so that the lower third of the stem is bare. Fill pots with cuttings potting mix, then insert the cuttings. Tent the pots with clear plastic bags, held in place with rubber bands (or you can just fold the open end of the bag under the pot). Keep them in a warm position – but out of direct sun – until well rooted, usually two to six weeks.

707 Which perennials can be propagated by stem-cuttings?

Arctotis
Argyranthemum
Dianthus
Diascia
Erysimum
Euryops
Felicia
Gazania
Helichrysum petiolare
Lotus berthelotii
Mimulus
Osteospermum
Pelargonium

Taking stem-tip cuttings

1 Take cuttings of healthy looking non-flowering shoots at any time during the growing season. Take several at different intervals.

2 Trim off the basal leaves, then insert the stems in pots filled with cuttings potting mix.

3 Cut a clear plastic drinks bottle in half and use this to create a mini-propagator for the cuttings.

708 How do I take basal cuttings?

Some plants produce clusters of new shoots from the base in early spring, and it is possible to create new plants from this material early in the season. Select strong-growing shoots from the outside of the crown and cut them from the plant. There should be a small piece of the old tissue (which may be slightly woody) at the base of each cutting. Trim off the lower leaves, then insert them into pots of cuttings potting mix. Tent the cuttings with a clear plastic bag. They should root within two to six weeks. If you keep them growing strongly, they should flower the same year.

709 Which perennials are propagated by basal cuttings?

Achillea
Anthemis tinctoria
Campanula latifolia
Chrysanthemum
Coreopsis
Delphinium
Lupinus
Monarda

710 How do I take root cuttings?

Dig up the plants while they are dormant in winter and wash the roots free of soil. Select roots of pencil thickness and cut them from the plant. (Remove only a few roots if you are intending to return the parent plant to the garden.) Cut the roots into lengths of about 5–10cm (2–4in). It is usually recommended that you cut the top of each cutting straight across, and angle the cut at the base. This is to make sure you insert the cutting the right way up in the potting mix. Fill a container with potting mix that is suitable for cuttings and make holes for them with a dibber. Insert the cuttings vertically so that the flat upper cut is flush with the potting mix surface. Cover them with a fine layer of horticultural grit, then place them in a cold frame. Leaves should appear in spring, when you can pot them up individually.

▲ **712** *Mint* (Mentha) *stems will root easily in a jar of water.*

711 Which perennials can be propagated from root cuttings?

Acanthus
Anemone
Campanula
Echinops
Eryngium
Geranium
Papaver orientale
Phlox
Primula
Pulsatilla
Romneya
Trollius
Verbascum

712 Can I root cuttings in water?

Many soft-stemmed plants can be rooted in water – try osteospermums, penstemons, fuchsias, mints and tradescantias. Fill jars with tap water, then take cuttings around 8cm (3in) long from the plant. Strip off the lower leaves so there is a clear length of stem at the base. To suspend the cuttings in the water, either place two cocktail sticks (toothpicks) over the jar to support the lower leaves or cut a piece of chicken wire to sit over the jar and hold the cuttings in place. Stand the jars on a windowsill, but shade them from full sun. Change the water every few days. They should root in two to three weeks. Roots produced in water may be brittle.

Taking root cuttings

1 Dig up the plant in winter and wash the roots clean of soil. Cut off roots of pencil thickness.

2 Cut the root into sections. Trim them straight across the top, angled at the base.

3 Insert them upright in pots of cuttings potting mix so that the straight upper cut is flush with the surface.

LAYERING

One of the simplest methods of propagating woody plants, as well as others such as climbers that have long, flexible stems, is known as layering. Stems form roots at points where they touch the soil. Some plants, such as strawberries and ivies, form layers naturally.

713 How do I propagate a plant by layering?

You can layer plants directly in the ground or prepare pots of potting mix (mixed with an equal volume of horticultural grit) that are placed near the plant. Choose a vigorous but flexible stem near ground level from around the perimeter of the plant. Bend it down to ground level and locate a point between two nodes or sets of leaves that will be in contact with the soil (or potting mix). Make a shallow cut in the bark on the underside of the stem (if the stem is very thin, for instance if you are layering a clematis, the cut is not necessary). Pin the stem to the ground (or the surface of the potting mix) and hold it in place with a short length of stout wire bent into a U-shape or with a stone. Turn the tip of the stem upwards and tie it loosely to an upright cane driven into the soil or potting mix to encourage upright growth.

▼ **715** Skimmia japonica *is one of a number of shrubs that can be propagated successfully by layering suitable stems.*

714 How long does it take the layer to root?

Layered stems can take anything between six to 12 months to form sturdy roots. To test for rooting, lightly pull on the stem. If you feel resistance, roots will have formed. Sever the stem from the plant, then pot the layer up or plant it out.

715 Which shrubs can be propagated by layering?

Andromeda
Aucuba
Carpenteria
Cassiope
Chaenomeles
Chionanthus
Corylopsis
Daphne
Elaeagnus
Erica
Fothergilla
Kalmia
Laurus
Magnolia
Osmanthus
Rhododendron
Skimmia
Syringa
Vaccinium

716 What is air-layering?

Air-layering is used where there is no suitable stem that can be pulled down to ground level. The stem is encouraged to produce roots well above ground level. It is often used for houseplants where conventional techniques can be difficult.

717 How do I air-layer a plant?

Select a suitable stem from the previous year's growth and strip off the leaves to create a bare length of 23–30cm (9–12in). Make a diagonal cut up to 4cm (1½in) long in the underside of the stem. Lift up the tongue of bark, then pack with damp

---

How to layer a plant

1 Find a flexible stem around the perimeter of the plant that can be bent down to ground level.

2 Hold the stem in place either with a piece of wire bent into a U-shape or with a heavy stone.

3 Insert a cane near the stem tip and tie the stem to this to keep it upright. Dig up the layer when the roots are well developed.

moss. Pack more moss around the stem and hold this in place with a plastic sleeve sealed to the stem at each end with insulating tape, lengths of wire or string.

To encourage rooting, it is necessary to exclude light – therefore, using black plastic should speed up the process. However, if you use clear plastic, you can see when – and if – the stem has produced roots.

718 How long does rooting an air-layered plant take and how do I deal with the new plant once there is a good root system?

It can take up to a year, but check periodically for signs of rooting. Try not to disturb the moss too much.

Check the plant in spring to see how good the roots are. If they are filling the plastic sleeve, you can sever the new plant from the parent, cutting just below the roots. Pot up the layer in a suitable potting mix, then trim back the topgrowth to create a balanced plant. Grow the plant on for up to year, then plant out in its final position.

719 Which plants can be air-layered?

Citrus
Dieffenbachia
Ficus
Hamamelis
Ilex
Kalmia
Magnolia
Monstera
Nerium
Rhododendron

▲ **719** Kalmia latifola, *the calico bush, is related to rhododendrons and can be increased by air-layering.*

How to air-layer a plant

1 Choose a vigorous, healthy stem on which the branches are well spaced.

2 Locate a point on the stem between clusters of leaves. With a sharp knife, cut through the bark.

3 Make a parallel cut farther up the stem, then peel away the collar of bark with the tip of the knife.

4 Wrap damp spaghnum moss around the stem to cover the cut area completely.

5 Wrap a piece of plastic over the moss to hold it in place and keep it moist.

6 Tie the plastic in position at each end with lengths of wire to seal in the moss.

Stooling a plant

1 Prepare a mix of equal parts garden soil, sand and peat or garden compost.

2 Mound this mix around the plant so that the bare parts of the stems are covered.

720 What are dropping and stooling?

These are two techniques used to propagate some soft-stemmed plants that tend to lose their leaves at the base of stems. Heathers (*Erica*) and woody herbs such as rosemary (*Rosmarinus*) and lavender (*Lavandula*) can be propagated by one of these methods. Both methods produce roots on an existing plant's bare stems to create secondary plants. As with layering, the techniques are very reliable as the new plants remain attached to the parent until well rooted – which can take up to one year. No further aftercare is required.

721 When should I propagate a plant by these methods?

Autumn is the best time for dropping or stooling, though it can also be done throughout winter, provided the ground is not frozen or waterlogged.

▲ **720** *Lavender plants can be propagated by dropping and stooling.*

722 How do I 'drop' a plant?

Dig up the plant and shake the roots free of soil. Dig a deeper hole that will accommodate the rootball and the lower, bare parts of the stems. Drop the plant in the hole. Leaf-bearing parts of the stem should be above ground level. Backfill with the excavated soil mixed with garden compost and sharp sand. New roots will form on the lower part of the stems that are under the soil.

723 Which plants are suitable for dropping?

Calluna
Daboecia
Erica
Lavandula
Rhododendrons (small)
Rosmarinus

724 How do I 'stool' a plant?

Prepare a mixture of equal parts garden soil, garden compost and sharp sand. Earth it up around the base of the plant so that all bare parts of the stems are covered. Leafy stem parts should be just above the mound. New roots will form part way up individual stems that are covered in earth.

725 Which plants are suitable for stooling?

Amelanchier
Cotinus coggyria
Hydrangea paniculata
Ribes
Salix

PROPAGATING BULBS, CORMS AND TUBERS

Some bulbs produce offsets that can be detached and grown on to flowering size, or they can be cut into sections and persuaded to produce several new plants. Most bulb propagation is best done when the bulbs are dormant.

726 What methods can I use to propagate bulbs?

You can increase your stocks of bulbs using a variety of methods. Many species are easily raised from seed. Depending on how the bulbs grow, you can either detach small bulblets or cut up a dormant bulb into sections or 'chips'.

727 What equipment do I need to propagate bulbs?

You need no special equipment for cutting up bulbs, but good hygiene is of paramount importance. All cut surfaces should be treated with a fungicide to prevent rotting. You can use either a fungicidal powder or a liquid. Wear rubber surgical gloves when handling the bulbs – this protects your hands (some people experience an allergic reaction) and also protects the bulbs from bacteria, which can cause rots.

728 What are offsets?

If you look at the base of a dormant bulb such as a daffodil, you will see that the roots emerge from a toughened disc – the basal plate.

▲ **726** *Dig up the daffodil bulbs that you wish to propagate and gently detach the bulblets with your hands.*

As part of its growth cycle, new bulbs emerge from around the basal plate annually, and in time the central bulb withers and dies back. If you dig up clumps of bulbs after flowering – but while they are still in full leaf – you should be able to tease them apart and separate the smaller bulbs. You can either pot these up for growing on or return them to the garden. Discard any old, withered bulbs.

▲ **729** *Choose congested plants to dig up. These Muscari are likely to have offsets.*

729 Which bulbs produce offsets?

Allium
Arum
Crinum
Crocus
Galanthus
Iris
Leucojum
Muscari
Narcissus
Nerine
Ornithogalum

Propagating tuberous begonias

1 In late winter, cut the tuber into sections, each with at least one bud.

2 Dust the cut surfaces with a fungicidal powder to prevent rotting.

3 Half bury each cut section in damp potting mix, in pots or trays.

730 How do I propagate bulbs by chipping?

Chipping is a good method for increasing stocks of bulbs that do not readily produce offsets, although you can also use this technique on these as well. Take a dormant bulb and trim back the growing tip. Also trim back the roots, but take care not to damage the basal plate. Holding the bulb upright, cut it in half with a sharp knife. Cut each half in half again. You can carry on dividing each section as far as is practical – you should get up to 16 chips, but it is important that each one has a scrap of basal plate at the bottom, as it is from this that the new bulblet will form.

Half-fill clear plastic bags with perlite or vermiculite, dampened with a little liquid fungicide. Dip each chip into a liquid fungicide, then put a few chips in each bag. Blow up the bags and seal them with rubber bands or wire ties. Shake them to distribute the chips. Keep the bags in a warm, dark place, such as an airing cupboard. Check them after about six weeks. Within 12 weeks, new bulblets should have formed on the basal plate and the chips themselves should be blackening. Remove the chips and snap off the bulblets. Pot them up and grow them on – they should reach flowering size within two to three years.

731 Which bulbs can I propagate by chipping?

Erythronium
Fritillaria
Galanthus
Hippeastrum
Hyacinthus
Iris
Narcissus
Nerine
Scilla
Sternbergia

732 What are cormels?

Technically, gladioli grow not from bulbs but from corms – a flattened disc of tough stem tissue that stays underground. Each corm produces little corms – or cormels – around the basal plate. To propagate using these, dig up the plants after flowering and as the foliage is dying back. Allow them to dry out in the sun, then store the corms in a cool, dry place over winter. In late winter to early spring, snap off the cormels from the base of the corm and pot them up. Grow them on in containers, protecting them from frost over winter. Two to three years later, they should have reached flowering size and can be planted out in the garden.

733 How can I propagate dahlias?

Dahlias grow from underground tubers – swollen roots like a potato. To increase your stocks, in spring, arrange the tubers on trays of potting mix, pressing them into it without burying them. When a tuber starts to shoot, lift it from the potting mix and cut it into sections with a sharp knife. Each section should have at least one shoot. Dust the cut surfaces with a fungicide, then pot up the sections and grow them on. Water and feed them well. They should be well enough established to plant out in late spring and should flower the same year.

734 How do I take basal cuttings of dahlias?

You can also propagate dahlias by cuttings. If they are to flower the same year, take them as early as possible. Coax the dormant tubers into life in late winter by arranging them on trays of potting mix, then keeping them warm at 15–18°C (60–65°F). When the shoots have two or three pairs of leaves, cut them from the tuber, with a small piece of tuber tissue at the base. Trim off the lower leaves. Pot up the cuttings, then place them in a heated propagator. Once rooted, pot them on and gradually harden them off. Protect the cuttings from frost. They should be ready for planting out in late spring.

Propagating dahlias

1 In late winter, place dahlia tubers on trays filled with moist potting mix.

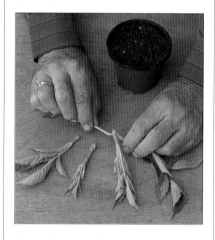

2 Use the new shoots as cuttings. Each should have a tiny section of the tuber at its base.

3 Treat the base of each cutting with a hormone rooting compound, then plant them up in plastic pots.

PROPAGATING LILIES

Lilies are much more diverse than other bulbs, some being adapted to sun, shade, acid or alkaline soils. As you might expect, they can be propagated by a number of methods, all of which are easy and reliable.

735 Can I grow lilies in all types of soil?

No – some have specific requirements as to acidity/alkalinity. When propagating and potting on, therefore, choose a suitable potting mix. Use a soil-based type for those that tolerate alkaline soil, such as *Lilium davidii* and *L. candidum*, and an ericaceous one for acid-lovers, such as *L. lancifolium* and *L. rubellum*. The following lilies tolerate a range of soil types in the garden: *L. amabile*, *L. martagon*, *L. pyrenaicum* and *L. regale*.

736 How do I grow lilies from seed?

Seed is an excellent method for raising new lilies – from species only, though. Most produce seed in copious amounts and the new plants will be guaranteed virus free. Detach the seed capsules from the tips of the stems of the parent plants when they are fully dry and just beginning to split open, usually towards the end of summer. The seed is best sown fresh but can also be stored dry over winter in

▲ **736** *Unlike other lilies, the Madonna lily* (Lilium candidum) *needs shallow planting if it is to flower correctly.*

paper envelopes in a cool, dark place. Sow the stored seed the following spring. Fill small pots with seed potting mix (or ericaceous for acid-lovers) mixed with sharp sand or perlite. Water well and allow to drain. Surface-sow the seed, then top with a layer of horticultural grit or sand. Place the containers in a cold frame.

737 How long does it take the seed to germinate?

Most lily seed should germinate within a few weeks, but some species are slow and may not emerge until the second season after sowing. Leave pots undisturbed until you see signs that the seeds have germinated.

738 How do I deal with seedlings?

Lily seedlings produce a single upright leaf. Water and feed well while they are growing. The seedling will behave like a mature bulb – after a few months the leaf will die back below the potting mix surface (where a little bulb is forming). Keep the pots dry over winter. The following spring, knock the potting mix out of the pots and locate the bulblets. Pot these up in fresh potting mix, burying them to twice their depth. When new growth appears, start watering and feeding. Repeat this procedure annually until the bulbs reach flowering size – three to five years, when they can be planted out in their final positions.

Growing lilies from seed

1 Fill pots with seed potting mix mixed with sharp sand or horticultural grit. Sow the seed thinly on the potting mix surface.

2 Spray with water to ensure good adhesion between the seed and the potting mix surface.

3 Top the potting mix with a layer of horticultural grit. Place the pots in a cold frame outdoors.

▲ **743** *The tiger lily readily produces small bulbs that can be propagated.*

739 What is scaling?

This is a simple and reliable method of increasing your lily stocks, and is suitable for both species and hybrids. The procedure involves removing scales from a bulb and encouraging them to produce bulblets. The best time to take scales is between late summer and spring.

740 How do I scale a lily bulb?

You can scale newly bought dormant bulbs, or dig up bulbs from the garden. For success, bulbs must be plump, firm and healthy. Snap off as many scales as necessary, as close to the base as possible. Either scale the whole bulb or remove a few outer scales, then replant the parent bulb.

741 What should I do with the scales?

Dust the scales with a fungicidal powder to prevent infection. Place them in a clear plastic bag half-filled with a mixture of peat or coir and perlite or vermiculite moistened with a little liquid fungicide. Inflate the bag, label and seal it, then shake it to distribute the scales within the potting mix. Place the bag in a warm, dark place such as an airing cupboard.

742 When will the new bulbs form?

Check the bag after six weeks. Within two to three months, a bulblet should appear at the base of each scale. Remove the scales from the bag, snap off the bulblets, then discard the withering scale. Pot up the bulblets, covering them to twice their own depth with potting mix. Keep potting them on in spring until they reach flowering size. After two to three years they can be planted in the garden.

743 What are bulbils?

The tiger lily (*Lilium lancifolium*) and its hybrids are well known for an interesting phenomenon – little bulbs appear on the stems in the leaf axils. You can snap these off in summer and pot them up, covering them to twice their depth with potting mix. Treat as for scales until ready to plant out.

744 What are bulblets?

Many lilies produce small bulbs on the portion of the stem below ground level. Dig up the lilies towards the end of summer and detach any bulblets. Pot them up individually, covering them to twice their depth with potting mix. Overwinter them in a cold frame or sheltered spot. Pot the bulblet on each spring. After two to three years they can be planted out.

745 Can I hybridize lilies?

Yes, the reproductive parts of lily flowers are prominent and accessible. It is easiest to do if the parent plants are in containers that you can bring indoors – this will prevent pollen from other plants blowing on to the receptors. Choose two lilies that are in flower at the same time. If you look at the open flower, you should easily be able to identify the central style (female) and the surrounding pollen-bearing anthers (male). Decide which is to be the seed parent and cut off the anthers, leaving the central style intact (this prevents self-pollination). Using a clean paintbrush, gather some pollen from the anthers of the other parent. Brush this on to the sticky surface of the stigma at the tip of the style. If the crossing is successful, once the flower fades, the ovary containing the seeds will begin to swell. Wait for the seed case to ripen and dry out, then sow the seed as normal.

Dealing with lily scales

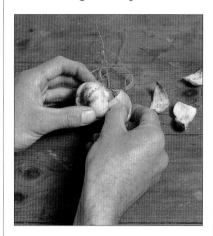

1 Take a clean, dormant lily bulb and snap off some of the outer scales, as close to the base of the bulb as possible.

2 Put some powdered fungicide in a plastic bag and place the scales in this. Give the bag a shake to coat the scales with fungicide.

3 Half-fill another bag with a mix of peat substitute and perlite, lightly moistened. Place the scales in the bag, inflate it, then seal.

CHAPTER EIGHT

PRUNING AND TRAINING

Many trees, shrubs and climbers benefit from pruning as it not only keeps them from getting out of control but can also improve their health and vigour, as well as increase their crops of flowers and fruits. Training plants has a different but related purpose. Not only are trained plants decorative in themselves, but the bending of stems encourages good flower and fruit production. Although many gardeners would confess to being baffled by pruning, the basic principles are actually very logical and the techniques simple – it is all a matter of getting the better of the plants. Some plants are best left unpruned. Watching how they grow and taking note of when they flower provide the best clues to how to proceed. And remember that you can seldom kill a plant outright through incorrect pruning.

PRUNING

PRUNING TREES, SHRUBS AND HEDGES

PRUNING AND TRAINING CLIMBERS

PRUNING AND TRAINING ROSES

PRUNING AND TRAINING FRUIT TREES

PRUNING SOFT FRUITS

◀ *Roses and clematis need training and pruning to be productive.*

PRUNING

The pruning needed to keep a plant productive and in good health can be reduced to a few basic principles. These should always be at the forefront of your mind before reaching for the secateurs and trimming your plants.

746 What are the aims of pruning?

One of the aims of pruning is to relieve congestion in a shrub. Certain plants can develop masses of crowded, twiggy growth. If air circulation is poor within the body of the plant, mildew and other fungal diseases can easily take a hold, especially during mild, damp weather in early autumn. Pruning also allows you to remove weak-growing material, which is always susceptible to disease. Finally, pruning encourages new growth – young growth is always more vigorous, productive and disease-resistant than the old.

747 Can I use pruning to make a big plant smaller?

Pruning stimulates growth. If you want to keep a plant within bounds with pruning, you will need to clip it regularly during spring and summer. It is best to think of pruning as a task

▼ **750** *The new growth buds here are arranged opposite each other on the stem. Prune just above the buds with a single clean cut. The growth above the buds will die back, and the young buds should continue putting on strong growth, unaffected by the pruning.*

that will refresh a plant and improve its flowering or fruiting performance or that will enhance some other decorative feature.

748 Are there any plants that do not need pruning?

Some plants do not respond well to pruning. Others achieve a good shape naturally without any interference. They include magnolias (though *Magnolia grandiflora*, responds well to pruning and training), ornamental cherries (*Prunus*), Japanese maples (*Acer japonicum, A. palmatum*) and all the daphnes.

Many trees and shrubs do not require regular pruning, but you should always keep a look out for any growth that is dead, diseased or damaged. This should be removed promptly, whatever the time of year. Cut back affected growth to strong, healthy wood.

749 Are there any basic pruning principles I should follow?

It is important to remember that pruning stimulates vigorous new growth, which emerges from the point at which you cut the stem. If you want the plant to produce new stems at the base, you must cut at ground

◀ **752** *Pinching out side shoots just below a flower bud produces bigger but fewer flowers.* .

level. Prune vigorous stems only lightly, weak-growing stems much harder to produce a balanced plant.

750 How do I know where to cut the stems?

If you examine the stems of a range of garden shrubs, you will see that the leaves are carried in one of two possible arrangements – they are either held alternately on each side of the stem (as in roses) or in pairs opposite each other on the stem (as in the spotted laurel, *Aucuba japonica*). Make pruning cuts just above a bud or pair of buds. If you cut above a single bud, the new shoot will grow out in the direction the bud is facing – your aim in pruning these plants being to produce a vase-shaped plant with an open centre. If you cut above a pair of buds, two new shoots will appear, more or less at right angles to each other – the result being a more compact, bushier plant.

751 How far away from the buds should I cut?

You should cut just above the bud (or pair of buds) in question. Cut too far above it, and you will leave a stub of wood that – because it cannot grow – turns black and dies back, potentially killing the whole shoot. Cut too close to the bud or buds, and you may damage the emerging growth.

752 What is pinch pruning?

Pinch pruning involves the removal of the soft growing tips of plants such as fuchsias, chrysanthemums and pelargoniums. It encourages bushy growth. Use finger and thumb to remove the tip of each stem just above a leaf or pair of leaves.

PRUNING TREES, SHRUBS AND HEDGES

Many gardeners are worried that trees may grow too large – or there may already be large trees in the garden that are casting too much shade or causing other problems. Most trees, shrubs and hedges respond well to pruning.

753 When is the best time to prune a shrub or tree?

Prune spring-flowering shrubs such as forsythias immediately after flowering. Summer-flowering shrubs such as roses, fuchsias and *Buddleja davidii* can be pruned in late winter to early spring just as new growth is emerging. Many gardeners like to prune deciduous shrubs in winter, when it is easy to see the structure of the plant and it is possible to reach into the base of the plant.

754 What action do I need to take after I have pruned a shrub?

After pruning, feed and water the plant well, then mulch. (This does not apply to autumn pruning – wait until the following spring when the plant comes back into growth.)

755 Which shrubs need little or no pruning?

Berberis
Callicarpa bodinieri
Crataegus
Cytisus

▼ **753** *Camellias respond well to pruning or can be left to grow into large shrubs. Prune after flowering, if necessary.*

Daphne mezererum
Phlomis
Rhododendron
Salix helvetica

756 What is meant by reversion?

Sometimes, shrubs with variegated leaves (usually evergreens such as euonymus), throw up a shoot that has reverted to the original green leaves of the parent species. If this shoot is ignored, it will gradually take over the whole bush and the variegation will be lost. So, it is essential to cut out this green shoot at the base.

757 How do I prune to increase the coloured stems of *Salix* and *Cornus*?

The decorative, coloured stems of willow (*Salix*) and dogwood (*Cornus*) are at their best in winter when they can be most clearly seen and add interest to an otherwise barren garden. If the shrubs are left unpruned, they become large and the stem colour is confined to the short growths at the tips of the branches. However, if they are cut to the ground each year in spring, they will quickly throw up a mass of thin shoots, each with a strong colour. They are fully grown by the following winter, but are unlikely to flower.

758 How do I prune a hydrangea?

Hydrangeas have quite specific pruning requirements. It is best to leave the faded flowerheads on the plant over winter – especially in cold areas – to protect the new spring growth from frosts. Cut off the flower heads in early spring. Shorten any thin or old shoots to the lowest strong bud. You can cut back all stems on *Hydrangea paniculata* to within two buds of the base. The climbing hydrangea (*H. paniculata*) needs minimal pruning – simply remove the faded flowers, if practical.

Pruning a fuchsia

1 Leave fuchsias unpruned over winter – the old stems will protect the crown from frost.

2 In early spring, cut back all the previous year's stems to the base of the plant, where new shoots should be visible.

3 After pruning, the new shoots have more access to the light and should grow away strongly.

759 What is coppicing?

Coppicing is a traditional technique that was used to encourage the growth of whippy shoots suitable for baskets and fence-making. The leader is cut back to near ground level in late winter to early spring. This stimulates the production of quantities of flexible shoots. Cut these back hard the following late winter to early spring. Over time, a stubby 'stool' develops, to which you cut back annually (or in alternate years, if you prefer). Nowadays, the technique is used for ornamental effect – the stems, often vividly coloured, are particularly attractive in winter and are used in floral design.

760 What is pollarding?

Pollarding is a similar technique to coppicing, but instead of cutting the stems down to ground level, allow the tree to develop as a central leader tree with a head of side branches. Once the trunk has reached the desired height, cut all the stems back to their point of origin in late winter–early spring. Repeat the process every year or every two or three years. It is an effective means of keeping in check what would otherwise be a large tree. Pollarded trees look effective if there is room to plant them in avenues.

761 Which are the best trees for coppicing and pollarding?

Acer pensylvanicum 'Erythrocladum'
Catalpa bignoniodes
Cornus
Corylus avellana
Eucalyptus
Paulownia tomentosa
Populus x *candicans* 'Aurora'
Salix
Tilia
Toona sinensis 'Flamingo'

◀ *762 Some large trees may stop natural light from getting to the house.*

762 My tree is shading the house – what can be done about it?

It may be necessary to do no more than thin the canopy. However, it is advisable to contact a tree surgeon, who can assess the tree, and then carry out any necessary work. It is not always possible to reduce the size of tree significantly – in some cases, complete removal is the best option. After the tree has been felled, you may need to hire a stump grinder to remove the lower trunk and roots.

763 Can I prune a tree that has a preservation order on it?

Contact the local authority for permission to prune a tree that has a preservation order on it. A reasonable request would not normally be refused, though you may get consent for no more than a partial prune.

764 How do I remove a large branch from a tree?

A saw is needed to cut branches from trees. It is tempting just to cut straight down through the branch from above. This, however, is risky – once you have cut half way through, the weight of the branch may tear it from the

▼ **759** *Coppicing involves the annual cutting down of a tree to a low framework close to ground level.*

▼ **760** *A pollard is effectively a coppice that is formed on a tall trunk. Pollarding looks brutal but is effective.*

▼ **760** *Regular pollarding results in quantities of whippy stems. Cut back regularly to keep up production.*

▲ **760** *An avenue of pollarded trees can make an attractive feature.*

▲ **767** *Many trees can be successfully grown in large containers.*

tree, leaving an untidy break that may not heal easily. To prevent this, make a cut in the underside of the branch first, opposite the proposed downward cut. Then make the downward cut. This will enable you to remove the branch cleanly.

765 Do I need to treat the stub?

It was once recommend that you treat any large cut surface on a tree with wound paint to prevent disease, but this is no longer considered necessary. Clean cuts should callus over rapidly and the tree will come to no harm. Cuts heal fastest during periods of dry weather, so aim to cut the stems then.

766 What can I do about a tree that has grown too large?

Large trees growing too close to house or boundary walls are sometimes best removed. You can reduce the size of other large trees, but check with the local authority first as preservation orders may be in place. It is also possible to lift a tree canopy if it is too dense. All major pruning jobs should be carried out by a qualified tree

surgeon, as the cuts should be made so that the tree will regrow into a balanced shape. Tree surgeons also have the necessary equipment, including scaffolding, that enables them to carry out work with power tools at height safely.

767 How do I prune a tree in a container?

Trees grown in containers need pruning to keep them in proportion to the container. Prune immediately after flowering (but taking care not to remove any cropping stems on a fruit tree), then again in mid- to late summer. If practical, you can also root-prune the tree. Remove it from the container, ideally in autumn, wash old compost from the roots with a jet of water, then lightly trim the roots. Return the tree to the container, backfilling with fresh compost. If you do not mind the tree growing larger, repot it in a larger container.

768 How do I renovate a shrub that has not been pruned for many years?

Remove dead, damaged, diseased or dying wood. Also remove any suckers around the plant by cutting them away below ground level where the

shoot joins the root. Remove any weak growth and any branches or stems that rub against or cross over each other. Up to one-third of the oldest wood can be taken out to stimulate fresh growth. Several of the oldest stems should be cut back to any new growth, starting from near the base. Repeat this process over the next three years until the shrub has completely renovated itself. Some shrubs, such as *Ceanothus*, are reluctant to produce new growth from old wood. In this case, either omit this stage or remove and replace the plant.

769 My hedge has grown tall. What can I do to ensure it can cope with high winds?

If the hedge is a large, thick one, it is advisable to taper the hedge so that it is narrower at the top than it is at the base. This is called a batter. This brings two advantages. It allows the lowest stems more access to the light, so they are less likely to die back. Secondly, it makes the hedge less top-heavy and more able to withstand severe weather such as strong winds and gales and heavy snowfalls.

Pruning a hedge

1 To make quick work of clearing up trimmings lay down a cloth under the area you are going to clip.

2 When using shears keep the blades flat against the plane of the hedge to get an even cut.

3 When trimming the top of a formal hedge, use canes and string as a guide to help you get it flat.

4 Keep the blades flat when you cut the top of a hedge. Use steps if the hedge is tall.

5 Power trimmers are much faster than hand shears, and in consequence things can go wrong more quickly.

6 Some conifers are slow growing and produce few stray stems. Cut these off with secateurs (pruners).

770 When do I clip a hedge?

To keep a hedge neat, twice yearly clipping is needed. Shear over the hedge in mid-spring, when all danger of frost has passed, and then again in late summer, when the plant has put on significant growth. Do this before the first frosts of autumn. Fast-growing hedges, such as Leylandii conifers (*Cupressocyparis leylandii*) need clipping more regularly – at least four times a year, at equally spaced intervals between mid-spring and late summer.

771 How can I keep a straight line when I cut?

You can maintain a straight line by stretching a cord between two uprights driven firmly into the ground. Pull the cord tight and check the level with a spirit level.

772 When can I prune a wildlife hedge?

Wildlife hedges should be clipped only lightly so as not to remove too much flowering and fruiting growth. If you clip in summer, you should be able to identify the fruiting branches, as the developing fruits should be already visible. Remove some of the older wood in winter. Ensure that any nesting birds have flown the nest before embarking on such a pruning project. Local authorities may have guidelines on appropriate times to prune and renovate.

773 My hedge is thin and straggly. How do I coax it back to life?

A hedge that has not been regularly trimmed – especially during the early years – will often show thin areas and uneven or bare patches. In these cases, cut the individual plants back hard in early spring. New growth is likely to be vigorous. Cutting the stems back ensures that the plant puts on growth lower down the stem to thicken up the base of the hedge. Shorten any new whippy stems to encourage them to branch out, thus producing denser growth. Trim the new growth again in mid- to late summer. The harder you cut, the thicker the growth will be. But beware, if you cut too far back, the hedge may not recover. Established hedges need trimming twice a year, in spring and mid-summer, both to keep them in check and to maintain dense growth. Most conifer hedges do not respond well to such treatment, however, apart from yew. If a conifer hedge has become very straggly, it may be necessary to replace it entirely.

PRUNING AND TRAINING CLIMBERS

Climbers are vigorous plants that can easily get out of hand without regular pruning. But it is
a simple matter to keep them in check, provided you keep a watchful eye on their growth,
although neglected plants can also be brought under control.

774 How do I train a climber?

On planting, cut out any dead,
diseased or damaged stems and
lightly trim back the remainder.
Fan them out and tie them loosely to
the support. As the plant grows, train
in the stems as close to the horizontal
as possible. This diverts the plant's
energies away from overly vigorous
upright growth, encouraging it to
produce shorter, lateral stems that will
be flower-bearing.

775 How do I make sure that a climber grown up a post will flower all the way up?

A pergola over a path creates a
delightful shady walkway if covered
in climbers. Where space is limited,
climbers can be grown on posts at the
back of a border. To ensure that the
posts or pergola are covered in flowers
all the way up, attach upright wires to
two opposite faces of the post or parts
of the pergola. As the climber grows,
wrap the stems around the uprights,
attaching them to the wires where
they touch.

776 I want the climber to cover a wall. Should I use trellis?

Unless the climber is a self-clinger,
you will need to attach some sort of
support to the wall against which to
train it. Although trellis panels can be
used, most climbers will not attach
themselves unaided and will need to
be tied in. If you opt for trellis, rather
than attaching it directly to the wall,
mount it on upright battens (up to
5cm/2in deep) screwed to the wall.
Nailing trellis to battens brings certain
advantages. Firstly, if you need to gain
access to the wall – either to repoint
or paint it – you can simply detach
the panel and lay it flat on the ground,
climber still attached. Secondly,
mounting the panel allows air to
circulate behind the plant which is
important if the plant is not to
succumb to mildew late in the season.

777 What are the alternatives to trellis?

Leaf-stalk and tendril climbers are
much happier attaching themselves to
thin wire (though they will still need

▲ **775** *You can make an instant support
for a climber simply by driving several
bamboo canes into the ground.*

guidance). You can screw upright
battens to the wall, then create a
system of horizontal wires stretched
between vine eyes. Alternatively, vine
eyes can either be screwed or
hammered into the wall and are
available in a range of sizes.

Fixing a trellis to a wall

1 Trellis should be mounted on
battens. Drill holes in the wall, then
screw the battens to it.

2 Nail the trellis to the battens. It is a
simple matter to remove the trellis
later if you need to paint the wall.

3 Train in the stems of the plant
horizontally, tying them in with
short lengths of wire or string.

Growing a climber through a shrub

1 Prepare the ground beside, not under the shrub, otherwise the climber might be starved of water.

2 Plant the climber in the prepared soil and tie its shoots to one or more canes, leading them into the shrub.

3 Water the ground around the shrub thoroughly and then apply a mulch to the same area.

778 What are vine eyes?
Vine eyes, traditionally used for training grapes but suitable for all plants, are of two types. One is designed to be screwed into a wall. Drill a hole of suitable diameter first and tap in a plastic rawl plug before screwing in the vine eye. The flat type, more convenient to use, but possibly less stable, can simply be hammered into the mortar between bricks. Both are available in sizes up to 15cm (6in).

779 How do I prune a climber?
Prune early-flowering climbers immediately after flowering, and late-flowering ones at the start of the growing season. Once the climber has filled its allotted space, shorten overlong shoots and remove any crossing stems. Cut back thick, old stems to ground level. You can then shorten side shoots, if necessary.

780 My climber is completely overgrown and is just a mass of stems. What can I do?
A plant that has really got out of hand can be given a new lease of life by renovation, or drastic, pruning. In late winter, cut back all the stems to near ground level. Feed the plant well, water it, then mulch. Given that climbers are vigorous plants, recovery is usually swift – though the plant may not flower the first year after.

▼ **780** *If a climber is neglected, it rapidly turns into a mass of congested stems that do not flower well.*

◄ **778** *Vine eyes are hammered into the mortar between bricks in order to secure them in place.*

781 Why are clematis divided into three groups?

Clematis is a large genus comprising many species and literally hundreds of hybrids. For convenience, they are divided into three groups according to their flowering season, each group having different pruning requirements. Group 1 clematis flower in late winter to spring. Group 2 clematis flower in two flushes, the first in mid-spring, the second later in summer. Group 3 clematis flower in summer.

782 How do I prune a Group 1 clematis?

Group 1 clematis need no regular pruning, but can be clipped after flowering, if necessary. If pruned hard, *C. montana* may not flower the following year.

783 How do I prune a Group 2 clematis?

Group 2 clematis comprise many popular varieties with large flowers, some having double flowers. What distinguishes them from varieties in the other groups is that they flower twice, first in mid- to late spring, then again in summer (although

▼ **782** Clematis armandii *is one of the few evergreen clematis. It produces its scented white flowers in mid-spring.*

▲ **784** *'Huldine' is a Group 3 clematis, a dainty* viticella *type that can be pruned hard in late winter.*

▼ **783** *Clematis 'Lasurtern' is a Group 2 clematis that needs careful pruning to produce its two flushes of large flowers.*

double-flowered ones produce only single flowers second time round). Thin congested growth in late winter, cutting back old, woody stems to the base, and shortening others, bearing in mind that these will carry the first crop of flowers. You can leave some vigorous ones unpruned. Simply aim to reduce congestion. Deadhead after flowering. Popular varieties include 'Lasurstern', 'Nelly Moser' and the double 'Vyvyan Pennell'. Against a warm wall, the slightly tender *C. florida* 'Sieboldii' is very desirable.

784 How do I prune a Group 3 clematis?

Some of the most popular large-flowered hybrids belong to this group, including 'Hagley Hybrid' and 'Star of India'. The yellow-flowered *Clematis orientalis* is also a member, as are the many hybrids derived from *C. texensis* and *C. viticella*. Pruning is straight-forward – simply cut all stems down to fat buds near the base in late winter. They can also be left unpruned, provided growth is not too congested.

Training a wisteria

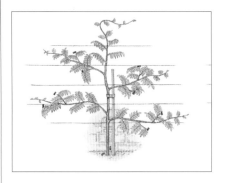

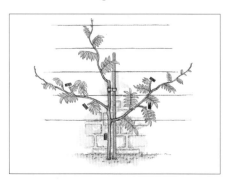

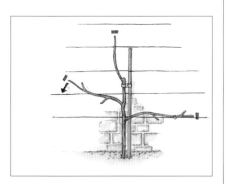

1 Year one, plant the wisteria in winter or early spring. Cut back all side shoots and cut the leader to about 1m (40in).

2 Year one, summer. Select two strong shoots and tie these into the wires. Also tie in the vertical leader. Remove all other laterals.

3 Year two, winter. Gently pull the two laterals down to the horizontal. Cut off the leader about 75–90cm (30–36in) above the laterals.

4 Year two, summer. Repeat the process that you completed in the previous year, this time adding a second tier of new laterals.

5 Established pruning, summer. Once the wisteria is established, prune any new shoots that are not required to fill a space back to five or six leaves.

6 Established pruning, winter. Each winter cut back all the shoots pruned in the summer to two or three buds. Cut out any shoots that cross.

785 How do I prune a wisteria?

Prune in late summer, cutting back any of the current year's growth that exceeds the allotted space and tying in new stems. Once established, in late summer cut back all stems that are growing outside the framework. Shorten laterals to five or six leaves. In mid-winter, cut these back to two or three buds. These are the spurs that will carry the flowers.

786 How do I train my wisteria?

Wisterias are vigorous plants. Rigorous pruning is needed to divert their energies into flower production. Poor soil can be beneficial – rich soil only encourages leafy growth.

◄ **786** *Train wisterias against a warm wall for prolific flowering.*

PRUNING AND TRAINING ROSES

Roses have their own particular needs, and nearly all benefit from pruning every year.
This not only encourages them to produce beautiful flowers in greater quantities but also
helps keep them healthy and vigorous.

◀ *787 A rose that is in full bloom looks stunning, creating a lavish focal point in the garden. Pruning helps to produce the best results from the plant, keeping it healthy and productive.*

early spring to tidy up their shape and to remove any dead, damaged or diseased stems.

790 I have an old garden rose that is very straggly and does not flower well. Can I revive it by pruning?

If an old garden rose is not performing well, you can usually revive it with drastic pruning. In late winter to early spring, cut back the oldest stems to ground level and others to within 15–30cm (6–12in) of the ground. There will be plenty of strong growth the first year, with flowers the year after that. Do not prune at all in the first year, or you may remove flowering wood for the following year.

▼ *790 Cutting a neglected rose to near ground can produce excellent results.*

787 When should I prune my roses?

Many roses are pruned in spring, when the buds are swelling but before much of the new growth has emerged. It is difficult to judge exactly the best time. If you prune early, you will encourage early growth. This soft growth will be susceptible to late frosts. Any severely frosted stems will blacken and start to die back, meaning you have to prune again. Many gardeners are in favour of autumn pruning for roses. At the end of the growing season, many roses have developed as fairly large, twiggy bushes. Strong autumn winds can lift them from the ground. Pruning minimizes the risk of this happening. On the down side, if the autumn is mild, the rose may start into growth,

and this growth will be vulnerable to winter frosts. If you do decide to prune, cut stems back by about a half.

788 Why am I so often told to prune 'to an outward-facing bud'?

Growth buds on roses lie in an alternate arrangement, on opposite sides of the stem. If you prune to a bud that faces outwards then the shape of the bush will grow outwards, producing a healthy plant that is not congested in the centre and is less prone to disease.

789 How do I prune an old garden rose?

Old garden roses generally flower on wood that is two years' old or more. They need only very light pruning in

▲ **791** *Pruning a rose low down the stem will result in vigorous new growth.*

791 How do I prune a hybrid tea rose?

In late winter to early spring, cut out all obviously dead and damaged shoots. Also remove badly placed or crossing shoots. Thin any congested growth in the heart of the plants. Prune out or shorten very thin, straggly shoots. Trim back stronger shoots by up to half their length, cutting just above an outward-facing bud.

792 How do I prune a floribunda rose?

Floribundas often look more twiggy than hybrid teas. Start by cutting out dead or diseased shoots. Remove any crossing or badly placed stems. Cut all the main stems back to about 45cm (18in), although they can be left longer on more vigorous varieties. Shorten any remaining side shoots by up to two thirds of their length, cutting to outward-facing buds.

793 How do I prune a patio rose?

Simply clip over the plant in early spring. In summer, trim off flowers as they fade.

▶ **795** *This weeping standard is a rambling rose grafted on top of a tall stem.*

▲ **794** *Prune congested areas of standard roses.*

794 How do I prune a standard rose?

Standard roses are actually rose bushes grafted on to a tall stem – they are artificially produced. You need to take care to create a balanced head. Shorten the main stems in the head to about six growth buds. Do not prune too hard, as this may stimulate over-vigorous shoots that could spoil the shape. Shorten remaining side shoots to a couple of buds to stop growth from becoming too congested.

795 Do I prune a weeping standard rose in the same way?

Most weeping standards are ramblers grafted on to an upright stem. Prune them in summer, immediately after flowering, cutting old stems hard back. Have a look at the plant the following spring. If the growth looks uneven, cut back the longest shoots to create a more balanced effect. Miniature climbers are also sometimes grafted to create standards. These are repeat-flowering roses, so simply prune to relieve congestion in early spring.

796 How do I prune a rose hedge?

Rather than pruning the plants individually, simply shear over the plants in early spring. If they are repeat-flowering roses, shear them over again in mid-summer after the first flowering. If they have decorative autumn hips, prune in spring only. You could use an electric hedge trimmer for this job, if the hedge is long.

797 Do I train a rambling rose with pruning?

Ramblers are prone to mildew if trained against a wall, but are ideal for training on free-standing systems of horizontal wire or over pergolas. They produce arching canes at or near ground level. Tie these in as they grow, as close to the horizontal as possible. On a pergola, wrap them around the uprights (rather than allowing them to grow straight up).

After flowering, cut back the oldest, woody shoots to ground level. You may need to take them out in sections. Tie in the new growth while it is still flexible as replacements.

798 Can I prune a rambling rose that has been trained into a tree?

If you have planted a rose to cover a large tree, it is usually impractical to prune it in the usual way. Use long-handled loppers to cut back overlong shoots that hang down.

799 I have a very congested rambler trained over an arch. What is the best way to prune it?

If the stems of the rambler are very congested, it can be difficult to remove the old stems. First, identify the stems you want to cut back, then cut them into short lengths. Remove them piece by piece.

▲ **800** *Properly trained, a climbing rose will cover a wall with flowers in summer.*

800 How do I prune a climbing rose?

Climbing roses need little pruning in the early years while you are building up the framework. Once this is established, prune in early spring. Leaving the basic framework intact, shorten flowered shoots by up to two-thirds of their length, cutting to outward-facing buds.

801 I have read that you should not prune a climber too hard – is this true?

Hard pruning will not cause lasting harm to most climbing roses, but you need to take care if the variety is a climbing form of a hybrid tea or floribunda (e.g. 'Climbing Iceberg'). Hard pruning can make these climbers revert to the shrub form.

802 How do I prune ground cover roses?

If you have a number of ground cover roses, simply shear over them in spring. If they are varieties that have attractive autumn hips, prune them selectively in mid-summer. This will encourage them to produce more flowers but without removing all the fruiting stems.

803 What should I do with the rose prunings?

Roses are prone to disease that can persist in woody growth. All rose cuttings should be burnt rather than shredded or composted.

▼ **802** *Ground cover roses need clipping like hedging if they are to continue flowering throughout the summer.*

PRUNING AND TRAINING FRUIT TREES

Pruning and training are an important part of fruit tree growing, both to ensure abundant crops and to keep the plants healthy and vigorous. It can take several years to train a tree against another structure, but the results are worth it.

804 How do I train a fruit tree?

Fruit trees are usually grown as central-leader trees, standards (or half-standards), bushes, pyramids, cordons, espaliers or fans. Nowadays, fruit trees can usually be bought ready trained, but it is a simple matter – and also rewarding – to train the plants yourself.

805 What are standards and half-standards?

Standards have a clear trunk of 2–2.1m (6–6½ft) and half-standards have a clear trunk of 1.2m (4ft). To develop the tree, allow a young plant to grow unpruned, clearing the trunk of laterals as for a central-leader tree. Once the main stem has achieved the desired height, cut it back, then prune the laterals as for a bush. Standard trees are grown on vigorous rootstocks and are usually too large for most gardens unless planted in isolation, almost as a specimen.

▼ **808** *Cordons allow you to grow many different varieties of fruit in a limited amount of space.*

▲ **806** *A mini orchard of fruiting trees is possible in a relatively small space if fruit trees are grown as bushes on dwarf root stock.*

806 What is meant by a bush where apples are concerned?

The bush is an excellent form for any garden where a number of fruit trees are grown, but they must be on dwarfing rootstocks. The aim is a bushy plant on a trunk 75–90cm (2½–3ft) tall. Prune the leader of a young tree or whip to stimulate branching low down. In winter, select the strongest laterals to form the framework and cut back the remainder. Shorten the remaining laterals to outward-facing buds to develop the desired open centre. The following winter, lightly prune these to encourage bushiness. Many apple and pear varieties can be grown in this way.

▶ **809** *A mature espalier has thickened horizontal 'arms' that produce copious fruit-bearing side shoots, which are easy to reach and to pick.*

807 How do I train a fruit tree into a pyramid shape?

A pyramid is a dainty tree, often used for pears and plums, built around a strong central leader. Staking is essential, as this form is less stable than a bush. The first winter after planting, shorten the leader to 50–75cm (20–30in). Develop the

lower branches first by cutting back suitably placed laterals to outward-facing buds on the undersides. This encourages a horizontal habit. Remove vigorous shoots on the upper portions of the leader. As the plant grows, tie in a replacement leader to the stake, removing all other vigorous upright-growing branches. Prune the upper branches in the same way as the strong laterals towards the base of the plant, cutting to outward-facing buds on the undersides.

808 What is a cordon?

A cordon, suitable for many apple and pear varieties, is a vigorous upright stem that has usually been trained at an angle, with stubby side shoots – ideal where space is limited. The aim is to build up a system of short, stubby 'spurs' the length of the stem. A cordon must be grown against a system of wires. The main stem is tied to a sturdy cane, and this in turn is tied to the wires. To maintain the cordon, remove overcrowded growth in winter and shorten overlong laterals to three or four buds. Shorten the leader, as necessary, in late spring. In summer, cut back any overlong, whippy shoots to the base.

809 How do I create an espalier?

In this form, lateral branches are trained strictly horizontally. An espalier is highly decorative, although high maintenance. Apples and pears can be trained in this way, either against a wall or free-standing on

◄ 805 A half-standard is a neat tree that will produce fruit at eye level, because of its short height, making harvesting the fruit very straightforward.

wires. Espaliers can be bought ready-trained. Alternatively, plant a whip and cut it back in winter to a strong bud just above the lowest wire. From the new growth, select the strongest as the new leader and tie this to an upright cane lashed to the wires. Select two strong laterals and tie these to canes that themselves are tied in diagonally to the wires. The next winter, bring these down to the horizontal and attach them to the lowest wire. Cut back the leader just above the second wire and continue this procedure in subsequent years until the espalier is complete.

810 How do I produce a fan?

A highly decorative form, also trained on wires, the fan is useful for fruit trees such as peaches and apricots, which are not commonly grown on dwarfing rootstocks and benefit from wall protection in cool areas. They can be bought ready-trained. Alternatively, choose a young plant with several strong laterals. On planting, cut all of these back apart from two that are suitably placed for training to the diagonal to either side of the leader. These form the 'arms' of the espalier. Tie them to canes that can be lashed to the wires. Cut back the leader to just above the upper arm. As suitably placed, strong side-shoots grow, tie them in to the wires, aiming for an even development on both sides.

811 Why are fruit trees and bushes sometimes trained on horizontal wires?

Growing fruit on a system of horizontal wires enables you to grow the maximum number of plants in the smallest space. It also makes gathering

▶ 813 This redcurrant is being trained vertically from three leaders in the crown of the plant. It is also held in place with wires fixed to the wall.

the fruit really easy – if the plants are properly trained the fruits will be easily accessible and you won't have to stretch your hand into a large twiggy bush to get at them. Tying stems in horizontally encourages the plant to produce short upright shoots all along the length of the stem, and these shoots will carry the fruits.

812 How do I train my fruit trees on a system of wires, and can I do this with any fruit tree or bush?

To create a system of wires for plants in rows, drive sturdy uprights into the ground, approximately 1.8m (6ft) apart. Run horizontal wires between them, using wire of a gauge that can bear the weight of the plant – thin wires are fine for raspberries but apples and pears will need a thicker type. The wires should be 30–45cm (12–18in) apart.

813 How do I train a plant against a wall?

To train a plant against a wall using wires, stretch the wires between vine eyes inserted into the wall 30–45cm (12–18in) apart. It is important that the plant is held away from the wall surface to ensure good air circulation around the stems. Plant the shrub 30cm (12in) from the wall in well-prepared soil.

▲ **815** *Step-over apples produce their fruit on a long stem that is trained horizontally near ground level.*

814 What should I use to tie the stems to the wires against the wall?

A number of materials can be used to attach stems to wires. They should be soft enough not to chafe young growth. Wire ties are useful as they can be bent easily to the appropriate shape. The best wire to use is the type coated with rubber, as this prevents the tie from cutting into the wood. Raffia is a natural material that can be cut to length. Though strong in the

▼ **816** *Malus pumila 'Dartmouth' is a spur-bearing apple tree carrying deep-red apples in autumn.*

short term, it rots after a year or so, and must be renewed regularly. Garden twine is strong and convenient to use but, like raffia, tends to rot in wet weather. Tie the stems loosely, so they can continue to grow and thicken. Check the ties regularly and loosen or replace them as necessary.

815 What is a step-over apple?

Step-over apples are similar to cordons in appearance, but the main stem is pulled strongly to the horizontal and is tied to a wire no higher than 30cm (12in) above the ground. Only apples grafted on to dwarfing rootstocks are usually grown in this way. To create a step-over, cut back a whip to within 30cm (12in) of the ground. Pull the new leader hard

down and tie it on a horizontal wire stretched between short uprights. Step-overs are effective as a decorative feature when used to edge beds in the vegetable garden.

816 What is the difference between a tip-bearing apple and a spur-bearing apple?

Apples produce their fruits either at or near the ends of shoots (tip-bearers) or on short knobbly 'spurs' that grow out of the length of the shoot (spur-bearers). New shoots on tip-bearers often contain fruit buds. Most apples are spur-bearers, but a few varieties, such as 'Jonagold', are both tip- and spur-bearing. Spur-bearing apples are suitable for training as cordons, fans, espaliers and as step-overs. The two types of tree are pruned differently, so recognition is important.

817 How do I prune a fig tree?

Although they are hardy, figs fruit best in warm climates – in fact, in warm conditions, they will bear two or three crops a year. In cold areas, only one crop will ripen each year and they need training against a warm wall for this to happen. All major pruning should be done in late winter to early spring while the plant is dormant. In warm areas, grow as a free-standing tree or shrub with minimal pruning.

▼ **816** *Malus 'John Downie' is a tip-bearing crab apple. The buds are nipped out to thin fruiting.*

In cold areas, fan-train against a warm wall. Shorten over-vigorous growth. Remove older branches and tie in suitable replacements. Small figs that develop towards the end of the growing season will overwinter and ripen as the following year's crop. Remove any new figs that appear in summer, as these will not have time to ripen and will divert the plant's energies away from the crop. At the same time, shorten any new growth that is shading the swelling figs.

818 How do I grow a fruit tree with a single stem and a balanced crown?

This type of tree can be used for a specimen planting. Allow a young tree or whip to develop with minimal pruning. Once the tree is established, after three to five years, remove the lower branches to create a clear trunk, 1.5–1.8m (5–6ft) tall. The main upright stem (the 'leader') is allowed to continue growing so that the tree achieves the dimensions it would do in the wild. Apart from mulberries, chestnuts and some other trees that do not respond well to pruning, few fruit trees are grown in this way.

819 I'd like to grow chestnuts. What factors do I need to consider?

Chestnuts are late-flowering, so need a long, hot summer if the nuts are to ripen fully. They make large, handsome trees. Allow them to develop naturally with minimal pruning. On mature trees, large, thick branches may pose a hazard, and should be removed by a tree surgeon. Chestnut trees grow very quickly and so are suitable for very large gardens, where they can be positioned at least one and a half times their ultimate growing height away from the house.

820 How do I prune and train hazelnuts?

In the early years of a newly established tree, prune the tree to create an open-centred bush, shortening a dominant leader if necessary to encourage lateral branching. On established plants, in

▲ **818** *This fig tree has a single leader from the base of the plant, and well-balanced top growth.*

late summer break longer stems mid-way along their length and allow the broken ends to hang down (this technique is known as 'brutting'). Shorten the broken stems in winter. This method encourages stronger flowers to form on weaker stems. These will be wind-pollinated. Ultimately a greater crop of fruit from the tree will ensue. Plants can also be grown as small trees with minimal pruning, but will not crop so freely.

▼ **819** *Sweet chestnut trees produce a spectacular display of chestnuts in the autumn months.*

▲ **821** *Walnut trees can be grown as specimen trees in a garden design, or to produce nuts.*

821 How do I treat a walnut tree?

No formal pruning and training is required. Trees should be allowed to develop with minimal attention. Any work required on mature trees should be carried out by a qualified tree surgeon. It is best to prune any walnut tree during the dormant season in winter. Stems bleed quantities of sap if pruned in spring or summer.

822 How do I maintain all the different forms of tree or shrub?

Regular pruning is needed to keep trained plants within their allotted space. In summer, trim back new growth to maintain the form and to expose the fruits to the sun. Cut back over-vigorous shoots to the base. For plants trained against a wall, pinch out any awkwardly placed shoots and those pointing into the wall. After harvesting the fruits of plants trained on a system of wires, cut back older, fruited stems and tie in new, suitably placed stems as replacements. These will flower and fruit next year.

Winter is a good time to assess deciduous plants. Thin over-crowded growth and remove entirely older, thicker stems that will be less productive than younger ones.

PRUNING AND TRAINING SOFT FRUITS

Soft fruits, or berries, have a short but keenly anticipated season; they are truly a taste of summer. They are produced on low- to medium-growing bushes that will crop abundantly if conditions are favourable and with appropriate pruning.

823 How do I prune a blackcurrant?

On planting, cut down all the stems to within 10cm (4in) of the ground. The new growth produced in the first year will not fruit. The following winter, remove straggly stems and others as necessary to create an open-centred bush – the unpruned stems will flower and fruit during the next growing season. Thereafter, in mid- to late winter, remove up to one third of all stems that have fruited the previous season. Old bushes can be renovated with hard pruning, at the expense of the following season's fruits.

824 How do I prune redcurrants and whitecurrants?

A young plant should have three or four strong stems on a short trunk. The first winter after planting, shorten these by a half. Allow new shoots to develop during the following season, then in winter reduce their number to eight to ten main branches, aiming to produce a balanced bush that is open at the centre, so that the air can circulate freely and to ensure harvesting the crop is easier to undertake. These stems form the main

▲ **824** *Redcurrants will produce vigorous growth if pruned in autumn.*

framework. Each winter after this, cut back all new shoots to one bud from the base to create a system of fruiting spurs on the framework stems. In later years, remove old stems that are not fruiting well, cutting back to a suitably placed replacement shoot. Feed well after pruning, water and mulch to conserve moisture in the soil and improve its structure.

▲ **825** *Gooseberry fruits are translucent when ripe in mid-summer.*

825 How do I prune a gooseberry?

In late winter, shorten the growth of new plants to create a bush on a short leg about 10cm (4in) in length with two or three strong laterals. Of the shoots that develop from these, select eight to ten to create a balanced framework with an open centre. These shoots will fruit the following year. Once established, each winter remove

Pruning established blackcurrants

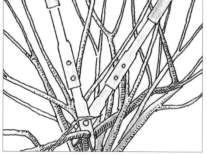

1 In mid-winter, when the stems are bare, cut back to the base older stems that fruited last year.

2 Thin the stems that are left as necessary, especially ones that cross, to create an open-centred bush.

3 Blackcurrants fruit on new wood. They will produce a prolific crop if well tended.

Pruning established gooseberries

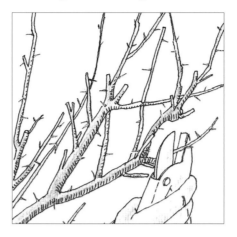

1 In winter, cut out stems that cross, as well as any pointing towards the centre of the bush.

2 To develop a spur system, cut back the previous season's shoots to one bud from the base.

3 Remove older branches, cutting them right back to near the base, to refresh the plant and improve fruiting.

older branches entirely. It is also possible to develop a spur system on the main framework, as explained for redcurrants and whitecurrants above. For smaller crops of larger fruits, thin the developing crop by up to a half in late spring to early summer.

826 How do I prune a blackberry?
Blackberries are vigorous plants that produce usually thorny canes from the base each year. Train the plants on a

▼ **827** *Raspberry plants will crop abundantly if pruned annually to produce vigorous new fruiting shoots.*

system of horizontal wires stretched between a series of uprights. Shorten the canes on planting. The shoots that develop in the first year will not fruit until the year following. As they grow, weave them into the wires, pulling them as close to the horizontal as possible. The following year, allow new canes to grow upright, tying them loosely to the upper wires. After fruiting, cut the fruited stems to the base, untie the new canes, then weave them on to the wires for fruiting the following year. Feed the plants after pruning, water well, then mulch.

827 How do I prune a summer-fruiting raspberry?
Plant raspberries in rows. As they grow, tie the canes to horizontal wires stretched between uprights. If the canes reach above the uppermost wire, arch them downwards and tie them in. On planting shorten the canes. The new canes will fruit the following year. After harvesting the fruits in summer, cut the fruited canes down to ground level.

828 How do I prune an autumn-fruiting raspberry?
Train the plants as described for summer-fruiting raspberries above. However, autumn-fruiting varieties

will crop on the current season's growth. Simply cut all canes down to ground level in spring before new growth begins.

829 How do I prune a blueberry?
Prune to create an open-centred bush. The winter after planting, remove straggly stems and others as necessary. Once established, prune annually in winter, removing some of the oldest branches entirely. Shorten others by up to one third to a half. Blueberries need acid soil – if your soil is alkaline, they will be perfectly happy in large containers filled with ericaceous potting mix. Feed and water them well to ensure good cropping.

830 My fruit bushes are not cropping well. What do I do?
Old, tired plants can often be given a new lease of life by hard pruning. To renovate a plant, cut down all stems to within 10cm (4in) of the ground in late winter to early spring. If the bush has a short trunk – for instance, a gooseberry – cut the main stems back to 10cm (4in) from the trunk. Feed the plant and water it well. New growth in spring should be vigorous. Prune thereafter as for a new plant. Flowering and fruiting is usually delayed for a couple of years.

CHAPTER NINE

GARDEN PROBLEMS

Pests and diseases are an inevitable part of gardening life, and a whole industry is devoted to their control, even if they cannot always be eliminated. However, most are easy to deal with, provided you get on top of the problem at the earliest possible stage, and the treatment does not necessarily involve using chemicals. Weeds present their problems to gardeners, too. Persistent weeds need perseverance to eradicate, while others are easily removed with a hoe. A garden is a mixed environment, and sometimes it is a matter of increasing the range of plants you grow to attract pest predators into the garden as well. Some garden problems are caused by poor growing conditions – too wet, too cold, dry or windy. Healthy plants usually repair themselves and many problems often disappear after you improve the soil or move a plant to a more suitable location.

GARDEN HYGIENE

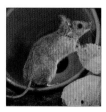
CONTROLLING PESTS

CONTROLLING WEEDS

INSECTICIDES AND FUNGICIDES

GREENHOUSE PROBLEMS

SPECIFIC PLANT PROBLEMS

FRUIT PROBLEMS

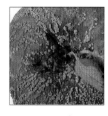
VEGETABLE PROBLEMS

PHYSIOLOGICAL PROBLEMS

◀ *Many plant problems are visible to the naked eye, but others can only be seen with a microscope.*

GARDEN HYGIENE

You can avoid a whole host of potential problems by observing good garden hygiene, which means removing and burning all diseased plant material and any other plant remains that can harbour pests and diseases.

831 What is good garden hygiene?

Good hygiene means clearing the garden of dead and decaying plant material. This is not only a breeding ground for fungal spores and bacteria, but also provides shelter for a host of overwintering pests. In autumn, clear up all dead leaves and either compost them or use them to make leaf mould. Material that is already diseased should be burnt. Prune shrubs and trees routinely to remove all dead, diseased and damaged growth. Burn all diseased stems and branches. Keep pruning tools clean – viruses are often spread on blades.

832 How do I keep my garden free of pests?

If you are to keep the use of garden chemicals to a minimum, then a garden should present a balanced eco-system with as wide a range of beneficial insects as possible. To attract these, grow a broad range of plants. Ideally, there should be plants in flower throughout the year to feed pollinators. If you can, grow native trees and shrubs (possibly as part of a wildlife hedge). These will support a host of invertebrates in their bark. Although plants will still suffer attack, pests will be present in much smaller numbers. It takes time to attract the predators of garden pests, but worth persevering.

833 Is it desirable to clear all debris from the garden at the end of the summer season?

A clean sweep of the garden, although theoretically a good thing, actually removes a lot of potentially valuable organic matter. Leaves that have fallen on the ground break down *in situ* to feed the soil. Windfall apples and pears will start to rot and feed wasps, which are an important predator and eater of caterpillars and aphids. Some low-growing plants may rot, however, if they are left covered in fallen leaves. You may need to be selective in your approach, keeping some areas of the garden free from plant debris while adopting a more *laissez-faire* approach elsewhere.

▲ **833** *In autumn, remove dead leaves from around ground-cover plants because they can attract rots as they break down, which then pass to living plants.*

834 How do I keep down the incidence of disease?

Practise good hygiene. Some varieties of plants are more susceptible to disease than others. When buying plants, look for guaranteed virus-free stock and varieties that have been specially bred for disease resistance. If a particular plant proves to be vulnerable in your garden, it can often be more practical to replace it.

Gathering leaves

1 On a deck, patio or other hard surface, sweep together leaves with a stiff brush.

2 Use two pieces of board to help you pick up the leaves in greater quantities, then bag them.

3 A rake with splayed tines will help you collect leaves on a lawn. Only collect leaves during still weather.

CONTROLLING PESTS

Many wild visitors, such as rabbits, squirrels and deer, are regarded as pests by many gardeners, while other wild creatures such as hedgehogs, frogs, toads and insects are encouraged because they feed on those pests that damage plants and carry disease.

835 Are birds sometimes regarded as pests?

Most gardeners have an ambivalent attitude to birds. On the plus side, they eat slugs, snails and insects. On the debit side, they peck at fruits (especially soft fruits and flower buds). Troublesome birds include blackbirds, bullfinches and starlings.

836 How can I protect fruiting plants from birds?

Vulnerable plants can be protected from birds with netting. Many gardeners grow their soft fruit in a dedicated fruit cage. The netting should be of a small enough gauge to prevent birds from getting trapped in it, but should allow access to pollinating insects and not shade out the sun. On trees, individual fruits (or fruit trusses) can be protected with netted bags.

▼ **835** *Birds can be garden pests if you grow soft fruit, but are worth attracting into the garden because they will eat plenty of insect pests.*

837 How can I attract birds to eradicate insect pests?

Birds need to be able to perch, so will appreciate a tree. An autumn-fruiting tree such as a sorbus or malus will provide food in the winter. Berrying shrubs should also be included, such as *Cotoneaster* and *Berberis*. If possible, place a few nesting boxes throughout the garden. Different styles will attract different birds. Bird feed helps but also attracts rats.

838 Are bats likely to be a problem?

On the contrary – they are valued by gardeners as they feed on molluscs, moths and other invertebrates that are active at night. In most areas, bats are protected species. You can buy special bat boxes for the garden in which they can shelter during the hours of daylight. Only in the tropics are bats a pest.

▼ **836** *A fruit cage will protect valuable crops of soft fruits from birds without excluding light and rainfall. They will still need protection from insect pests.*

839 Rabbits are eating all my plants – what can I do to deter them?

Rabbits are among the most serious garden pests – they will eat virtually anything (including tree bark), leaving a trail of devastation behind them. To keep rabbits out of the garden, erect a boundary fence at least 1.2m (4ft) high. To guard against burrowing, sink sturdy corrugated plastic or metal into the ground along the fence, to a depth of at least 45cm (18in).

840 How can I protect young trees from rabbits?

Rabbits will often gnaw at tree bark during winter when other food is hard to find. Their gnawing might kill a young tree. Use proprietary spiral tree guards around the base of newly planted trees. The guards expand as the tree grows and can be removed after about three years.

▼ **839** *Place a guard around young tree trunks to protect them from gnawing animals. The protection can be removed once the tree is established.*

▶ **842** *Squirrels are now commonly seen in urban areas as well as in woodland and can be a garden pest.*

841 How can I keep deer out of the garden?
Beautiful though they are, deer can be serious pests. They often browse at head height, ripping branches from trees and shrubs. A fence at least 1.8m (6ft) high is necessary to keep them out of the garden.

842 Can I control squirrels?
Squirrels are fast-moving, extremely agile animals, so it is difficult to keep them out of a garden. Not only do they eat flower buds, the soft young growth of plants, and fruits and nuts, they also strip bark from trees. They will also help themselves to food put out for birds. Protect vulnerable plants with wire netting (not plastic, which they can gnaw through), use squirrel-proof bird feeders and cover plantings of bulbs with chicken wire.

843 Mice are a problem in my garden – what can I do about them?
Mice will dig up and eat bulbs (especially those that have been recently planted) and peony roots and will also eat plant material in storage – tulip bulbs and dahlia tubers, as well as vegetables, for instance. Set traps or use mouse poison.

844 How can I kill slugs and snails?
Slugs and snails count among the worst garden pests. They will feed on nearly all young plant material – seedlings are particularly vulnerable. They can be controlled with poisons, usually in pelleted form. Sprinkle these sparingly around plants in early spring before the molluscs become active. If you mulch your plants, it is important that you apply the pellets to the bare earth before you put down the mulch, as the pests are active underneath the mulch. Alternatively, the poison can be applied as a liquid drench around the plant.

Many gardeners are cautious about using molluscides. Not only are the

slimy corpses unsightly, but there is a risk that the poison may affect any birds or frogs that then eat them. Further, these poisons actually attract the pests, so must be applied sparingly or you can easily create a worse problem than you had in the first place.

845 Are there any non-chemical ways of tackling slugs and snails?
Slugs can be controlled with a parasitic nematode that is watered around the plants. This, however, does not kill snails. Both slugs and snails can be picked off plants by hand. They are usually active at night, so many gardeners patrol the garden at night with a torch. You could try sinking a container of beer in the garden. Slugs will be attracted to the beer and will fall in.

▼ **843** *Mice eat bulbs, including those in storage, and nibble at greenery.*

846 I am told that hedgehogs will eat slugs – how can I encourage them into the garden?
Hedgehogs are among the gardener's best friends, as they feed on slugs and snails. To provide shelter for them, pile a few logs in an area of long grass or other secluded part of the garden. If you already have hedgehogs, resist the temptation to put out saucers of milk, which they cannot digest. Hedgehogs will eat dog or cat food, and you can buy food specially formulated for them, but bear in mind that any food you put out may attract unwelcome visitors such as rats and neighbours' cats.

847 Can I attract toads and frogs into the garden?
Toads and frogs also eat slugs and snails and other garden pests. The presence of a pond will act as magnet for them. It is illegal to remove spawn from the wild, but anyone who already has a pond will probably give you some spawn in spring. Piles of rocks near the pond will provide cool places for the amphibians to shelter during warm weather.

848 Can I grow hostas without using any form of mollusc control?
Contrary to popular belief, it is possible to grow hostas successfully without any means of mollusc control,

▼ **845** *Pick snails off by hand and destroy them.*

though it involves defying conventional garden wisdom. Hostas grow best in moist, humus-rich soil in shade – exactly the same conditions enjoyed by molluscs. Instead, grow your hostas in full sun in poor, gritty soil. Out of the many varieties, choose ones with thick, waxy leaves such as *Hosta sieboldiana*, 'Blue Moon' and similar types. These are much less palatable to the molluscs than thin-leaved varieties. Growing them in poor soil in sun further encourages tough growth. However, the leaves will be much smaller and less lush than on plants that are growing in shade.

849 Are all slugs bad news?

Perhaps surprisingly, no. Big slugs can be the gardener's friend. Not only do they eat up decaying plant material – usually a breeding ground for disease – but will cannibalize smaller slugs and snails. If you see snails on a garden path, stamp on them then leave them as food for large slugs.

850 How can I attract other wildlife into the garden?

If you have space, leave an area of the garden uncultivated, and allow the grass to grow long and weeds to seed themselves. A pile of logs can shelter stag beetles and other invertebrates, particularly over the winter. The long grass will be a home to small mammals such as shrews and dormice.

851 I have heard that flatworms cause problems. What are they?

Flatworms are orange-brown leech-like creatures up to 8cm (3½in) long. They are active mainly at night, and are found beneath stones, logs and other objects that are in contact with the soil. They prey on beneficial earthworms, so are considered a serious pest. Since they are introduced into gardens in the roots of bought container-grown plants, it is worth soaking newly purchased plants in water in order to encourage any flatworms to emerge. Destroy any that you find.

▲ *844 Slug pellets provide an instant remedy, but might also kill birds, which eat the contaminated slugs.*

852 How do I deal with greenfly?

Greenfly can be seen clustering on unopened rosebuds in spring. You can spray with insecticide or simply dislodge them with a strong jet of water. If you do this, you will have to revisit the plant every day or so, as the pest will return. Ladybirds help greatly in keeping down greenfly numbers. If you cannot see any ladybirds, larvae can be bought mail order and introduced into the garden.

853 How do I stop cats from using my garden as a toilet?

Cat repelling products are available, with differing success rates. If you have a newly dug bed of topsoil, cats

▼ *847 A pond will be a magnet for a whole range of beneficial insects.*

will be attracted to it because it is soft and easy to scratch around in. Put prickly twigs around new plantings to deter cats. If cats dig in the garden when you are around, a gentle shower of water from a garden hose will see them off. You could plant garlic in areas that cats are attracted to since the strong smell is unappealing to them. If you are prepared to tolerate cats (or have your own cat), sprinkle cat litter in an area that you do not mind them using. It contains a chemical that attracts them. Wear gloves when removing cat faeces.

854 Are foxes a problem in the garden?

Foxes thrive in urban as well as rural habitats and are a frequent visitor to gardens. Loved and loathed in equal measure, a fox can steal chickens and rabbits, scavenge household waste for food and damage lawns and vegetable beds in pursuit of food. Foxes are carriers of parasites that can affect the health of humans as well as other domestic pets, but the presence of a fox does not necessarily pose a danger to humans. To deter a fox, clear areas of wilderness in the garden in which a fox might choose to find a home. Clear up food waste and block any easy access points. Use a fox-repellent product, available from garden centres, and apply it with persistence.

▼ *848 Hostas attract slugs and snails, causing damage to the leaves.*

CONTROLLING WEEDS

Dealing with weeds is an important part of keeping the garden in good health. Weeds attract many pests into the garden and are often hosts for fungal and other diseases, which then spread to other plants.

855 What is the difference between an annual and a perennial weed?

Many weeds are annuals – they complete their growth cycle within a year. These are relatively easy to control, but it is important to do so before they set seed. If they have already shed their seed, this will germinate and grow to produce a fresh crop of weeds. Perennial weeds are more difficult to eradicate. Some, such as ground elder, disappear under ground in winter but form dense mats of roots. Woody weeds, such as brambles and elders, can also prove troublesome. Tap-rooted weeds can be difficult to eradicate, as any scrap of root left in the soil will regenerate.

856 Do I need to get rid of all weeds?

Weeds are a problem in all gardens. Not only are the majority of small ornamental merit, but they will compete with your plants for moisture and nutrients. They are a food source for many common insect pests, which will then move to other plants. Some are also prone to mildew and other fungal diseases, so it is best to get rid of as many as you can.

▲ *855 Weeds can quickly colonize areas of the garden if not controlled.*

857 How do I deal with annual weeds without weedkillers?

Hand weeding is time-consuming but a highly effective way of dealing with weeds. At the seedling stage in spring, simply hoe over them to sever the topgrowth from the roots. You can leave them on the soil surface to break down – the roots will break down under ground. Larger weeds will need to be removed individually.

White vinegar can be used to kill young weeds. Heat the vinegar first for the best results. Repeated applications may be necessary.

858 I have heard that weeds can be killed by excluding light. How do I do this?

If you have a large area to treat, you can cover it with thick black plastic or pieces of old carpet. To be effective, all light must be excluded. It can take up to year, or even two or three, for weeds to be killed by this method.

859 What are weed-suppressing membranes?

Weed-suppressing membranes are sheets of material that are spread over the soil and prevent weeds from coming through. They are permeated by tiny holes that allow free passage of moisture and air. For maximum effectiveness, the ground should already be weed-free before a membrane is laid – the membrane can really only prevent weed seeds from coming into contact with the soil and germinating. They are usually most effective on flat ground.

860 How do I use a membrane?

Clear the site of weeds, then rake over the soil to level it. Lay over the membrane and cut it to fit, if necessary. Secure it at the edges either by weighing it down with stones or bricks or dig a trench with a spade into which you can tuck each edge. To plant, cut crosses in the membrane for each plant, fold back the edges and excavate a suitable planting hole. Once the plant is in position, fold back the edges. Top the membrane with grit, pebbles or chipped bark to hold it in place.

▼ *858 Spreading black plastic over the soil can prevent weed seeds from germinating.*

▼ *860 Cutting crosses in the membrane will allow plants to grow while suppressing weeds around them.*

861 I am trying to be more environmentally friendly. Is there any justification for using garden chemicals?

Chemicals still have a place in gardening, even though there are far fewer available today than previously. Used wisely, they play an important part in keeping the garden healthy, provided their use is localized.

862 How do weedkillers work?

Any weedkiller that is applied to a plant is carried around it in the same way that all plants take up water from the ground.

863 What are contact weedkillers?

Weedkillers work in a variety of ways. Contact weedkillers – sometimes called spot weedkillers – have to be sprayed or painted on to the leaves by hand. They kill only the part of the plant with which they are in contact. They are useful where isolated weeds have to be removed from among other plants and hand-weeding is impractical, but can also be used over a wider area. Annual weeds are usually killed outright, but perennials may need two or more applications, and often regrow strongly, as the roots are not affected.

▼ *863 A contact weedkiller is painted on to the leaves of a weed but does not affect any surrounding plant material.*

864 What are systemic weedkillers?

Systemic, or translocating, weedkillers enter the leaves of the plant and are then carried through the plant's entire system. Depending on the vigour of the weed, more than one application may be necessary.

865 Will these weedkillers stay in the soil?

Nowadays, nearly all weedkillers, both contact and systemic, break down on contact with the soil. They do not leach out of plant roots into soil. Once the site is cleared, the ground can therefore be replanted straightaway.

866 What are soil-acting weedkillers?

Highly effective, soil-acting weedkillers are seldom used today because of concerns over the environment. They are applied to soil and enter weeds through the roots, killing all types. However, they persist in the soil for months, in some cases up to a year. You will therefore not be able to replant for a considerable time. If you buy a new-build property with areas of bare soil in the garden, check with the contractor whether the soil has been treated with such a weedkiller.

▼ *868 Spray weedkillers are best used on still, dull days, when the product will not blow on to neighbouring ornamentals.*

▲ *867 Special attachments can be fitted to watering cans to distribute diluted chemicals evenly.*

867 When is the best time to apply weedkillers?

It is best to apply chemical weedkillers during periods of good growth when the sap is moving around at a higher rate and the chemical will be taken with it. Weedkillers are most effective at the seedling stage for all types of weeds and since most weeds spread by seed, applying the weedkiller before flowering and the plant sets seed is essential. Biennial weeds are more easily treated in their first season, as seedlings or small rosettes. For perennial weeds that are difficult to control, an application of a systemic weedkiller in the autumn can be very effective. Plants under stress such as those in areas of waterlogging, drought or low temperature are less susceptible to the weedkiller as they are growing poorly.

868 What are the best conditions for applying weedkillers?

Choose a dry, still day. Avoid use during windy periods – the wind will blow the product on to other plants, which may themselves be killed.

INSECTICIDES AND FUNGICIDES

Some garden chemicals are formulated to kill insects and the fungal spores that cause plant diseases. They should all be applied as soon as you spot a problem on a plant – this will actually cut down on their use.

869 How do insecticides work?

Contact insecticides kill the pest on contact – therefore, you need to spray the pest directly, during the period when it is active. Systemic insecticides are sprayed over a plant. The plant absorbs the insecticide and the insect ingests it as it feeds.

870 When and how should I spray plants?

Spray plants when the pest is active – either when you have seen it or seen evidence of the damage it causes. For complete effectiveness, spray both surfaces of the leaves.

871 Why should some insecticides be applied only in the evening?

If you want to spare pollinating bees, which are active during warm, sunny weather, spray in the evening when they will be resting. This method will only be effective on pests that are active at night.

872 Are there any alternative methods of discouraging insects?

In many cases it is possible to remove pests by hand. Winged insects are tricky to catch, but their grubs are usually slow-moving, so can be picked off and destroyed. Greenfly and other aphids that cluster on stems and buds of plants can usually be dislodged with a jet of water delivered from a hose or spray gun.

873 What are organic treatments?

Some garden chemicals are derived from naturally occurring sources. However, they tend to be less effective than chemical controls and need to be applied more frequently.

874 What is a biological control?

Biological control is a method of introducing predators into the environment, which then prey on the

▲ **874** *A biological control hanging from a greenhouse plant indicates if problem pests are in the environment.*

pest. Biological controls are often used in greenhouses to control red spider mite and whitefly.

875 What are pheromone traps?

Female insects emit pheromones when they are fertile, to attract males. Pheromone traps, which contain a sticky landing stage, mimic the scent – the males are attracted and are caught on the glue. The traps do not control pests, but they do indicate that egg-laying females are present. Further steps then need to be taken to control future generations of the pest.

876 Can I mix chemicals – such as an insecticide with a fungicide?

You should not mix different products. Some chemicals can react with each other, creating a toxic cocktail that can be dangerous.

877 Are garden chemicals less effective than they used to be?

Most legislation aims to limit products available to the amateur gardener to those that are stable and safe in use – extensive use of safety equipment should not be necessary. Therefore, many of the more potent products that were freely used by an earlier generation are no longer available.

▲ **878** *Lacewings are beneficial insects that eat aphids. Attract them to the garden with wild carrot plantings.*

Because the market share for garden chemicals is tiny compared to that for commercial/agricultural use, it is not worthwhile for manufacturing companies to invest in developing new products to replace them.

Much research is being done into genetic modification. It is possible, for instance, to switch off the gene in carrots that is responsible for the scent in the leaves that attracts carrot fly. Virology is also likely to play a part in pest control – certain viruses can be introduced into plants that cause no harm to the plant (or to humans) but prove fatal to insect pests. All such research is for the commercial agricultural market, but it is likely that such controls will filter down to the gardening market in time.

878 What is a beneficial insect?

There are many beneficial predators that can be encouraged to visit your garden and help to control populations of pests. Predators such as ladybirds, hoverflies, lacewings and wasps feed on pests directly, while parasitic insects lay their eggs in a pest species. When the eggs hatch, the larvae feed on the pest insect and kill it. The majority of these pests are tiny wasps, flies and mites.

GREENHOUSE PROBLEMS

Some pests seem to occur only in greenhouses – where the closed environment effectively shields them from predators such as birds and other beneficial insects. Diseases can also proliferate in the warm, humid conditions under glass.

879 How can I minimize the risks of problems occurring in my greenhouse?

To lower the risks, open greenhouse windows and doors on warm days. Remove all fallen leaves and other plant debris from the floor and staging because these can harbour disease and provide shelter for insect pests. In autumn or winter, clear out the greenhouse and hose it down. If you store empty pots in the greenhouse, check whether they are sheltering slugs and snails.

880 What is honeydew?

As insects feed – often on the undersides of leaves – their excreta drips down on to the upper surface of leaves below, creating a shiny, sticky deposit. This deposit is known as honeydew, which in itself does not damage a plant, but it attracts moulds and, being sweet (hence the name), is a food source for ants. The ants do not damage plants, but, as they move from plant to plant in search of the honeydew, they transfer the pest's eggs to new plants. If you have a honeydew problem, you may discover you have an ant problem as well.

▲ **882** *Red spider mite can be controlled with a parasitic mite.*

881 How do I control whitefly?

Whitefly are tiny, white, moth-like insects that suck sap from a range of plants. They are usually seen on the leaves. When disturbed, they fly from the plant, but quickly return. They excrete honeydew and are a common pest under glass (and also sometimes outdoors). Some strains have developed resistance to chemical insecticides, but they can be effectively

▼ **879** *Keep the greenhouse well-ventilated during hot periods in summer to prevent a build-up of humidity in which fungi can multiply.*

▲ **883** *You can try scraping off the scales with a stiff brush.*

controlled with the parasitic wasp *Encarsia formosa*. Lemon balm and parsley also attract the parasitic wasp.

882 What are the symptoms of glasshouse red spider mite?

Red spider is a tiny mite that is usually unseen – you will detect its activity through the presence of fine webs between leaves and stems. The mite causes considerable damage – leaves show mottling, then dry up and fall, and the cropping of fruiting plants can be much reduced. They proliferate during warm, dry conditions, so mist plants well to raise the humidity.

883 What are scale insects?

Scale insects are tiny insects that are usually found on plant stems and the undersides of leaves. The young insects (called crawlers) find a suitable location on the plant to feed. They then coat themselves in a waxy, woolly or hard coat and cling to the plant like barnacles. Their coating makes them highly resistant to insecticides. Since they feed on hidden parts of the plant you may only be aware of their presence once you spot the honeydew they excrete on the surface of leaves. Lacewings and hoverflies eat scale insects.

SPECIFIC PLANT PROBLEMS

Some problems affect specific plants or families of plants and are particularly noticeable.
These are some of the most common and are easy to recognize. Most are easy to eradicate;
others are caused by the extremes of the weather.

884 What causes diseases in plants?

Diseases are caused by fungi or pathogens – a bacterium or virus – that attack plant material. Some are benign, but many create serious problems for gardeners. Crops can be ruined and flowers spoilt – in some cases, the plant itself may die.

885 Why do the leaves on my hellebores turn black?

Blackening of the leaves on a hellebore is a sure sign of botrytis or grey mould. You will normally spot the problem around or just after flowering time. It is usually the older leaves that blacken – the fungus has probably entered the plant as a result of frost damage. Cut back all affected leaves, then feed the plants, water and mulch to improve the soil structure and keep the plants growing strongly.

886 The leaves on my rose have large circular holes in them. What is the culprit?

The leaf-cutting bee cuts regular round or oval holes in rose leaves. This solitary bee resembles a stouter honey bee and causes no lasting harm to plants – in fact, it is valued as a pollinator. Either do nothing, or swat away the insect when you see it. Lilacs and camellias can show similar damage.

887 What is rolling up the leaves on my roses?

Adult female leaf-rolling sawflies lay their eggs on rose leaves in late spring. Their secretions cause the leaf to wrap around the egg, which hatches into a small green caterpillar. You can control the pest either by spraying with an insecticide or picking off the leaves by hand as soon as they start to roll up – before the grub can do any damage.

888 What is rose canker?

Rose canker is a fungal disease that enters the plant through wounds, often as a result of pruning. The fungus grows down stems from the cut edge, resulting in die-back. If the plant is growing vigorously, this die-back is not too severe. Other symptoms include spotting on and cracking of the stems. To treat, cut back affected growth, then feed and water well to encourage recovery.

889 The leaves on my roses are covered in spots. What are they?

While spots on leaves can be caused by any number of factors, the likeliest suspect is black spot on roses, a fungal disease that proliferates on poorly growing specimens. Initially brown/black spots appear, then the area around the spots turns yellow. The whole leaf discolours and is shed – in severe cases, plants can be completely defoliated. The disease varies in its impact. In some areas, outbreaks are few, and the weather also seems to play a part. To control the disease, cut back all affected growth and burn it. Collect up fallen leaves from the soil and burn them,

then spray the plant with a fungicide. A foliar feed can help speed up recovery. Some rose varieties are known to be resistant to black spot, and these should be favoured if the disease is common in your area.

890 My variegated holly has produced a few plain cream shoots. What made it do this?

While all variegated shrubs have a tendency to throw out plain green shoots from time to time, rather less common is the habit of variegated hollies of producing plain cream shoots. They usually appear in winter, probably as a result of a sudden cold snap or other brief change to the growing conditions. Simply cut them out – flower arrangers value them for their decorative appeal. Unfortunately, plain cream shoots cannot be used for propagation because they contain no chlorophyll (green pigment) and the cuttings are incapable of rooting.

If you notice a plain green shoot on any variegated shrub, you will see it is much stronger than the others. Left untreated, the green growth will take over. (This phenomenon is often seen on neglected hedges of variegated

▼ **884** *Blight and mildew are some of the most common plant problems.*

▼ **886** *The holes in these rose leaves were made by a leaf-cutting bee.*

▲ **889** *Black spot, a very common disease, is clearly noticeable on these rose leaves.*

▲ **890** *A sudden cold or very cold spell can make a holly (Ilex) push out plain-leaved shoots.*

▲ **891** *To trap earwigs, scrunch newspaper or straw into a container and place it upside down on a bamboo cane.*

privet that show increasingly large patches of plain green.) Cut out the non-variegated shoots at the base as soon as you notice them, reaching right down into the shrub.

891 Earwigs are ruining my clematis flowers. How can I trap them?

You can make a highly effective earwig trap by stuffing a flowerpot with newspaper or straw, then inverting it on a cane driven into the soil in the vicinity of damaged plants. The earwigs will shelter in the straw overnight. Each morning, remove the pot from the cane and knock out any earwigs. Burn the straw and replace it after a couple of days to destroy any eggs that may have been laid.

892 I pruned my apple tree last year and it has produced masses of upright, twiggy shoots that show no sign of flowering. What went wrong?

The tree has been overpruned. To remedy the situation, remove around half of the shoots, then lightly shorten the remainder to encourage branching. Next year, remove a further half of the upright branches, which should be starting to thicken. Lightly shorten the remainder to encourage further branching. Thin any congested growth in the middle of the crown. By year three, the tree should be beginning to flower and fruit.

893 Why don't my peonies flower?

A peony that is growing strongly with lush foliage but no flowers is probably planted too deep. In spring or autumn, dig up the rhizomes – very carefully, as they are brittle and easily broken – and replant them only 2.5cm (1in) below the soil surface. To further encourage flowering, give the plants a dose of a potassium-high fertilizer in early spring as the leaves emerge from below ground. Soil that is rich in nutrients will produce plants with dense foliage.

▼ **894** *Pelargoniums can be grown in pots and will make an attractive display.*

894 How can I overwinter my pelargoniums?

To overwinter pelargoniums, you need to induce dormancy in autumn. Gradually withhold water, then cut back the topgrowth to leave a woody framework. Keep the plants dry over winter, in a shaded situation, and in a cool but frost-free place – a garage or spare bedroom that you keep unheated is ideal. In late winter, coax them back into growth by raising the light level – though they should be out of direct light – and water sparingly. If the plants are very woody and tree-like, use new growth as cuttings material.

FRUIT PROBLEMS

Fruit trees and shrubs are subject to a range of problems, as both the flowers and fruits are a food source for insects and birds. As the garden pests eat holes in them, they allow disease to enter the plant.

895 What is codling moth?

This serious garden pest causes damage to both apples and pears. The adult is a grey-brown moth that lays its eggs on or near small fruits. Emerging larvae tunnel into fruits, pushing out a crumbly brown excrement as they feed. You need to deal with the pest before egg laying takes place. A pheromone trap indicates the presence of fertile females. Spray trees and/or tie special bands around branches to deter crawling larvae. Collect and destroy any affected fruits that have fallen to the ground.

896 How do I recognize apple sawfly on the fruit?

Apple sawfly produces unmistakeable scarring in a broad, brownish spiral on the surface of fruits. The adult female sawflies lay their eggs on open flowers. The larvae are white maggots that tunnel through the developing fruits, causing the scarring. To prevent damage, trees should be sprayed within seven to ten days of petal drop, when the females are laying. Some varieties are more susceptible than others.

▼ **895** *The codling moth tunnels into fruits, especially apples and pears.*

897 My apples have dimples and lumps on them – what is the cause?

Most probably these lumps are caused by the apple capsid, a pale green insect that sucks sap from developing fruits and leaves. Mild infestations can be tolerated, as neither the fruit nor its keeping quality are adversely affected, though the lumps are unsightly. 'James Grieve' seems particularly susceptible. To guard against the pest, spray in early spring as the new growth emerges.

898 Why are my apples rotting?

A number of related fungi can cause fruits to rot, and these are particularly troublesome during a wet season. The rots enter the plant through wounds caused by birds, wasps or caterpillars. You will notice the problem on fruits as rings of buff or grey fungal spores. The fruits turn brown and soften. Sometimes they are shed by the tree, or hang on over winter. To prevent the disease, spray with sulphur when the blossom turns pink in spring, then again before harvesting. Collect and destroy all mummified fruits. Store only perfect, dry, undamaged fruits.

▼ **896** *Apple sawflies leave a tell-tale trail on the skin of the fruit.*

899 What causes russeting on the skins of my apples?

Russeting is a natural condition of certain apple varieties, although the appearance of rough patches on the skin of smooth-skinned varieties is unsightly. Russeting is most likely caused by frost damage when the fruits are developing, or by powdery mildew or nutrient deficiencies in the soil. Since the fruits are still edible, control is not usually necessary – or even possible – but practise good cultivation to keep trees growing strongly to minimize the risks.

900 Why does my apple tree shed its fruit in early summer?

The June fruit drop is a natural phenomenon that does not affect the health of the tree or the quality of the crop – the plant is merely shedding excess fruits that it does not have the energy to develop fully. No measures need to be taken to prevent this. However, if fruits are shed at other times, it is worth cutting them open to check for any pest damage. Poor growing conditions, such as excessive dryness at the roots, can also cause fruit drop.

▼ **898** *Rots on fruits can be encouraged by a variety of factors.*

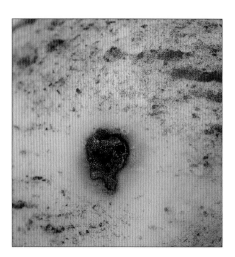

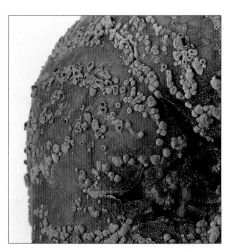

901 Why are my apples speckled with brown inside and out?

This is bitter pit. Sunken pits appear on the skins of apples, the flesh immediately beneath the pitting is brown and there are also brown areas throughout the fruit. The problem usually develops on fruits in storage, but can also be observed on fruits still on the tree. Seriously affected fruits are inedible. The usual cause is lack of calcium, usually arising as a result of irregular watering. Too much potassium and/or magnesium in the soil can also cause bitter pit. To prevent the problem, keep trees well watered during periods of drought when the fruit is developing and spray with calcium nitrate throughout the summer.

902 Why does my apple tree produce fruits only in alternate years?

Biennial bearing is an interesting phenomenon – trees fruit heavily one year, then have a year off, with some varieties being more prone to this than others. You can get round this by reducing the amount of blossom in spring. Remove up to nine in ten flower clusters so that the plant produces only a moderate crop, putting the rest of its energies into developing buds for fruiting the following year. Biennial bearing may also be the result of poor pruning.

▼ **901** *Bitter pit – sunken patches on the skin – is a common problem of apples.*

903 What causes my pear tree to produce misshapen fruits?

Misshapen pears are often the result of a boron deficiency in the soil; the fruits also usually show brown patches. To prevent the problem, spray the trees with sodium tetraborate (borax) at petal fall.

904 My fruit tree flowered well, but there are no fruits. What happened?

Unfortunately for gardeners, blossom time often coincides with cold, frosty nights. If blossom is affected by frost, to which all fruit trees are vulnerable, fruits cannot develop. Keep an eye on the weather and be prepared to throw a length of horticultural fleece over flowering plants whenever frost is threatened. Cold weather can also deter pollinating insects. On plums, peaches and apricots, it is often worth pollinating the plants by hand to ensure good cropping.

905 My plum tree is exuding sticky resin – what is the cause?

Gumming is a particular problem of plum trees – and of the related peaches, cherries, plums and apricots. Although no permanent damage usually results, the trees lack vigour. On a young plant, this can prove fatal unless dealt with promptly. Cut off lumps of hardened resin, if necessary, but it is more important to keep plants well-watered, fed and mulched.

▼ **903** *Distorted pear fruits indicate some mineral deficiency in the soil.*

906 What is silver leaf curl?

Silver leaf is a serious fungal disease of plums (especially 'Victoria'), cherries, peaches and apricots (and the ornamental forms of the same). All these belong to *Prunus*, a particularly susceptible genus, though other plants can also show symptoms. It is common in areas that experience mild, wet winters. The leaves turn silver, then brown, and curl up. Since the disease, carried in rainwater, often enters the plant through pruning wounds, it is usually recommended that all pruning of vulnerable plants should be done during warm, dry weather in early to mid-summer – at this time of year, the wounds should heal quickly. This is therefore the time to cut back affected growth, using sterilized tools. Feed, water and mulch the plant after you have pruned it to encourage recovery.

907 My raspberry fruits are drying out on the plant. What causes this?

The female raspberry beetle lays her eggs on open flowers. The emerging larvae eat the developing fruits from the inside. Blackberries, loganberries, tayberries and other hybrid cane fruits can also be attacked. You need to spray plants when the flowers are open in the evening to avoid harming pollinating insects. There is no biological or organic control for this pest.

▼ **905** *Plums often exude a sticky gum, both on the fruits and on the stems.*

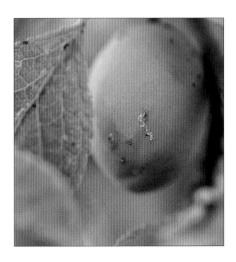

VEGETABLE PROBLEMS

While home-grown vegetables are a delight, if your carefully raised plants are to perform well throughout the growing season you need to keep a look out for potential problems that can spoil the crop before you get a chance to enjoy it.

908 What causes potato blight?

If your potato plants collapse and you find that the tubers are rotting underground, blame blight, probably the worst (and possibly commonest) disease of potatoes. It's a fungal problem that tends to strike during humid weather, especially when warm days follows cool nights. To reduce risks, look for resistant varieties and make sure you plant at the recommended depth. Earth them up regularly as the plants grow. Spray maincrop potatoes in summer with a fungicide. When you are lifting tubers, check that they are firm – the disease can spread from one to the other while they are in storage. The disease can also affect related plants such as tomatoes.

909 My potatoes are full of tunnels. What's causing the damage?

Wireworms are a common potato pest. The adults – click beetles – lay their eggs in the soil, and the emerging larvae feed under ground, making tunnels in potato tubers. One of the most effective methods of controlling the pest is to dig over the soil regularly. This brings the larvae to the surface, where they either dry out or are eaten by birds.

▼ **912** *The Colorado beetle is a serious pest of potatoes and related plants.*

▲ **909** *Wireworms tunnel into the potato flesh.*

910 My potato plants are cropping poorly. The leaves are yellow and, when I dig them up, I find cysts on some of the roots. What causes this?

Cyst eelworms spend most of their lives feeding within plant roots. Mature females burst through the root walls, producing characteristic cysts. Since the eelworms (nematodes) are capable of going dormant in soil when there is no food source, it's important to practise crop rotation so that their numbers do not build up in any one piece of ground. Some varieties are known to be resistant to the eelworm, so look out for these if you have already experienced the problem. Tomatoes can also be affected.

911 What are nematodes?

Also called roundworms, nematodes are microscopic organisms that live in the soil. Most are benign, but some are capable of entering plants and causing disease. They sometimes cause galls and cysts to appear on plant stems and leaves. However, some nematodes have a valuable part to play in biological controls. For instance, *Phasmarhabditis hermaphrodita* is a nematode that

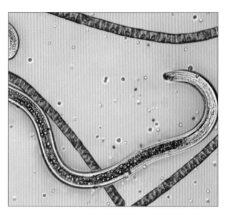

▲ **911** *Nematodes (magnified) are microscopic creatures that live in the soil.*

parasitizes slugs. It enters the slug as it feeds, then eats the slug from the inside, causing its death. It is one of the most effective means of slug control available. It is applied as a spray on soil where slugs are active.

912 What is the Colorado beetle?

The Colorado beetle, as its name suggests, is native to North America, but it has been introduced into Europe, where it is a notifiable quarantine pest. The adults are yellow-orange and black striped beetles about 1cm (¾ in) long. Both they and their larvae eat the leaves of potatoes, causing extensive

▼ **914** *The asparagus beetle should be dealt with before it lays any eggs.*

defoliation. Contact your local government agriculture department if you spot one.

913 When I dig up my potatoes some of them have black spots while others are almost completely rotten. What causes this?

Bacterial soft rot, sometimes called blackleg, can affect potatoes, especially if they are grown in cold, wet, poorly drained soil. Sometimes the topgrowth of the affected plants collapses. This is not usually a serious problem, as only isolated plants are affected and the disease does not spread from plant to plant or persist in the soil. Dig up and destroy affected plants. Make sure that any tubers you dig up for storage are disease-free, as healthy potatoes can be affected by contact with a diseased one. Improve the soil if it drains poorly. Some varieties are resistant to the disease.

914 How do I deal with the asparagus beetle?

Unlike most vegetable crops, which are annuals, asparagus are perennials that need a permanent home. Asparagus beetles – the adult is black with yellow blotches – can cause a great deal of damage. The best way to deal with them is to pick them off by hand, ideally before the adults have laid their eggs, as the larvae – dull cream in colour – also feed on the plants. Spraying with pyrethrum can also give some measure of control.

915 How can I control carrot fly?

Adult carrot flies lay their eggs in the topgrowth of young carrots. The larvae then tunnel down into the roots, turning them brown and ruining the flavour. Carrots in storage can also be affected if the larvae have already entered the roots. The fly also attacks celery, parsley and parsnips. The adults are attracted to the scent of the leaves. Sow seed as thinly as possible so you do not need to thin the seedlings – in handling the plants it is difficult to avoid bruising the leaves, and this

releases the oils that appeal to the flies. The females fly low over the ground, so you can also protect crops with a physical barrier. Either throw horticultural fleece over the plants or erect a 60cm (2ft) clear plastic barrier around the bed.

916 What causes the skin of my tomatoes to crack?

This is a common problem of tomatoes – deep cracks appear on the surface of the fruits. A number of factors can cause this, but the likeliest is an irregular water supply while the fruits are forming, either too much or too little. Keep plants well watered when they are in full growth, especially when the fruits are forming. Make sure that any containers you are using drain properly – plants do not like to sit in water.

917 There's a silvery marking on the pods of my pea plants – what has caused this?

The pea thrip is a sap sucker that feeds on pea plants. It thrives in hot, dry conditions. You can treat the plants with an insecticide, but to deter the pest, make sure that plants are well watered during dry spells and less appealing to the pest.

918 What is a notifiable disease?

Some diseases – usually those potentially affecting agricultural crops or conservation areas – are so serious that you are legally required to inform your local government agriculture department if you suspect an outbreak in your garden. Sudden oak death is one of the most recent to emerge.

▲ **916** *Tomato fruits can crack if the plants are over- or under-watered.*

919 Which conditions favour fungal diseases in the garden?

Many fungal spores are carried in water, including rainwater. Excessive damp is thus the enemy of nearly all garden plants. It encourages plants to put on soft growth that is a breeding ground for fungal spores. Various mildews are among the commonest. In late summer to autumn, ideal conditions for their proliferation often occur. The temperature falls, so more moisture is held in the air. If plants are congested, air stagnates around the stems, so take this into consideration when planting out crops. Dryness at the roots of the plants compounds the problem.

▼ **915** *Carrot fly is a flighted insect whose grubs damage the roots.*

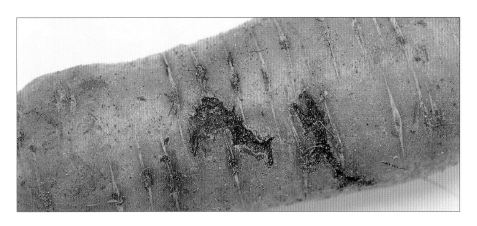

920 What is honey fungus?

Honey fungus is a serious disease that is caused by a number of related fungi. It often results in the death of plants, since it is usually undetected until an affected plant dies. Honey fungus is the commonest cause of die-back in woody plants, although soft-stemmed plants are also vulnerable. Symptoms include die-back and discoloration of the leaves, failure of new buds to open in spring, fan-shaped, honey-coloured fungal growths at the base of trunks and, if you dig around the roots, bootlace-like growths underground. Prevention is difficult, as the disease goes unnoticed until plants are already dying, but the problem is often associated with dead roots left in the ground after trees and shrubs have been felled or moved. In the event of an outbreak, try to trace any of the underground growths back to the original dead plant that harboured the disease, then dig up and destroy any remaining plant material. Also dig up and destroy any newly affected plants, with as much of the root mass as possible. Treat the soil with a

▼ **920** *Honey fungus can cause die-back and can even result in the death of a plant.*

fungicide or replace it up to a depth of 1m (3ft) before replanting with new plants.

921 What are viruses?

A virus is a primitive, microscopic organism that lives in the cells of another living thing. Viruses are difficult to classify because of their ability to mutate. They infect many plants, often causing serious damage – affected plants may have to be destroyed, since the viruses cannot be treated. Viruses enter plants through wounds, often caused by insects, but

◀ **922** *Leafhoppers are tiny insects, up to 3mm (⅛in) long. They are active in spring, after overwintering as eggs on the host plant. Leafhoppers are specific to a group of plants, from which they suck sap, causing damage.*

sometimes inflicted by gardeners during the propagation or pruning process. Common viruses include the mosaic viruses seen on cucumbers, turnips and orchids (especially cymbidiums). If possible, choose virus-resistant varieties. Viroids are similar to viruses but lack a protein coat.

922 What are vectors?

Many viruses are spread by insects and other invertebrates which introduce the virus into the plant as they feed. Although an affected plant may die, you can protect the rest by identifying the vector and controlling it. Leafhoppers are common vectors of a number of viruses and can be controlled with insecticides. Apply these as soon as they become active.

923 What is grey mould/botrytis?

This is a very common fungus that can prove fatal to plants. You'll notice either a greyish brown fluff on plants and fruits, or blackened areas on leaves and other parts of the plant, or a general spotting. Different varieties of the disease attack different plants. Grey mould is easily passed from plant to plant, especially under glass where high temperatures and high humidity occur at the same time. The best advice is to cut back the affected parts, then think about thinning the plants – congested growth encourages the mould. Take care when watering plants, especially soft fruits – a jet of water can damage fruits, opening them up to disease. Fungicides can be effective, but only if you improve cultivation as well.

◀ **923** *Powdery moulds often appear on leaves and stems in late summer to autumn. Affected stems need to be removed and destroyed.*

PHYSIOLOGICAL PROBLEMS

Many plant disorders are often caused by the growing conditions themselves – whether too hot, too cold, too wet, too dry – rather than by any pest or disease. Deficiencies in the soil can also lead to plant growth problems.

924 What soil problems are there that I should be aware of?

Plants derive the nutrients they need from minerals dissolved in the soil. Nitrogen (N), potassium (K) and phosphorus (P) are major nutrients required. Other elements, known as trace elements, are present (and needed by plants) in much smaller quantities. If soil is deficient in any of these minerals and nutrients, the plants in the soil will be affected adversely in some way.

925 What are the symptoms of a potassium deficiency?

Potassium is needed for reliable flowering and fruiting. If a plant fails to perform as expected, there may well be a deficiency. Roses in particular have a heavy demand on potassium, so rose fertilizers are high in this element. You can use a rose fertilizer on other flowering shrubs to improve their flowering (the plants do not know it's a rose fertilizer). Apply a

▼ **925** *Potassium deficiency is treated by digging in rose fertilizer.*

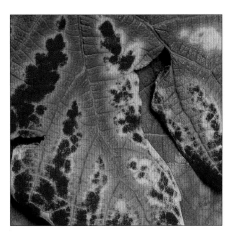

▲ **924** *Yellow on a leaf can be the result of a number of factors, including manganese deficiency.*

rose fertilizer in early spring, then again in summer. A dose of potassium at the end of the growing season will firm the growth of all woody plants and make it less vulnerable to frost – important on slightly tender plants such as fuchsias. Tomatoes also need potassium for good fruiting, so tomato

▼ **926** *Nitrogen deficiency shows as a yellowing of the leaves.*

feeds are always potassium-high and need to be applied regularly throughout the growing season.

926 How would I recognize a nitrogen deficiency?

Nitrogen is required for lush, leafy growth. If plants fail to grow strongly or look a bit yellow it may well be worth feeding them with a nitrogen-high fertilizer such as seaweed extract.

927 How would I know if the soil is low in phosphorus?

Few soils are ever low in this element, but purple or brown spots on leaves and poor cropping can be indicators. The problem is likeliest to occur on heavy soil in areas of high rainfall. To combat the deficiency, fork in bonemeal or other phosphorus-high fertilizer around plants, ideally in autumn. Fruit trees benefit from applications of superphosphate every two or three years to keep them cropping successfully.

▼ **927** *A shortage of phosphorus in the soil leads to poor growth.*

CHAPTER TEN

GROWING UNDER COVER

People who love plants want to grow as many as possible. You can easily extend the number of different types you grow by investing in a greenhouse, conservatory or polytunnel. Greenhouses are ideal for summer crops of tomatoes, peppers and cucumbers, and, if unheated, can also be used to shelter alpines from excessive wet. Conservatories are attached to the house and often function as a complete indoor garden, filled with an array of tropical and subtropical plants, literally bringing the garden indoors. A large polytunnel with adequate headroom will enable you to grow quite large plants as well as giving protection to edible overwintering crops. A living room with a low light level can provide a home to a range of houseplants. All these options will provide a suitable environment for raising plants from seed and giving young plants protection from the worst of the weather.

CHOOSING
HOUSEPLANTS

GROWING
HOUSEPLANTS

EPIPHYTES

ORCHIDS

CACTI AND
SUCCULENTS

GREENHOUSE
GARDENING

GREENHOUSE
CROPS

◀ *Many plants, such as miniature roses, are grown specifically as houseplants.*

CHOOSING HOUSEPLANTS

Houseplants bring something of the garden into the home, so it is possible to enjoy greenery, even flowers, indoors when it is too cold to venture outside. While some have very specific needs, several are very easy to grow.

928 Which are the best flowering houseplants?

Moth orchids (*Phalaenopsis*) have been bred to do well in centrally heated living rooms where the air stays warm and dry. Cut back the flower trusses as they fade, cutting just above a node, and new flowering shoots should appear. Clivias (*Clivia miniata*) are easy to flower and seem to thrive when pot-bound. Repot them only when absolutely necessary. African violets (*Saintpaulia*) and sinningias are also popular, but need a fairly moist atmosphere for success.

929 Which are the easiest foliage plants to grow as houseplants?

Aspidistra elatior is often called the cast iron plant, because it is so difficult to kill and seems to thrive on neglect. (Actually, it is more or less hardy, and even worth trying outdoors in a sheltered spot.) The weeping fig (*Ficus benjamina*) is a shrubby plant or small tree that is also tolerant of a range of conditions indoors.

930 Which plants will do well in a damp bathroom or kitchen?

We tend to think of cacti as desert plants, but the so-called Christmas cactus (*Schlumbergera*) is a rainforest dweller that likes cool, preferably humid, conditions in relatively low

light. The bird's nest fern (*Asplenium nidus*) should also do well in similar damp conditions.

931 Which plants do well in low light levels?

Woodland ferns and other plants with tough leaves tolerate parts of the home that receive little direct light. *Chamaedorea*, *Fatsia*, *Aspidistra elatior* and ivies (*Hedera*) will do moderately well.

932 Which plants do well in a warm, dry living room?

In a well-lit position, cacti and succulents, which are adapted to drought, will do well. Away from direct light, try orchids such as phalaenopsis which have been bred to tolerate dry air. *Epidendrum* hybrid orchids are also very tolerant.

◀ **928** *African violets* (Saintpaulia) *have flowers in a range of jewel-like colours and fleshy, dark green leaves.*

▲ **930** *Choose houseplants for specific rooms of the house, noting the plants' requirements for light levels.*

▼ **931** *Ivies grow indoors as well as outside in poor light. Use them in bowls in combination with other plants.*

GROWING HOUSEPLANTS

To get the most out of your houseplants, they need care and attention in the same way as plants in the garden. But their needs are different, as they are growing in an artificial environment. A regular routine of maintenance will help keep them in top condition.

933 How do I care for my houseplants?

Dead growth on a plant attracts pests and diseases, and a build-up of dust on leaves prevents normal leaf function – leaves should be able to 'breathe'. Remove dead leaves as a matter of routine, either with scissors or with your fingers. You can clean leaves either by wiping them with a cloth dipped in a mild soap solution or, in summer, by taking the plant outside and hosing it down with a pressure sprayer filled with a soap solution. Ready-mixed spray leaf cleaners are also available. Whatever you opt for, handling the plant is beneficial – physical contact toughens leaves.

934 Can I make my own leaf shine?

You can give clean leaves a polish with semi-skimmed (low-fat) milk, mayonnaise, or 1:8 mix of vegetable oil and water. Mayonnaise gives the glossiest finish but inevitably smells of itself. And there is no doubt that ready-made sprays are easier to use if you are tackling a large leafy plant such as a weeping fig (*Ficus benjamina*).

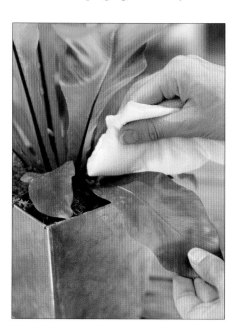

▲ **933** *When placing your plants, pay attention to light levels. Most houseplants will thrive near a window.*

935 How do I care for houseplants over winter?

Most houseplants are found in the wild in tropical and subtropical regions of the world – where the year is divided into two seasons, wet and dry. If conditions are favourable, they can be in growth virtually throughout the year. In temperate zones, it is necessary to induce dormancy during winter. From late summer onwards, gradually reduce the frequency of watering and do not feed. Place your plants on a sunny windowsill so that they receive maximum light. Many cacti and succulents can be kept completely dry. Other plants should be kept barely moist. The following

◄ **934** *Glossy leaves give a plant a healthy appearance, but most leaf-shining products are purely cosmetic; they do not contain fertilizers. If you do decide to use these, it is important to clean the leaves first, otherwise any dust on the plant can get sealed in.*

spring, begin watering and feeding, and shade the plants from direct light (but not cacti and succulents).

936 Should I place my houseplants outdoors in summer?

Putting your houseplants outdoors in summer brings certain advantages. Being exposed to the elements helps toughen the foliage, while the presence of a much wider range of invertebrate life than is found in the home can help control pest damage that they may be prone to. Houseplants can usefully be incorporated in summer containers and hanging baskets.

937 What is the best position for houseplants outdoors?

Houseplants do not like extremes of temperature, so should be placed in light shade with shelter from strong winds. An enclosed courtyard – possibly outside a basement flat – can provide ideal conditions.

▼ **936** *Putting plants outdoors in summer can help firm the growth and expose them to more light.*

938 Which potting mix should I use for my houseplants?

Although you can buy special houseplant potting mix, most plants will do well in a soil-based potting mix (John Innes No.2) or a soil-less one, such as a multi-purpose potting mix. But some types of plants have very specific needs. Orchids need a special potting mix that is low in nutrients, fibrous and swift draining. Cacti need a compost that is low in nutrients but high in minerals. For these plants, it is best to buy the products that are specially formulated for them.

939 When should I repot my houseplants?

Most houseplants should be repotted when their roots are filling the pot – the appearance of roots emerging from the draining holes at the base is a sure give-away. There are some exceptions, such as cymbidium orchids and clivias (*Clivia miniata*), which seem to thrive on being pot-bound. Repot these only when absolutely necessary. The best time for repotting is early spring, when the plants are just beginning to emerge from their winter dormancy.

940 How do I repot my plants?

If you want the plant to keep on getting bigger, repot it into the next size pot up (potting on). If you want the plant to stay the same size, it is a matter of replacing the potting mix it is growing in (repotting). In both cases, remove the plant from its container and shake the roots free of excess soil. To pot on, line the base of the new container with crocks and a layer of potting mix. Put in the plant – the top of the rootball should be about 2.5cm (1in) below the pot's rim to allow for watering. Feed potting mix around the rootball and lightly firm it down as you do so. Water the plant to settle the potting mix.

To repot a plant, wash all the potting mix off the roots and give them a light trim. Wash out the container thoroughly. Return the plant to the container, using fresh potting

Repotting a houseplant

1 Line the base of the new container with crocks to aid drainage. Cover the hole to retain the potting mix.

2 Slide the plant from its existing container. Place the plant in the centre of the new one.

3 Feed fresh potting mix into the gap between the rootball and the side of the pot.

4 Firm the potting mix lightly with your fingers, then water well and allow to drain.

mix, again allowing a gap of 2.5cm (1in) between the compost surface and the pot rim.

941 Some of my houseplants are too big for repotting. What should I do about them?

If you have a large houseplant you may find it impractical, or impossible, to repot it because of its size or shape. In this instance, lay a sheet of newspaper near the plant, lean the pot to one side, then scrape out as much of the old potting mix as you can with your fingers, being careful not to damage the roots. Replace it with fresh potting mix. The new potting mix will contain nutrients that will feed the plant when it is watered. The old potting mix can be added to the compost heap.

942 What potting mix should I use for repotting citrus?

Citrus – a large group that includes oranges, lemons, kumquats and a host of attractive ornamental plants – like slightly acid conditions. Rather than using straight ericaceous potting mix, which is too acidic, it is best to mix equal parts of this with a soil-based one – either John Innes No.2 or 3.

943 Will my citrus produce fruits if I grow them in a conservatory?

Citrus are often sold bearing flowers and fruits. Fruits can take up to nine months to ripen on the plant even in warm climates, so they are unlikely to produce fully ripened fruits under glass in cool areas. Low temperatures impair fruiting – so such plants are best treated as ornamentals.

944 What is the function of the clay pellets that are often seen for sale with the houseplants in garden centres and in florists' shops?

Lightweight clay pellets are sometimes used as trims around plants, but they actually have a practical function. Place them in the drainage trays to absorb excess water as it drains through. Many houseplants – those that originate from rainforest areas – appreciate a certain amount of humidity. You can also fill trays with the pellets, then pour water over to dampen them. Placed near your plants, they will release the water as a vapour around them. Top up the water as and when the pellets dry out.

945 What is hydroponics?

Hydroponics, or more properly hydroculture, is a system of growing plants in a clean, inert medium – such as expanded clay pellets – that support the roots. Nutrients are delivered to the plants dissolved in water. A water-level indicator shows when the level of the water needs to be topped up.

946 What are the advantages/ disadvantages of growing plants hydroponically?

Since the growing medim is inert, it is clean and stays weed- and odour-free. Plant growth tends to be vigorous and plants are generally less troubled by the usual pests and diseases. However, only a limited number of plants are suitable for growing hydroponically and maintenance costs can be high.

947 Which plants are suitable for growing hydroponically?

Anthurium
Chamaedorea
Cissus
Codiaeum
Dieffenbachia
Ficus benjamina
Hedera
Hyacinthus
Monstera
Nephrolepis
Saintpaulia
Schefflera
Spathiphyllum
Streptocarpus
Yucca

948 Which indoor plants can I grow from seed?

Campanula
Cobaea
Cyclamen
Impatiens
Pelargonium
Primula
Senecio
Thunbergia

949 Can I get my amaryllis bulbs to flower again?

After flowering, remove the faded flowers to prevent the plant from setting seed. Leave the stem in place – it will help build up the bulb as it dies back. Feed every two weeks with a potassium-high fertilizer, until the plant starts to show signs of die-back – typically in late summer-autumn, when the leaves will soften and start to turn yellow. Stop watering and feeding and allow the topgrowth to wither. Once it has turned brown, pull it away from the bulb. Remove the bulb from its pot and dust off any potting compost. Store the bulb on its side over winter– it must be kept dry, then pot up in early spring in fresh potting mix. Keep just moist until the first signs of new growth appear, then water regularly. Bulbs may need two years to build new flowers.

950 I have heard I should 'rest' my cyclamen – what does this mean and why should I do it?

Indoor cyclamen are valued for their winter flowers, in shades of pink and red as well as white (some have scented flowers). As the plants begin to die back after flowering, stop watering and allow the potting mix to dry out. There is no need to remove the tubers from the pots. Set the pots on their sides and store them in a dry, lightly shaded situation, such as under the staging in a cool greenhouse. Allow the tubers to remain dormant for eight to 12 weeks. Then start checking for signs of regrowth at the top of the tuber. Once you see shoots, bring the pots back into a lightly shaded position and begin watering and feeding the plants. In winter, you can place the plants in full light.

▼ **943** *Citrus plants thrive when grown in containers. Keep them in good light levels in a warm environment.*

▼ **948** *Most primulas are hardy plants, but some of the tender ones make delightful subjects for growing indoors.*

EPIPHYTES

The word 'epiphyte' comes from the Greek word *epi*, meaning 'upon', and *phyton*, meaning 'plant'. In the wild, these are often found in rainforest areas, clinging to the branches of large trees. Epiphytes make unusual and attractive houseplants.

951 What is an epiphyte?

Unlike the majority of plants that grow with their roots in the ground (known as terrestrials), epiphytes have a method of attaching themselves to host plants, usually by means of special roots that wrap themselves around tree branches.

952 How does an epiphyte gain its nutrients?

An epiphyte receives its nutrients mainly in the form of bird droppings and plant debris that wash over the plant in rainfall. However, loose matter similar to that found on the forest floor also accumulates in tree clefts, and the epiphyte's roots often find their way into this material.

953 Which epiphytes are commonly grown as houseplants?

Several plants that are epiphytic in the wild can be successfully grown in containers as houseplants. The group includes some of the bromeliads, such

▲ **951** *Many plants of the bromeliad family grow epiphytically.*

as *Aechmea*, *Guzmannia* and Spanish moss (*Tillandsia*), the rainforest cactus *Schlumbergera* and many orchids.

954 How do I grow epiphytes at home?

Epiphytes like to have air around the roots, so many of the potting mixes formulated specially for them are

loose in texture and they drain freely. Roots should never be allowed to sit in water. Epiphytes are also accustomed to very low levels of nutrients, so should be fed with a special feed or general fertilizer applied at half to a quarter strength. They benefit from a foliar feed sprayed directly over the leaves at two-weekly or monthly intervals during spring and summer (but not when in flower).

955 How do I water an urn plant?

The urn plant, *Aechmea fasciata*, is an attractive houseplant, with a rosette of leathery, grey-green leaves that look as though they have been brushed with silver. In its natural environment the leaves can grow to 1m (3ft) long. After flowering, keep the 'well' at the centre of the plant topped up with water, allowing this to dry out during winter when the plant is resting. In spring, when the plant is growing, add a small amount of fertilizer to the water.

▼ **951** *Many epiphytes have spectacularly beautiful flowers.*

▼ **953** Schlumbergera, *the Christmas cactus, is an epiphyte and houseplant.*

▼ **955** Aechmea fasciata *should be watered regularly.*

ORCHIDS

Orchids are surely the most glamorous of indoor plants, with spectacular flowers that can be produced over several weeks or even months. Contrary to popular belief, many are surprisingly easy to grow. Providing the correct light and heat levels are essential.

956 Which are the easiest orchids to grow?

Moth orchids, or phalaenopsis, have been bred to thrive in the conditions found in most houses. Many orchids like cool and damp conditions, but these orchids do well in dry, centrally heated living rooms. Ballerina orchids (*Epidendrum*) are also easy to grow.

957 Can I grow orchids on a windowsill?

Many orchids can be successfully grown on a windowsill, provided it is not in direct light in summer.

958 What conditions do orchids need in order to thrive?

Most of the orchids that are commonly grown as houseplants are complex hybrids and it is not necessary to replicate tropical conditions in the home to grow them successfully. However, they do have certain temperature requirements.

▼ **956** *Epidendrums have smaller flowers than many other orchids but are worth a place in collections.*

They are usually divided into three groups depending on the climate in which their parent species are grown. Cool-growing orchids originate from high altitudes where nights are cool, often dropping to 10°C (50°F). They need a minimum temperature range of 10–13°C (50–55°F) and a maximum of 21–24°C (70–75°F). Intermediate-growing orchids, from slightly warmer areas, need a minimum temperature of 14–19°C (57–66°F), with a maximum of 30–33°C (86–91°F). Warm-growing orchids, originating from steamy rainforests, have a minimum requirement of 20–24°C (68–75°F) and a maximum of 30–33°C (86–91°F).

Orchids from near the equator are adapted to light levels that remain more or less constant throughout the year. In regions far from the equator, day length fluctuates widely between summer and winter. To persuade the plants that they are nearer home than they are, it is usually necessary to shade them in summer to protect them from hot sun and from scorch – under glass, temperatures can soar much higher than they would in the plants' natural habitat. Conversely, in winter, most orchids need maximum light, and the shading should be removed.

959 What is the difference between an epiphytic and a terrestrial orchid?

Epiphytic orchids grow on trees – their roots have a grasping rather than a feeding function. Terrestrial orchids grow in the ground like other plants. Both need special potting mixes that are formulated to meet their separate needs.

▶ **958** *Orchids need the perfect site in order to thrive as a houseplant – a light spot, not in full sun.*

960 Can I grow epiphytic orchids in ordinary flower pots?

Yes, but plastic is preferable as it is important that the pots drain quickly – terracotta tends to hold on to moisture. Orchids are often sold in clear plastic pots, because the roots – unlike those of most other plants – are adapted to being in the light.

961 What are pseudobulbs?

Many orchids produce their leaves from swollen growths above potting mix level at the base of the plants. These are referred to as pseudobulbs. Like true bulbs, they act as storage organs for the plant.

962 Some of the pseudobulbs of my orchid have become leafless. What is the problem?

This is how orchids grow. Each year, new bulbs are produced at the base of the plant and older ones go dormant – when they are known as back bulbs – or shrivel. But if the pseudobulbs look congested, it may be time to divide the plant. Healthy back bulbs can be removed and used for propagation.

CACTI AND SUCCULENTS

It is easy to get attracted to growing cacti and succulents – children are particularly interested. They are as fascinating as alpines. Most are slow growing and stay small for many years, so even a large collection need not take up much space.

963 What is the difference between a cactus and a succulent?

The answer is strictly botanical – not, as might be expected, the presence of spines, as certain euphorbias have spiny stems but are classified as succulents. The distinction is actually the presence of an areole, a small depression on cactus stems (or pads or leaves) from which the spines protrude. Not all cacti actually have spines – rainforest types such as the Christmas cactus (*Schlumbergera*) have stems that are composed of flattened, swollen leaves (but they still have areoles).

964 Why are so many cacti grafted?

Many cacti species are very rare in the wild, so only a small quantity of seed is ever available. Additionally, they can be reluctant to flower in cultivation – some flower only at night, and the flowers may be open for only a short

▼ **963** *Cacti vary in their appearance just like any other group of plants. They all have specific requirements.*

period of time. To ensure that enthusiasts can obtain these rare plants, therefore, seedlings are often grafted on to other species. This boosts growth and produces flowering plants more quickly, although it can also lead to some distortion.

▲ **965** *Cacti thrive in centrally heated rooms in shallow containers with sufficient drainage material.*

965 Which are the best containers to use for cacti and succulents?

Most of these plants have shallow root systems and they all need good drainage. The best containers to use, therefore, are shallow pans that are wider than they are deep. Mixed plantings can be effective.

Some cacti and succulents have a recumbent or trailing habit and can be displayed to advantage in hanging baskets that raise the plants to eye level. Make sure that the potting mix can drain properly. All of the following are worth trying in hanging baskets:
Aporocactus flagelliformis
Echinocereus pentalophus
Epiphyllum oxypetalum
Hatiora salicornioides
Hoya
Kalanchoe
Rhipsalidopsis
Schlumbergera
Sedum morganianum

Repotting a cactus

1 Fold a piece of paper into a strip 30cm (12in) long to help you handle the cactus.

2 Wrap the strip around the cactus. Holding the ends firmly, ease the cactus out of its pot.

3 Shake the roots free of the old potting mix, teasing out any lumps with your fingers.

4 Still using the strip, put the cactus in the new pot and feed in potting mix around the roots with a spoon.

966 I need to repot a cactus, but because it is prickly, what is the best way of handling it?
Fold a piece of paper into a strip and wrap this round the plant to protect your hands from the spines. Support the plant by the roots.

967 Can I grow cacti from seed?
Easily. If you are an enthusiast, you will probably be able to get hold of the seed of certain species over the Internet. You can buy packets of mixed seed in garden centres – fun to sow, as you do not know exactly what you will be getting. If the seed is very fine, mix it with a little sand to make it easier to sow. Fill small pots with cactus potting mix and surface sow the seed. Lightly cover with fine sand. Keep the pots in a propagator at 19–27°C (66–81°F). Once the seed has germinated, remove the pots from the propagator and keep them at a temperature of 10°C (50°F). Leave the seedlings undisturbed for a period of three months while the roots form. Pot them up individually when large enough to handle.

968 Can I grow cacti outdoors?
Several cacti are surprisingly hardy. A couple of species of *Opuntia* can survive several degrees of frost, provided the climate is dry – what kills them is cold, wet weather. In a sheltered, sunny garden, they can be grown outdoors even in cold climates, but the soil must be gritty and free-draining.

969 Can I make a miniature cactus garden?
Many cacti are small and slow-growing. It is perfectly possible to grow several together in a single container, as they do not spread to encroach on each other like many other types of plant. Use a wide, shallow container and be sure to use cactus potting mix (free-draining and mineral rich). Top-dress with horticultural grit or sand.

970 How do I take care of cacti?
Water cacti only during spring and summer, allowing the potting mix to dry out between waterings. Feed them monthly with a cactus fertilizer. In winter, they can be kept dry. Mist them occasionally if they start to look shrivelled.

▼ **968** *Cacti suit hot climates and are adapted to dry conditions. Growing them outside in cooler conditions is possible, but special care will be needed to maintain plant health.*

GREENHOUSE GARDENING

A greenhouse has a multitude of uses. Not only can you use it to grow tender crops, such as aubergines and chilli peppers, but it also makes an excellent place to shelter container plants over winter and for raising seedlings in spring.

▲ **972** *A greenhouse is fundamentally a work space, so it is a good idea to place it in a working area of the garden.*

971 What types of greenhouse are there?

Greenhouses are available to suit every pocket and every size of garden. A wide range of designs are available incorporating a wide array of materials, some of which are more long-lasting than others. The most expensive types are free-standing. Lean-to types are designed to attach to a house or garage wall. These generally receive less direct light than the former, but benefit from residual heat reflected from the wall. Tomato houses are small but tall enough to accommodate fully grown tomato plants. They should be fixed against a wall. Some models include optional shelves so can also be used for smaller plants. Polytunnels comprise a series of metal hoops over which is stretched heavy duty plastic. They are commonly used for vulnerable crops grown directly in the ground or for overwintering large container plants.

▲ **972** *Plants naturally grow towards the light. If you site the greenhouse in sun, the plants will have a balanced shape.*

972 Where do I site a greenhouse?

Site a free-standing greenhouse in an open, sunny position, ideally sheltered from strong winds. If you are getting a lean-to type, fix it to a wall that is in sun during part of the day, but is also shaded at other times. If the lean-to adjoins too sunny a wall, the temperature is likely to be too high in summer for many plants.

973 How do I keep the greenhouse warm in winter?

A thermostatically controlled heating system, though expensive to install, can prove cost-effective in the longer term, as the heating will come on only when the temperature drops to a certain level. It might be worth the investment if you intend to use your greenhouse all year around. To reduce costs, insulate the glass with bubble plastic attached to the framework inside the greenhouse. Move all the plants that require supplementary heat

to one end of the house and separate this with a curtain of bubble plastic. Heat just this section for your tender plants, and leave the rest unheated. Remove the plastic in spring.

974 Can I cut down my greenhouse heating costs?

Chances are, you only need to heat a small area of the greenhouse in winter, as you will probably be growing fewer

▼ **973** *You can insulate a greenhouse – or part of the greenhouse – with plastic bubble wrap.*

plants than in summer – no tomatoes, for instance. Plus, some of your plants may be more tolerant of low temperatures than others.

Soil-warming cables, attached to the mains and controlled with a thermostat, are laid in a layer of sand that underlies the potting mix in a raised bed. They are useful if you are doing a lot of propagating to raise the temperature around seedlings and cuttings.

975 How do I keep the greenhouse cool in summer?

On sunny days, the temperature under glass can rise dramatically to a temperature that is damaging to nearly all plants. Aim to maintain a maximum temperature of no more than 22°C (72°F). Open the vents as necessary. If you need to keep the door open, screen the lower portion of the opening to keep out slugs, snails and mice that may seek shelter. Hose the greenhouse floor morning and evening to lower the temperature as the water evaporates and also to provide a humid atmosphere that suits many tropical and subtropical plants.

976 What else can I do to protect my plants in the greenhouse in hot summer weather?

To prevent the leaves of plants from scorching in summer, make sure that they do not touch the glass.

▼ **975** *Glass magnifies light, so to protect your plants, stretch a screening fabric over the panes in summer.*

Move the plants away from the glass, or, if this is not possible, trim back any growth that touches the glass. Turn pot plants as necessary to keep them growing evenly.

977 What is a maximum-minimum thermometer?

A maximum-minimum thermometer records the highest and lowest temperatures reached. Positioned in the greenhouse, it will help determine at which point in the year any heating needs to be switched on.

978 How do I control humidity in the greenhouse?

As the temperature rises in summer, the air dries out. Plants lose excess water from their leaves and can scorch. The growing medium dries out, leading to wilting. To maintain adequate humidity levels and to keep the temperature down, hose down the hard surfaces on hot days during the evening and early morning.

979 How can I control the light levels in the greenhouse?

Light intensity varies throughout the year and glass magnifies its intensity. In summer, it will almost certainly be necessary to shade the glass, both to lower the light level and to help keep the temperature down. You can shade plants by applying a special wash to the outside of the glass

▼ **976** *Open the greenhouse vents in summer to keep the temperature inside down – plants can easily scorch.*

▲ **978** *Watering the greenhouse floor increases humidity and helps lower the temperature.*

at the start of summer (this wash is then wiped or washed off in autumn). Alternatively, blinds can be installed on the outside of the roof – some powered versions can be linked to a thermostat so that they are automatically lowered when the temperature rises above a certain point. Fabric meshes can also be fixed to the outside of the glass.

If you wish to germinate seeds or force plants for exhibitions, growing lamps can be used to raise the light level. Use them in conjunction with a heating system.

980 How do I maintain a healthy environment in the greenhouse?

Good garden hygiene is essential if fungal and other diseases are to be kept at bay. Cut off any dead or decaying leaves and flowers, and remove dead plant material from the potting mix surface, from the greenhouse staging and from the floor.

▲ **981** *Greenhouse smokes can be used to control pests and diseases.*

Not only can they harbour fungal spores and rots, but they can also provide nesting sites for insect pests. Clean all pots after use. Store them where they cannot shelter slugs and snails. On sunny days stand plants outside, as far as is practical, to expose them to outdoor pest predators.

981 How do I use smoke?

Insecticide smoke cleans the greenhouse of all pests and diseases, particularly in hard to reach areas. For a smoke to be effective, close all vents in the greenhouse. Follow the manufacturer's instructions, taking

▼ **982** *Clean pots thoroughly before storing them.*

care not to inhale the smoke. Some smokes also have a fungicidal action and are useful for maintaining the appropriate hygiene level. Do not enter the greenhouse to retrieve anything until the time allocated for the smoke to work has expired. The smell of the smoke will linger.

982 When should I clean the greenhouse?

Warm, still days in summer and autumn provide a good opportunity for cleaning the greenhouse. Move all the plants out of the greenhouse, then sweep and wash down all the staging and the floor with a household disinfectant cleaner or a mild solution of bleach and washing up liquid in warm water. Wash the glass, being sure to remove all algal deposits that tend to build up where the panes overlap. A paint- or car-windscreen ice scraper can be useful for this.

983 What is a cold frame?

A cold frame is a small, closed case that is usually positioned in the lee of a wall, out of direct sunlight. It is used for growing on seedlings, cuttings and other young plants that have been raised under cover. The lid can be opened during daylight to harden off plants being kept in it. Traditionally glass, modern types are usually made of toughened plastic held in a metal frame. You can also improvise a frame with bricks and sheets of glass.

▼ **983** *A cold frame can protect small plants, seedlings and cuttings.*

Cleaning the greenhouse

1 Wash the windows with a mild detergent dissolved in warm water and a soft cloth.

2 Algae can build up where the panes meet. A pressure washer can help dislodge this.

3 Scrub down greenhouse staging with warm water. Add a few drops of bleach and washing-up liquid to the water.

GREENHOUSE CROPS

Some popular fruiting plants need greenhouse protection in cold areas. Aubergines, cucumbers, peppers and some tomatoes will all thrive in containers and produce bumper crops in the additional heat.

984 Which are the best sorts of tomato for greenhouse growing?

In a greenhouse, it is best to grow cordon types that are trained into an upright plant on strings or canes, rather than bush types that sprawl on the ground.

985 How do I grow cucumbers?

F1 hybrid varieties are the best to use, as they produce only female flowers. Fruits that are fertilized by male flowers are bitter tasting. Sow individual seeds into 8cm (3in) pots in early spring, then transplant the seedlings about eight weeks later into 30cm (12in) pots. You will need to erect something for them to climb up, for example, bamboo canes at an angle, or wires or strings attached to the greenhouse roof. Nip out the main growing shoot after five or six leaves have appeared and attach the shoots to the support.

986 How do I grow bell peppers?

Several different types of pepper can be grown in the greenhouse, including chilli peppers and sweet peppers. They need a minimum temperature of 12°C (54°F) to grow properly, so are ideal for growing undercover. Sow the

▲ **984** *Harvest tomatoes as they ripen on the vine. The skins should be evenly red.*

seed indoors in mid-spring in 8cm (3in) pots and keep at a temperature of 6–21°C (60–70°F) until germinated. When they are well developed, transplant the seedlings into 20cm (8in) pots. As sweet peppers ripen, they change colour from green to red, yellow, orange or dark purple, and become sweeter. Let hot chilli peppers ripen fully before harvesting; they should be a bright even red.

▼ **986** *Bell peppers ripen from green to red or yellow, orange or purple, depending on the variety.*

▲ **985** *Cucumbers can be harvested while still small for pickling.*

987 How do I grow aubergines?

Aubergines, or eggplants, need a lot of warmth to do well. Sow individual seeds in 8cm (3in) pots in early spring. Soak the seeds in warm water for a day before sowing to speed up germination. Transplant the seedlings into 20cm (8in) pots when 10cm (4in) tall, and pinch out the growing tips to encourage bushiness. Support the growing plants with canes.

988 What is a tomato house?

If you have no room for a greenhouse it is possible to grow them in a tomato house. These occupy limited ground space – usually enough to hold a couple of growing bags or large containers – but are tall enough (up to around 1.2m/4ft) to house the fully grown plants. They should be attached to a warm wall. Most are made of glass, perspex or clear plastic. Some models have shelves, which means that they can be used for other plants. At the end of the season use them for overwintering cuttings and other young plants.

▼ **987** *Aubergines can be successfully grown at home under cover, in grow bags or in containers.*

CHAPTER ELEVEN

GARDEN EQUIPMENT

Keen gardeners are always looking to invest in good tools because they make any garden job easier and are a pleasure to use. Simple hand tools – garden fork, spade, hoe, rake and trowel – are classics that have barely altered in centuries. Pots and trays are now manufactured in a range of materials, some biodegradable. Large tools, such as lawnmowers, hedge trimmers, strimmers and shredders, can be powered by petrol, diesel or electricity, and using these can cut down on the time it takes to do many garden jobs. Choosing the right potting mix for specific tasks can be a minefield too. The various types are discussed here, along with ways to recycle household materials as well as save water, for the benefit of the garden and the environment.

HAND TOOLS

PRUNING AND TRIMMING TOOLS

TOOLS FOR LAWNS AND MEADOWS

OTHER TOOLS

POTS AND POTTING PRODUCTS

HEALTH AND SAFETY

WATER CONSERVATION

RECYCLING

◀ *Having the right tool for a specific task makes the work easier and more enjoyable.*

HAND TOOLS

Whatever the technological developments, there will always be a need for hand tools. The design of these has remained largely unchanged over the centuries, and they are as useful today as they have ever been. A trowel and hand fork are essentials for many gardeners.

989 What should I look for when choosing new tools?

To be effective, garden tools should be well made. The shaft should be firmly attached and the handles comfortable to hold. Check the weight of the tool – heavy tools are resilient but can be tiring to use over long periods. Think of tools as investments; they should last a long time.

990 What is the best material for garden tools?

Most digging tools are made of carbon steel, which can be sharpened, and are reasonably priced. More expensive is stainless steel, which is rustproof, but cannot be sharpened. Some tools have a non-stick coating so that soil does not stick to the blades. Shafts can be wooden, metal or sturdy plastic (sometimes a combination of two of these materials). Hand tools are often made solely of sturdy plastic. Many gardeners buy cheap hand tools as they are so easily lost in the garden.

▼ **993** *Gardeners with back problems often use tools with extra-long handles.*

▶ **989** *These garden tools are classics. A fork and spade are essential for most gardens, while a half-moon cutter is useful. Choose tools that are appropriate for your height.*

991 How do I keep my garden tools in good condition?

Clean the metal parts of tools after use with an oily rag. Carbon steel types should be sharpened annually (more often if you use them frequently). Oil wooden handles with linseed oil to prevent cracking.

992 Can I hire garden tools?

Power tools – electric or petrol-driven – are expensive to buy, especially when your need for them occurs only once or twice a year. Fortunately, most are available for hire. Many hire shops will deliver very heavy tools such as shredders. Check whether a transformer is required for electrical tools – if so, the shop should be able to supply one with the tool.

▼ **993** *Gather windfalls with a rake, to save your back from aching.*

993 Are there tools that make digging less back-breaking?

Many gardeners enjoy digging for the physical exertion it requires, but it can be hard work, especially if the soil is heavy. Instead of driving the tool in with the ball of your foot – as seems natural – try using your heel instead. This straightens the spine and can make the job a lot easier. Use smaller tools that move less heavy earth.

An automatic spade has a lever attached, which you operate with your foot. This throws soil forwards and so cuts down on bending. It may make the job of digging easier.

994 What is a hoe used for?

Hoes are used for weeding. Keep the blade sharp and it will cut through weed seedlings in spring with ease. A hoe can also be used to make drills for seed sowing in the vegetable garden.

995 What types of hoe are there?

A digging hoe has two blades. Wield the tool as you would a pick axe to break up clods of soil during the cultivation process.

A hand hoe, sometimes also referred to as an onion hoe, has a conventional hoe head but is mounted on a much shorter handle so that it can be held in the hand. It is ideal for dealing with weed seedlings around established plants, particularly onions and other closely growing plants.

996 What is a shrub rake?

A shrub rake is a small rake that is designed to be held in the hand. Use it in places where a full-size rake is impractical – for instance, to weed or rake up fallen leaves from in-between shrubs and other plants that are tightly packed together.

997 Should I invest in a potting mix scoop?

Many gardeners use a trowel for scooping potting mix out of the bag, but a scoop has definite advantages, if you have a lot of containers to fill. The scoop's deeper bowl means you are less likely to spill the potting mix and this cuts down on wastage.

▼ *995 Use a hand hoe where a conventional hoe would be impractical.*

▶ *1000 A long-handled hand fork has several features that make it a valuable tool for less-able gardeners. The long handle means less bending is required. It is also made of lightweight material and has a handle coated with an easy-grip rubber coating.*

998 What is a claw cultivator?

A claw cultivator is a long-handled hand tool with three prongs or tines that are bent over like claws at one end. It is an excellent tool for breaking up and aerating hard-packed soil in a restricted space where digging is not appropriate.

999 Are there any special tools for digging out weeds?

While hand forks and trowels are suitable for the removal of many garden weeds, some tap-rooted weeds – such as dandelions – can prove intractable, especially if they have seeded in the cracks in paving. In these situations, it is more practical to use special tools such as a daisy grubber. These have long, narrow and narrow blades that are often forked at the tip, which makes the job much easier. Equally, an old kitchen knife can be just as effective, provided the blade is firm – flexible blades can snap, if they bend as you are prising the weed out of the soil.

1000 I find it tiring to use conventional trowels and hand forks – are there any alternatives?

Many gardeners find using trowels and hand forks tiring on the wrists, especially when working on heavy soil. Look out for long-handled models. The extra length in the handle gives you greater leverage, so less strength is needed.

1001 What is a cultivator?

There are a number of special tools designed for helping break up garden soil. It can be worth investing in a cultivator if you have an allotment or are a keen vegetable gardener and find a conventional fork does not do the job to your satisfaction. Some have three or more bent prongs held in a claw-like arrangement at the end of a long or short handle. A star-wheeled cultivator is designed to create a tilth on previously dug soil. Many models are available.

◀ *999 A hand fork is mainly used for working the soil around your plants. A trowel could be used just as easily for this task.*

PRUNING AND TRIMMING TOOLS

There is a multitude of tools designed for the purposes of pruning and trimming plants.
Mostly, they are designed to carry out specific tasks, so make sure you select the right tool
for a particular job, and keep tools maintained regularly.

1002 What tools do I need?

A good pair of secateurs (hand pruners) is essential. They are used for cutting all stems up to pencil thickness. Loppers (some with extending handles) will cut thicker stems and allow you to prune overhead without using a ladder and at ground level without excessive bending down. Use a folding saw with a serrated blade for thick, woody stems. Topiary shears, or sheep shears, are ideal for use on low box hedges, but will cut only soft stems. Stout scissors can be used for trimming isolated soft stems. Use shears for trimming hedges.

1003 Are there different kinds of secateurs?

Different styles of secateurs can be used for different jobs in the garden. By-pass secateurs have a sharp upper blade that cuts against a thicker lower blade in a scissor-like action.

▼ **1002** *Topiary shears are the best tool for trimming soft growth on box (Buxus) and other dwarf hedging plants.*

They are excellent for most pruning jobs in the garden, cutting stems up to pencil-thickness. Anvil secateurs also have a sharp upper blade, but this cuts against a flat lower blade. These are good for cutting through firmer, woody growth. Thicker stems can be cut with parrot beak secateurs that have two sharp blades. Some manufacturers produce special secateurs for left-handers.

1004 How do I keep my secateurs clean?

After use, wipe the blades with an oily rag. This should be enough to keep them clean, provided they are kept closed. Also wipe over any ratchets and other metal parts of the tool that could rust in storage.

1005 Should I have my cutting tools professionally sharpened?

Have secateurs sharpened regularly. When you prune a plant, you are

▼ **1002** *Some loppers have extending handles that allow you to trim branches above head height.*

effectively wounding it – the plant has to repair itself. Clean cuts made with sharp blades heal quickly. Blunt and/or rusty tools snag wood and can produce ugly tears in the bark. Not only are these slow to heal, but they provide an opportunity for disease to enter the plant's tissues.

1006 What are tree pruners?

Tree pruners have long, usually extendable, handles and are used for cutting stems above head height, avoiding the need for ladders. Some have bags attached near the blades for gathering fruit on apple and pear trees.

1007 Which saws are suitable for garden use?

Saws are used for cutting through mature, thick branches on trees and shrubs. Most garden saws have folding blades. You will need a small one for working in a restricted space – for

▼ **1003** *Standard secateurs will cut stems of pencil thickness only. Keep the blades clean and sharp.*

▲ **1011** *A powered trimmer will make short work of cutting a long or tall established hedge.*

instance when cutting through old wood at the base of a mature shrub. A Grecian saw is curved and cuts only on the pull stroke. Larger saws, with flexible blades, are useful for removing tree branches. If you need to fell a tree, use a bow saw – it can be held parallel to the ground in both hands.

1008 Should I invest in a garden knife?

Some gardeners would be lost without their garden knife – others do not see the need for one, preferring secateurs for most cutting jobs. However, a knife is essential for such jobs as trimming cuttings and grafting. Keep it well sharpened.

1009 What are topiary shears?

Topiary shears are similar in design to the hand shears that are traditionally used for clipping sheep and are used one-handed. They are excellent for fine work and for maintaining a sharp, clean edge on low-growing plants such as box. However, the blades will cut only soft growth produced during the current season. For firmer growth, you will need to use secateurs or hedging shears.

1010 What types of hedging shears are available?

Most hedging shears have straight blades, but there are some models with wavy-edged blades. These are good for trimming thicker stems, for instance on a mature beech or hornbeam (*Carpinus*) hedge, but are more difficult to sharpen.

1011 What are rechargeable hedge trimmers?

If you have a large hedge to cut, powered hedge trimmers are an absolute boon. There are attendant

problems, however. Petrol-driven models are heavy and tiring to use at or above head height. Electric models designed to be plugged into the mains may require an additional extension lead in use, and there is a real danger of cutting through the flex by accident (though the majority of models incorporate safety features that minimize the risk of electric shock to the user). Battery-powered models that are recharged through a special unit plugged into the mains are much easier to handle. However, they may not be able to cut through very thick shoots and need regular recharging.

1012 What is a brushwood cutter?

A brushwood cutter, usually petrol-driven, is a hand-held tool with a rotating blade designed to slash through woody weeds and coarse grass. It is essential to wear ear defenders and goggles when using one of these. Many gardeners find these tools uncomfortable to operate over extended periods (say longer than half an hour), owing to the vibration. Electric models are lighter in weight, but are usually only suitable for grass cutting.

1013 Chainsaws look and sound dangerous – are they?

Chainsaws – petrol-driven or powered by electricity – are used for tree felling and for removing large, thick branches from mature trees. A good sense of balance and a head for heights are essential. They are heavy in use and should really only be used by qualified tree surgeons (especially if the work required is above ground level). However, many horticultural colleges run short courses in their use, with an emphasis on the health and safety issues involved. This includes the wearing of appropriate protective clothing and the use of harnesses. Professional tree surgeons sometimes work in pairs or teams.

◀ **1012** *A strimmer or brushwood cutter cuts with a rotating nylon blade.*

TOOLS FOR LAWNS AND MEADOWS

If you take pride in your lawn – or even if you just want to keep it looking reasonably good –
you will appreciate using the right tools. For the best results, you will need more than a
lawnmower, though it is worth the investment if you have a large lawn.

1014 What types of lawnmower are there?

There are many types of lawnmower available, and choice will depend on budget and how much grass you have – not to mention to what extent you actually enjoy the job. Cylinder mowers, with blades that rotate around a horizontal axis, produce the finest cut. They can be manual or powered by petrol or electricity. Rotary mowers, with a single blade that rotates parallel with the ground, are bigger and suitable for dealing with areas of rough grass. As they tend to be heavy machines, most are petrol-driven. Most lawnmowers have a detachable hood or bag that collects the grass clippings – essential if you do not want the task of raking cut grass. Ride-on mowers are usually only worth considering if you have a large area to mow. All these types of mower usually incorporate a roller that rollers the grass as you cut.

▼ **1014** *There are many different types of lawnmower – choose one that suits your lawn size and that is easy to handle.*

1015 How does a hover mower cut the lawn?

Hover mowers are lightweight and powered by electricity. They float on a cushion of air, while a rapidly rotating nylon cord or plastic blade cuts the grass. Hover mowers are ideal for cutting the grass on a bank or any other area of uneven grass. On the downside, these mowers will not produce such a close cut as the types described above and the clippings tend to accumulate on the underside of the machine. You need to make sure that the machine is switched off when you remove this. The blade or cord will need replacing regularly.

1016 How should I maintain my lawnmower?

All lawnmowers should be cleaned before storage. Check metal blades regularly to make sure they are still sharp. Oil any moving parts so that the blades will turn easily when in

▼ **1014** *Many lawnmowers are fitted with a grass box that collects the clippings as you mow.*

use. Drain any excess fuel before storage and keep in a special can, bearing in mind that this is a potential fire hazard. Petrol-driven mowers should be serviced annually – most garages will do the job for you.

1017 Do I need to invest in a garden roller?

Garden rollers are almost a thing of the past, and are no longer generally recommended on established lawns because they tend to compact the ground, impeding drainage. Hire one if you want to ensure the ground is thoroughly flat before turfing.

1018 What is a strimmer for?

A strimmer is similar in design to a brushwood cutter, but instead of a blade it has a rotating nylon cord. It is usually smaller and lighter. Strimmers are used for cutting soft growth, either grass in awkward corners that cannot be reached with a

▼ **1017** *Rolling a lawn helps keep it perfectly flat – which also helps with mowing.*

▶ **1020** *Neaten the edges of a lawn with a half-moon cutter, which is the ideal tool.*

standard mower or ground cover plants and weeds. The cord has to be replaced periodically.

1019 What are lawn shears?

Lawn shears differ from ordinary shears in that the handles are at right angles to the blades. Although you can use hedging shears to trim long grass, it is easier to trim close to the ground with lawn shears and produce an even cut.

1020 What is the best tool for trimming the edge of a lawn?

A half-moon cutter is a special long-handled tool with a semi-circular, flat blade. The cutter is designed for trimming the edges of a lawn and can also be used for cutting turves – for instance, if you need to create a new flower bed within an existing lawn.

1021 What is a scythe?

A scythe is a traditional agricultural tool with a long, curved blade, which is used for slashing through long

▼ **1018** *A power strimmer is ideal for tidying an area of rough grass at speed, or for grass that has grown too long.*

grass, and a long handle designed to be held with both hands. Once you become adept at its use, this remains an effective tool for use in a wild garden or meadow planting – any situation where the vegetation is allowed to grow tall, but then must be cut to near ground level. It is essential to keep the blade sharp for maximum effectiveness.

1022 What is a sickle?

A sickle is similar to a scythe but is smaller and designed to be held in one hand. A sickle allows you to bunch stems with your free hand, then cut all the stems with one swing of the blade – useful if you need to be

▼ **1019** *Lawn shears have long arms and blades set at right angles, so that the lawn edge can be trimmed while standing.*

▲ **1022** *A sickle is an old-fashioned gardening tool.*

selective with your cutting (for instance, when deadheading or cutting clumps of plants in a large border).

1023 Is there a special tool I can hire to aerate the lawn?

Aerating a lawn is a tiring job if you are going to do it – as is perfectly possible – with a garden fork. It is possible to hire special rolling tools that make the job easier. A hollow-tined aerator lifts long, narrow plugs of soil from the lawn, while a slitter cuts small slits in the turf. Both improve drainage.

1024 What is a scarifying rake?

A scarifying rake has long, flexible tines held in a fan-like arrangement. It is used for raking thatch – dead grass and other plant material – from around the blades of grass. A lawn scarifier is effectively a rake on wheels. This can just be rolled over the lawn. While easier to use than a scarifying rake, it does a less effective job.

1025 What is a lawn lute?

If you want a smooth finish to your lawn, investing in a lawn lute is worthwhile. These are designed to level even slight undulations in the soil prior to sowing or to achieve a perfect level when applying top-dressings. They are made in a range of sizes, the smaller ones being suitable for most domestic situations. Large lutes, up to 4m (13ft) wide, are used professionally on bowling greens.

OTHER TOOLS

All gardeners make use of different tools and each can often be used for more than one purpose. As your gardening knowledge grows and the range of plants you nurture increases, you may find that additional tools make light work of some tasks.

1026 Do I need to wear gloves?

It is advisable to wear gloves but not essential. For women of child-bearing age, wearing garden gloves in a garden frequented by cats is essential. Cat faeces can carry a parasite that is harmful to an unborn baby.

1027 Do I need a fertilizer spreader?

Spreaders are designed to distribute fertilizer at a set rate over a given area. Most gardeners would never have the need for one of these, but they have their uses if you have to deal with a large area – prior to sowing a lawn, for instance. They are also useful for distributing fertilizer.

1028 How many watering cans do I need?

It makes sense to have two cans. Two full cans are easier to carry than one, and puts less strain on the back. It is also a good idea to keep a special can for applying weedkillers.

▼ **1026** *Heavy-duty gardening gloves are essential for work with thorny-stemmed plants such as roses.*

1029 What different watering can roses are there?

You can use a watering can without a rose when delivering a fertilizer root drench and when you want to make sure the water reaches right to the roots of a plant – but there is always an attendant risk that the weight of the water will compact the soil. Roses attached to the spout distribute the water like rainfall over a larger area, albeit with some wastage. Circular roses that fit flat on over the end of the spout usually deliver a fairly heavy spray. Oval types that point upwards deliver a lighter spray over a bigger area. Dribble bar attachments are useful for applying weedkillers and algae killers over patios and decking.

1030 Should I install a water butt?

Most gardeners are aware of the need to conserve resources, including water. Rainwater is the best water to use on plants, and a water butt attached to

▼ **1029** *Fit your watering can with a rose that will deliver the right kind of spray over your plants.*

the roof guttering offers the best way of collecting it. It is important that the guttering is plastic – not iron, lead or any other metal that can contaminate the water. The butt should be fitted with a lid to keep out insects and other debris that can foul the water. It is most practical to raise the butt above the ground on blocks, then it is easy to place a watering can underneath the tap at the butt's base. If you have space to house more than one water butt, kits are available to link them together.

1031 What types of garden hose are there?

Garden hoses are either round or flat. Flat types take up less space when wound up for storage. For good water flow, it is important that there are no kinks in the length used. Hoses on reels are easiest to manage. You can use connectors to join shorter lengths, while a range of nozzle attachments will allow you to deliver the water either as a jet or a spray of varying degrees of fineness. Seep hoses or trickle hoses deliver water to specific plants (or areas of the garden or greenhouse). A garden hose or tube that is perforated along its length is placed on the soil surface in borders. Depending on the angles of the holes, the water emerges either as a fine upward spray or a downward dribble. You need to check the pipes regularly to make sure the holes are not blocked with soil.

1032 Should I use a timing system?

To avoid wasting too much water, irrigation systems are usually used in conjunction with a timer that delivers the water only at specific times of the day. These are particularly useful if you have plants that need to be watered when you know you will be away from home.

around the site. Garden carts, with two or more wheels, are more stable than wheelbarrows but are not so easy to manoeuvre.

1034 What is a bulb planter?

A bulb planter is a tool that is used to remove large plugs from lawns. Individual bulbs are placed in the holes, then the plug is put back, minus a small amount of earth.

1035 What is a bulb auger?

Drifts of spring bulbs under deciduous trees can be highly effective, but it can be difficult to dig around old and congested roots to plant them, especially if you are looking to plant bulbs in quantity. A bulb auger, which looks like a large drill bit, attaches to a large drill to create holes around 5cm (2in) in diameter while cutting through tough or fibrous roots. Any soil is whisked away from the edge so it does not fall back into the hole.

The auger can be used for making holes quickly for transplants or for making holes around fruit trees for adding fertilizer.

1033 What types of wheelbarrow are there?

Wheelbarrows are made of sturdy plastic or rustproof metal and have a single wheel at the front. They are usually easy to manoeuvre provided the weight is well balanced. On some types – usually somewhat larger – the wheel is replaced with a ball. These are useful for carrying heavy loads,

▲ *1033 You will probably put a wheelbarrow to heavy use, moving plants, garden compost and other materials.*

especially if you are working on uneven ground. Builder's barrows are larger and heavier than ordinary garden wheelbarrows and have inflatable tyres. They are useful if you need to move heavy building materials

▼ *1030 If you are interested in water conservation, install a water butt that is linked to the guttering system.*

▼ *1031 A garden hose should be wound up when not in use to prevent it kinking and cracking.*

▼ *1034 A long-handled bulb planter can make the back-breaking task of bulb planting easier if you have many bulbs to plant, or have back or mobility problems.*

1036 What is a dibber used for?

Dibbers are usually narrow, pointed tools that are used to make holes in potting mix, either for seed sowing or for cuttings. Many gardeners find a pencil does the job just as well. Some dibbers are more bulbous, with T-shaped handles, and these are useful outdoors, both when sowing seed and for planting out seedlings – especially in the vegetable garden. The deeper you drive the tool into the soil, the wider the hole.

1037 Do I need to invest in a shredder?

Shredders are used to chop woody growth, usually hedge prunings, which can be spread around plants as a mulch. They are expensive, but can be hired. Some allotment societies or garden clubs join together to buy a shredder for the use of the members. Many models are electric, but larger ones are petrol-driven.

1038 What is a garden blower?

A garden blower is like an outdoor vacuum cleaner, but it can be switched between suction and blowing mode. Blowers are used to clear up fallen leaves and other debris. In suction mode, the material is collected in a large bag. They are powered by either electricity or petrol.

▲ *1036 A dibber is used for making holes in potting mix for seeds and seedlings and for pricking out.*

1039 What are the best plant labels to use?

White plastic labels are the most widely used and can be written on with a pencil. Most gardeners are happy to use these for labelling seedlings and cuttings. If you like to label plants in the garden, they can be obtrusive, and here it can be preferable to use black labels, for which special silver markers are available. Copper labels are the traditional choice for labelling shrubs,

▼ *1038 A garden blower has a separate attachment that is used to suck leaves and debris into a bag.*

▲ *1039 Label all seeds and cuttings – many plants look very similar when in the early stages of growth.*

as they can be hung from the branches. Terracotta and lead labels are also sometimes seen. These are much more expensive, though also more durable, than the other types.

1040 How do I stake a tree?

There are various schools of thought concerning tree staking, but most gardeners nowadays agree that a short stake is best. This allows the upper portion of the trunk and the crown to move in the wind, which produces

▼ *1040 When staking a tree, choose a stake that is around the same thickness as the trunk.*

▲ **1041** *You can buy rubber plant ties or simply use short lengths of string, wire or twine.*

stockier growth. Angle the stake so that you drive in the point about 30–45cm (12–18in) from the trunk. Take care to avoid damaging the root system. The stake can be removed after three years.

Use a stake that is a similar thickness to the tree's trunk. For young, sappy trees a bamboo cane, inserted upright just next to the trunk, is perfectly adequate.

1041 What are tree ties?

Tree ties are made of rubber or similar soft material. Most are designed to be tied tightly to the stake, and have an adjustable extension that is secured only loosely around the tree. You should be able to slip a couple of fingers between the trunk and the tie, thus allowing the plant to grow and thicken. Check the tie regularly and loosen it as necessary. The tie should not be in contact with the bark all round, or chafing can occur.

1042 How do I stake perennials?

Some highly bred perennials – peonies, delphiniums and dahlias – have large flowers that weigh down the stems. They have to be staked to keep them upright. Tall-growing delphiniums and dahlias can be staked with individual canes. Ring stakes – suitable for peonies – comprise a mesh circle that is held horizontally on (usually) four

uprights. Place the circle near the ground as the plant emerges in spring. Coax the stems through the mesh, then raise the circle at intervals as the stems grow until the flower buds swell.

Eye injuries are all too common in the garden. Special rubber or plastic caps are available for fitting over the tips of canes.

1043 What are pea sticks?

Pea sticks are thinnish stems used for supporting sweet peas (*Lathyrus odoratus*). Cut bare stems about 1–1.2m (3–4ft) in length from hazel bushes or birch trees in mid-winter and drive them into the soil next to sweet pea seedlings when you plant them out. Either use them in rows or make them into 'wigwams', tying them at the top with garden twine or wire. Wigwams can also be used for other annual climbers and less vigorous clematis varieties.

1044 When would I need to use garden twine?

Horticultural string is coarse and brown. Short lengths can be used for attaching plant stems to supports. Since it is a natural fibre, it tends to rot over time, so the ties need replacing every year or so.

Synthetic fibres can be dyed in strong colours that show up well in the garden. Polypropylene twine is excellent for marking out areas in the garden for a variety of projects. Use it to define the area of a patio or lawn or on an existing lawn to show where a

pool or flower bed is to be dug. You can also use it to indicate parts of a lawn that need treating with weedkiller/fertilizer or for bulb planting. The twine can be stapled to short stakes or tied to lengths of bamboo driven into the ground.

1045 I have seen bundles of raffia for sale – what is this used for?

Short lengths of raffia can be used to tie the soft stems of climbers such as sweet peas or clematis – as the material is soft, there is less risk of chafing. Raffia is unobtrusive, but as it is a natural fibre it rots after a few months, so has to be replaced.

1046 What are the best brooms for garden use?

A stiff brush is good for sweeping down a patio or deck, while a traditional besom broom, usually made of birch twigs strapped around a central pole, is the perfect tool for sweeping up leaves and other plant debris in autumn, as well as drying the lawn before a cut. Most domestic brooms are unsuitable for use in the garden. A soft brush can be used to push sand into patio crevices.

▼ **1043** *Hazel twigs can be used as an informal support for annual climbers. They will not show once the plant grows.*

POTS AND POTTING PRODUCTS

For successful container gardening, you need to use the appropriate pots and potting products. Some types of container are used for permanent plantings, others for the shorter term, such as for growing seedlings and cuttings at different growth stages.

1047 How do I choose a container for my plant?

Choose a pot that is slightly bigger than that the shrub or plant you intend to pot-on currently occupies. Choice of material is entirely personal. Terracotta pots are heavy to lift and can become damaged by the weather. Some gardeners find them visually more appealing than plastic. Good reproductions of classically shaped pots are available in plastic, which are lighter in weight and more durable.

1048 What are sweet pea tubes?

Sweet peas (*Lathyrus odoratus*) develop long roots and are believed to resent disturbance, so, rather than sowing the seeds in trays (then pricking them out when they germinate), it is best to sow them individually in containers that can easily accommodate the developing roots, then plant them out when they are well grown. Sweet pea

▼ **1047** *Terracotta pots are available in a wide range of sizes and styles from traditional and decorative to sleek and contemporary. Terracotta is heavy, but many gardeners prefer it to plastic.*

tubes are tall, narrow containers specially produced for this purpose, often made of a biodegradable material, so that the whole thing can be planted out. You can improvise by fashioning some from newspaper folded and rolled so that it is sturdy.

1049 What are long tom pots?

Long toms, however, are deeper than they are wide, and are designed for growing on tap- and deep-rooted plants, such oak seedlings. In comparison, a standard garden pot is as deep as it is wide.

◀ **1051** *You can make your own biodegradable pots from newspaper sheets wrapped around a broom handle, then folded tightly.*

1050 What are modules?

Modules are square plastic cells, intended for the sowing of seeds that are large enough to be sown individually. The seedling can stay in the module until well developed, then can be planted into a larger pot or directly into the garden, if conditions are suitable. Flimsy types are best supported in a tray of the same size – they are easy to cut with scissors. Modules can also be used for small cuttings – such as those of fuchsias and tender perennials.

1051 What are biodegradable pots?

Biodegradable pots are made of paper. They are ideal for growing on seedlings. Once the seedling has

▼ **1052** *Plastic pots and trays are cheap and made in all sizes for all purposes. They are usually brown, green or black. Choose an appropriate size for the plant that you are potting on.*

reached an appropriate size – when the roots begin to push their way through the sides – the whole thing can be planted out in the garden, minimizing disturbance to the plant. However, you have to be careful not to overwet these pots when watering, as they can disintegrate. For this reason, they are unsuitable for seeds that take a long time to germinate.

1052 How do I know whether to use trays, pots or modules?

Trays are useful for sowing very fine seed, for instance of tobacco plants (*Nicotiana*). Use modules for larger seeds that are easy to handle individually, for instance of nasturtiums (*Tropaeolum*). Once roots fill the modules, the little plants can be knocked out of each module for potting on. If the seedlings will be staying in the container longer term – for instance, if you are growing lilies from seed – use a conventional flower pot. Trays are also useful for striking large quantities of small cuttings, for instance of box (*Buxus sempervirens*) to provide material for a dwarf hedge.

1053 Should I stand my pots on special feet or put them in saucers?

Pots are often sold with matching trays that stand under them and catch excess water as it drains through. This water should then be discarded or used on other plants – and not allowed to stagnate. Few plants like to stand in water, and the water itself can attract fungi and bacteria. However, it is difficult to manoeuvre large plants in heavy containers, so it is more practical to stand these on small supports that hold them above the ground. Excess water can then drain through easily. Standing heavy containers on wheeled supports also makes them easier to move around the garden, or to clean behind and around them.

▶ **1053** *Place saucers under containers to catch excess water. Empty full saucers so that the plant's root system does not rot.*

▲ **1055** *Mix horticultural grit with potting mix and use it to fill containers that will hold bulbs and bedding plants. Add a top dressing of vermiculite or perlite around the collar of the plant.*

1054 What is rockwool?

Rockwool, also known as stone wool and similar in appearance to fibreglass, is made of molten stone and is much used in the building industry as an insulating material. As it is able to hold both moisture and air, it has certain applications in gardening. It is a good material for striking (cutting) cuttings, is often used in hydroponics and can be used for potting cymbidium orchids. However, as the material contains no plant nutrients, these have to be supplied as a root drench or foliar feed.

▲ **1055** *For ease of handling, moisten perlite so that it clumps together lightly before using to provide a top dressing over seed potting mix, or to lighten hanging basket potting mix.*

1055 What are perlite and vermiculite?

Perlite and vermiculite are granules of lightweight volcanic material that are added to potting and cuttings potting mix to improve drainage. Unlike horticultural grit, they are extremely lightweight, so are useful for hanging baskets which need to be kept as light as possible if they are not to impose too much strain on their fixings. Being light, they are apt to blow about, so dampen them slightly in the bag to make them easier to use. These materials have limited use in the open garden.

HEALTH AND SAFETY

The garden can be a dangerous place. Of all domestic accidents, a large proportion occur outdoors, usually through falls and the misuse of garden equipment, or doing too much work without adequate levels of fitness. Take all precautions necessary to avoid accidents.

1056 Should I wear any special protective clothing?

Many domestic accidents occur in gardens through falls, electric shock or injuries from the misuse of equipment. It is important to pay attention to health and safety issues when creating and working in a garden if the risk of these is to be minimized.

Most modern ear defenders are lightweight and pleasant to wear. Use them whenever you are using power machinery, such as hedge trimmers, motorized lawn mowers or the cutting tools that are used for tree felling or slab cutting.

Eye injuries are common in the garden. Protect your eyes with goggles (in conjunction with ear defenders, if using powered tools) when shearing hedges, felling trees and cutting slabs and paviors. It is also worth wearing goggles if you need to move a large conifer – the needles are sharp and it is easy to jab your eye with a stiff stem in the process of handling the plant. Wear gloves to protect against thorny or poisonous plants.

▲ **1057** *Working at height in a garden always has risks. Make sure that ladders are stable and erected correctly before beginning work and do not be tempted to over-reach.*

▼ **1056** *Protecting eyes from flying debris and ears from noisy machinery is essential when using powered equipment.*

1057 Is it safe to use ladders in the garden?

Sometimes it is necessary to work at height in the garden – perhaps when picking apples and other top fruits, pruning, hedge trimming and carrying out other maintenance work to walls and fences. The use of ladders in such situations should be discouraged. They are not stable and falls are common. It is better to invest in a platform or scaffolding system that can be adjusted on uneven ground so that it stands perpendicular. This will enable you to work standing level. Most models incorporate a safety rail.

1058 Is a hard hat necessary?

To guard against potential head injuries, it makes sense to wear a builder's hard hat whenever you are working at height. Some special helmets combine a head covering with goggles and ear defenders.

1059 How do I avoid getting back problems?

Try not to bend your back when lifting, especially heavy objects. Keep your back straight and bend the knees. If you need to carry objects, aim to hold an equal weight in each hand rather than a heavy weight in one hand. It puts less strain on your back, for instance, to carry two smaller filled watering cans, one in each hand, than a single large can.

1060 What are the implications of using electricity in the garden?

The combination of moisture and electricity is always a potentially explosive one, and gardens are inevitably damp places. Electricity is often required in the least safe place of all – to power a fountain or waterfall in a pond. Irrigation systems are also generally powered by electricity. It is essential that all wiring is installed by

▲ **1058** *Wear a hard hat if you are cutting branches from trees at height or pruning tall shrubs.*

a qualified electrician. Outdoor sockets should be protected from the elements by waterproof housings. Where possible, use low-voltage types. This includes rechargeable equipment that is not connected to the mains when in use. Low-voltage and solar-powered lighting systems are available.

1061 How should cable be laid?
It is usually recommended that electricity cables be buried at least 60cm (2ft) down, where digging is unlikely to take place. Where possible, run it alongside a fence or wall (where the ground is unlikely to be disturbed) or under paving. (Laying under paving has the disadvantage that the cable is inaccessible should it become necessary to dig it up or replace it.) Electricity cables should be armoured to guard against damage from spades and other sharp tools that could sever them.

Lay a marking tape 15cm (6in) above the cable. This will come to light if you need to dig over the area at any point. If you sell the property, it will also alert the new owners to the presence of the cable lower down.

1062 How do I use an electric lawnmower safely?
Avoid mowing a lawn when it is raining or when the grass is still wet after a shower or when still dewy after a cool night. When mowing, make sure the cable runs behind you so that you do not cut towards it. It is a good idea to use a 'Power Breaker' which plugs into your mains socket and reduces the risk of electrocution. Before cleaning or making adjustments to your mower, always make sure it is switched off and unplugged from the mains supply.

1063 Are there any special considerations when using a petrol mower?
If you use a petrol mower you should always remove the spark plug cap. When using petrol-driven mowers or refuelling, keep well away from naked flames and do not smoke, as the fumes from petrol can ignite into a fire ball. Ensure that the mower is serviced regularly and store it in a dry place.

1064 Should I have a tetanus jab?
Tetanus, or lockjaw, is a serious infection caused by a bacterium that lives in the soil, especially manured soil. It enters the body through a cut or open wound. A tetanus jab will prevent, but not cure, it. Regular tetanus jabs are recommended.

1065 Are there any general tips that will minimize the risk of accidents occurring in the garden?
Keeping the garden a safe place is largely a matter of common sense. Design your garden to reduce the need for maintenance and lifting. Keep off paving if it is icy and slippery and fix uneven paving slabs to reduce the risk of tripping. Put the garden hose away after each use. Put all tools away after use, and clear away prunings. Use electrical equipment only during dry weather and always fit an RCD (residual current device) to prevent electric shocks. Keep all weedkillers and insecticides locked away from children. Wear all the recommended safety equipment when using machinery and tuck in loose items of clothing. Never leave a barbecue unattended and check it has been extinguished after use.

1066 How can I make the garden a safe place for young children?
As in the house, the garden is full of potential hazards and constant vigilance of young children is essential. Fence off and make inaccessible, or fill in, any ponds or similar water features. Make designated play areas for children that are interesting and appealing, with soft landing areas for play equipment. Keep play areas away from glass houses. Keep the garden boundaries secure and locked, if necessary. Identify and remove any poisonous plants from the garden. Prickly plants will quickly be respected. Remove any animal faeces with a trowel. Promote an interest in gardening by planting fast growing seeds that will keep children interested and content to be in the garden environment.

▼ **1066** *Fence off areas of the garden that you do not want to give children access to. Ensure the fencing is secure and cannot be negotiated by a child too young to understand the dangers.*

WATER CONSERVATION

Making the best use of available water is increasingly important to many gardeners. Not only does this save money in metered areas, but if rainwater has been allowed to collect in storage tanks it lowers the possibility of a serious shortage during hot periods in summer.

1067 Why should I conserve water?

Water is a precious resource. The climate is unpredictable, and periods of drought can occur even in temperate areas. For the good of the environment we should aim to use the minimum amount of water in our gardens and recycle what we do use to maintain an adequate reserve. Household appliances such as washing machines and dishwashers are wasteful of water – even up-to-date models that recycle some of the water used. It makes sense – both economically and ecologically – to collect as much of this water as possible for reuse in the garden.

1068 What is the best way to water plants when there is a hosepipe ban?

Attach water butts to household guttering to collect rainwater. To get the maximum value from any water you do use in the garden, irrigate

▼ **1070** *Water butts are easy to install to any downpipe on a house or garage wall, or even, as here, to collect the water from a pitched greenhouse roof.*

▲ **1069** *A thick mulch of slate chippings helps to stop water evaporating.*

plants only in the evening – less will be lost through evaporation – and use a watering can without a rose to deliver the water directly around the roots. (Using a hose or sprinkler is wasteful, as much moisture is lost.) Water plants thoroughly, then cover with a mulch of garden compost, bark chippings or grit. This will help keep the roots cool and moist.

1069 How can I cut down water use in the garden?

Mulch plants thickly in spring and autumn. One of the major benefits of mulching is that it cuts down the rate at which water evaporates from the soil, both by covering the surface and by keeping the soil at a cool temperature. You can also reduce the need to water by concentrating on drought-tolerant Mediterranean plants, especially if the soil is free-draining.

1070 How do I collect rainwater?

Rainwater can be collected in water butts that are attached to the house guttering. If you intend to collect rainwater, it is essential that the guttering is plastic. Lead or iron

guttering, as is sometimes found on older buildings, will contaminate the water. If you become really keen on collecting water, attach butts to garages, sheds and other out-buildings – any structure with a sloping roof to which a length of guttering can be fixed.

1071 What is grey water and how do I collect it?

Grey water, also known as sullage, is water that has been used in the house for personal washing, household cleaning and laundry. A number of systems are available that will divert waste water from dishwashers and washing machines for use in the garden. Once it has cooled, bath water can be siphoned off with a hose pipe into an outside trough.

1072 How harmful are cleaning agents dissolved in the water?

Traces of soap used in personal washing are unlikely to harm plants – in fact, they can be beneficial as they can facilitate a plant's uptake of the water. At the other end of the scale, water containing bleach is unsuitable for garden use. Sodium, chlorine and boron are all toxic to plants. Laundry products should be low in salt and phosphates and have a neutral pH. Look for eco-friendly products that break down rapidly.

Grey water can be used to water plants once it has cooled, provided it contains no toxic chemicals and is not used on plants in the kitchen garden that you intend to eat.

1073 Any other tips for saving water?

Wash vegetables before cooking in a large bowl rather than under running water. Not only will you use less, but the water you do use can be tipped directly on to garden plants.

RECYCLING

There are plenty of materials from the household shopping that can be reused in the garden. From empty plastic yogurt pots, to broken CDs and even old clothing, choosing to be green is often second nature to many gardeners.

1074 Can I make my own bird scares?

To make bird scares, string together old CDs and DVDs, metallic milk bottle tops and scrunched-up aluminium foil. Run the string between upright canes driven into the ground among your crops. If you have any old cassettes, remove the tape and stretch this between canes. This will vibrate in the wind, emitting a humming sound that will deter birds.

1075 Can I reuse food packaging?

Lightweight yoghurt pots and margarine containers can be used as pots for seedlings, cuttings and divisions – simply jab a few holes in the base for drainage. Clear plastic boxes with snap on lids in which fruit is sold can be used to store seed heads in autumn. (Clear plastic containers are unsuitable for growing plants in as they do not exclude light, an essential for root development.)

▼ **1074** *Stringing CDs on to wire and placing it taut across a newly seeded patch of ground is a good bird deterrent.*

▲ **1074** *A traditional scarecrow can make an attractive feature in the garden.*

1076 Can I reuse polystyrene packaging?

Polystyrene packaging from computers and white goods can be broken into pieces and used as bulk drainage material at the base of containers in place of stones or crocks.

▼ **1074** *Birds can be dissuaded from attacking your plants by stretching string and shiny foil over the crops.*

1077 Can I make use of clear plastic drinks bottles?

Cut empty plastic bottles in half to use as mini cloches to protect individual plants in the garden or to place over similarly sized pots in which you are raising seedlings or cuttings. The top ends of the bottles are particularly useful – you can regulate the humidity created by periodically removing the screw top.

1078 Why can I not recycle the black plastic pots that plants are sold in at garden centres?

While many councils have recycling schemes and will collect plastic containers in dump bins on site, black plastic is usually excluded. This is because black plastic is already made up of recycled plastic and further recycling is not possible. However, many garden centres will accept them for re-use and offer them to other customers for their own use.

▼ **1077** *Plastic bottles can be used to protect individual plant specimens in the garden from the worst of the weather.*

INDEX

ACKNOWLEDGEMENTS

Photographers: Peter Anderson, Caroline Arber, Sue Atkinson,
Jonathan Buckley, Sarah Cuttle, Nicki Dowey, Paul Forrester,
John Freeman, Michelle Garrett, Simon McBride, Robert Pickett,
Jo Whitworth, Mark Winwood and Steven Wooster.

Illustrator: Liz Pepperell

Thanks to the following picture libraries:
key t = top, b = bottom, l = left, r = right, c = centre

Corbis, page 16t and page 200tl.

Fotolia, page 16bm, page 65t, page 71bl, page 120bl,
page 138tr and b, page 200br, page 237bl, page 241tc and bl,
page 243t and bc.

GAP, page 63tl.

Istock, page 4bl, page 13bl, page 14tr, page 52t, page 68b,
page 86bc, 226t, bl and bc, page 229br, page 236t, page 237bc,
page 238c, page 239b, page 240l and r.